Chicago Public Library

C
P L

REFERENCE

Form 178 rev. 1-94

DISCARD

D1446059

MANUFACTURING FOR EXPORT IN THE DEVELOPING WORLD

In recent years much has been made of the success of developing countries, particularly in East Asia, that have achieved rapid economic growth by manufacturing goods for export.

This volume looks at the experience of a number of countries which have tried to effect a similar transition. It combines case studies of five countries with an introduction that considers the overall context and conclusions. The book uncovers serious potential difficulties in maintaining the pace of manufacturing for export in developing countries, and shows that there is no simple relationship between import liberalization and manufacturing for export.

G. K. Helleiner is Professor of Economics at the University of Toronto. He has published widely in international trade, finance and development and is at present the Research Coordinator for the Group of Twenty-Four – the caucus of developing countries in the international financial institutions.

UNU WORLD INSTITUTE FOR DEVELOPMENT ECONOMICS RESEARCH

(UNU/WIDER) was established by the United Nations University as its first research and training centre and started work in Helsinki, Finland in 1985. The principal purpose of the Institute is policy-oriented research on the main strategic issues of development and international cooperation, as well as on the interaction between domestic and global changes.

UNU World Institute for Development Economics Research
(UNU/WIDER)
Katajanokanlaituri 6 B, FIN-00160 Helsinki, Finland

MANUFACTURING FOR EXPORT IN THE DEVELOPING WORLD

Problems and possibilities

Edited by G. K. Helleiner

London and New York

First published 1995
by Routledge
11 New Fetter Lane, London EC4P 4EE

Simultaneously published in the USA and Canada
by Routledge
29 West 35th Street, New York, NY 10001

© 1995 United Nations University

Typeset in Garamond by
Ponting–Green Publishing Services, Chesham, Bucks
Printed and bound in Great Britain by
Mackays of Chatham PLC, Kent

British Library Cataloguing in Publication Data
A catalogue record for this book is available from
the British Library

Library of Congress Cataloging in Publication Data
A catalogue record for this book has been requested

ISBN 0–415–12387–9

CONTENTS

FIGURES

TABLES

CONTRIBUTORS

Ismail Arslan is an economist in the World Bank Resident Mission, Ankara, Turkey.

Merih Celasun is Professor of Economics at the Middle East Technical University, Ankara, Turkey.

Gerry Helleiner is Professor of Economics at the University of Toronto, Canada.

Patricio Meller is former Executive Director of CIEPLAN, Corporacion de Investigaciones Economicas para Latinoamerica, Santiago, and at present Director of the Master's Program in Public Policy, University of Chile.

Benno J. Ndulu is Professor of Economics, University of Dar es Salaam, Tanzania, currently on leave as Executive Director, African Economic Research Consortium, Nairobi, Kenya.

José Antonio Ocampo is Director of the National Department of Planning in Colombia, and previously was Senior Researcher at FEDESARROLLO and Professor of Economics at University de Los Andes, Bogotá, Colombia.

Jaime Ros, a Mexican economist, is Associate Professor of Economics and Fellow of the Kellogg Institute for International Studies at the University of Notre Dame.

Joseph J. Semboja is Senior Research Fellow, Economic Research Bureau, University of Dar es Salaam, Tanzania.

Leonardo Villar is Technical Vice-Minister, Ministry of Finance, Bogotá, Colombia.

FOREWORD

The interrelationship between trade and industrial development has been a key issue in economic research and development studies in the post-World War II era. Industrialization has played a crucial role in the national modernization policies of all developing countries. World trade has become a source of opportunities for many nations and at the same time the medium for the spread and the spill-over effects of economic growth in the field of output, and of disturbances caused by national policies, imbalances, or changes in competitive positions. Industrialization and trade have also been important factors in social and industrial changes. Many developing countries have gone through different stages of industrial development during the past decades. With the increasing role of industry in their economies, trade in manufacturing has also become an important channel for strengthening their position in the world economy.

For most of the twentieth century, changes in trade proportions have been strongly related to the increasing role of industry in the life of nations. The colonial division of labour – characterized by the flow of natural resources from the agricultural or raw-material-exporting countries to the industrialized world – which by and large dominated trade patterns since the industrial revolution, has been gradually replaced by a new pattern: the industrial division of labour. Comparative advantages related to natural resource endowments were replaced by 'acquired' advantages. In order to strengthen their international comparative position, nations and firms have been focusing increasingly on human resource developments, innovative capabilities, and new strategies in production and services.

Between 1950 and 1990, world trade in industrial products expanded almost twice as fast as did the output of manufacturing industries. During this period, major shifts occurred which corresponded to the impact of industries on production and consumption patterns, cost and price relations, comparative market positions, and on the regional locations of industry. The industrial division of labour and economies of scale also played a key role in bringing about changes in trade policies, the rejection of protectionism, the progress of economic integration, and the establishment of free trade zones and common markets, especially in Europe.

Three major developments have strongly contributed to the radical transformation of the patterns of relations between trade and industrial development on a global level since the early 1970s:

- *the new technological revolution*, which is the source of important structural and institutional shifts in the relations between production and services and in both the manufacturing and service sectors;
- *the redrawing of the techno-economic map of the globe* and the emergence of new competitors, and particularly the fast growth of manufacturing in the developing world;
- the changes in the goals of national policies and regulatory regimes of trade and capital flows (export orientation, deregulation, liberalization, privatization).

These developments in turn lead to new relations between trade and national economic development.

The 'trading system' as a factor in influencing the global distribution of income, wealth and employment opportunities has become a network of interactions of direct investments by transnational corporations, of trade in goods and services, of technology transfers in different forms, and of a number of regulatory structures. Many of the developing countries are facing new challenges and are finding it increasingly difficult to develop appropriate responses. In many cases the national institutionas are not prepared to deal with the new tasks, related to constant structural adjustment needs and other pressures, caused by the new forms of interconnectedness with the increasingly competitive global markets.

This volume, the third within the framework of the research project on the interrelations between trade and industrialization in the developing countries, reveals many of the new developments. It is an in-depth analysis of general processes and specific cases, showing the diverse patterns as well as the variety of the domestic and international policy implications of the more recent changes in the perspectives of five countries from three continents.

FOREWORD

Within the research project, this volume is the last one dealing with national experiences. I express the gratitude of UNU/WIDER to all the participants of the international research network, and also to the Swedish International Development Authority (SIDA), who supported the project. The former director of UNU/WIDER, Dr Lal Jayawardena, joins me in giving special thanks and appreciation to the director of this project, Professor G. K. Helleiner, for his invaluable professional contribution.

Mihály Simani
Director, UNU/WIDER
Helsinki

PREFACE

This volume is the latest in a series on trade and industrialization in developing countries, the product of a research project conducted under the auspices of the World Institute for Development Economics Research (WIDER) and financially supported by the Swedish International Development Authority (SIDA). The first volume, *Trade Policy, Industrialization and Development: New Perspectives*, edited by G. K. Helleiner (Clarendon Press, Oxford, 1991), prepared the ground for the project with a literature review and identification of some of the key issues requiring detailed research. The next volume, *Trade Policy and Industrialization in Turbulent Times*, edited by G. K. Helleiner (Routledge, 1994), presented reviews of experience in the 1970s and 1980s in fourteen developing countries. This volume focuses on one aspect of these experiences in an important subsample of these countries; its country studies have been undertaken by the same authors as in the previous volume, sometimes joined by new co-authors. The authors discussed drafts of their papers, as well as a wider set of other country papers on other aspects of trade and industrialization experience, at a conference at the OECD Development Centre in November 1992.

Project participants are, again, grateful to the Swedish International Development Authority (SIDA) for its financial support for the project and to WIDER for its sponsorship. They are also grateful to their conference host, the OECD Development Centre, Paris. Particular thanks are due to Lal Jayawardena, former Director of WIDER, and Hema Perera, its former Principal Research Fellow, for their continuing firm support for the project; to Barbara Tiede, the project's secretary, at the University of Toronto, who has maintained her cheerful and efficient management of the details of the project's business and effectively steered the manuscript to the publisher; and to Rodney Schmidt for his extensive assistance in preparing the papers for publication.

Toronto
August 1994

1

INTRODUCTION

G. K. Helleiner

During the past couple of decades the value of manufactured exports from the developing countries has grown rapidly. Their value now substantially exceeds that of total non-oil primary product exports from these countries. Manufacturing for export has become a major element in recent industrial growth in the developing world. At first, the bulk of these manufactured exports originated from a very small number of developing countries, most famously Korea, Taiwan, Hong Kong and Singapore. Thereafter, however, many more developing economies entered into successful manufacturing for export and even more are seeking to emulate them. Experience in the successful East Asian countries has attracted a great deal of recent research attention (e.g. World Bank 1993b; Amsden *et al.* 1994; Bradford 1994; Fishlow *et al.* 1994; Wade 1995). Both official and private plans for continuing and expanding industrial production in the developing countries typically rely heavily upon the prospect of manufactured exports.

This volume seeks to shed more light on the transition to successful manufacturing for export in the 1980s in a sample of five relative 'latecomers' (in some cases, it would be more accurate to say 'less well-known comers') among the developing countries that have embarked upon this new path – Colombia, Chile, Mexico, Tanzania and Turkey. By presenting a number of detailed case studies of countries' recent experiences, and analysing their differences and similarities, this volume aspires to assist policymakers and analysts who continue to grapple with the problems attendant on this transition. The studies build upon earlier, and more general, comparative analyses of trade policies and industrialization in these same countries (as well as others) in the 1970s and 1980s (Helleiner 1994).

From these broader earlier analyses emerged the desirability of more focused and detailed study of the transition to industrial exporting in a representative sample of those countries that had made significant progress, or tried to make it, in this sphere.

Three of the four middle-income developing countries studied in this volume – Colombia, Mexico and Turkey – experienced manufactured export 'booms' for periods in the 1980s or early 1990s (see Table 1.1). Chile, the other middle-income country, experienced a parallel boom in non-traditional exports, most of which were not, according to standard definitions, manufactured products, but which nonetheless involved processing activity and often important links to domestic manufacturing activity. The only low-income Sub-Saharan African country in the sample, Tanzania, also performed better in manufactured exports during this period than it had ever done before.

Table 1.1 Periods of rapid growth and annual rates of growth of manufactured and non-traditional exports in sample countries

Colombia manufactured exports, 1967–74: 16.4%; 1990–1: 29.5%

Chile non-copper exports, 1985–90: 15.4%

Mexico non-oil exports, 1981–92: 17.2%

Tanzania manufactured exports, 1986–90: 19.9%

Turkey manufactured exports, 1980–9: 27.1%

Sources: Country studies, this volume

Despite these similarities, the countries in the sample are varied both in their initial conditions and in their recent experience. Tables 1.2 and 1.3, drawn from standardized international sources to facilitate comparison, show the main relevant characteristics of the five countries. (The only significant difference between national and international data is, interestingly, in the definition of manufactured exports in Chile, about which more below.) Four of the five countries have manufacturing sectors accounting for over 20 per cent of their GDP. Over the past two decades, Turkey's manufacturing sector share has grown, Chile's and Colombia's have declined (Colombia's only slightly), and Mexico's has been stable. Tanzania's manufacturing sector accounted for only 10 per cent of GDP in 1970 and this share dropped to even lower levels in the 1980s.

All five countries experienced significant increases in the share of exports in GDP in the 1980s and all but Tanzania, which moved sharply in the reverse direction, also did so in the 1970s. Mexico and Turkey more than doubled their export shares over these two decades. (Data on export shares and on the composition of exports, which follow, must be interpreted cautiously during periods in which there were major changes in relative prices, e.g. in the domestic relative price of tradables following devaluation, and in world prices for oil, copper and other exports, which can significantly influence the measurement of their change over time. The dimensions of the changes described here are nonetheless remarkable.)

The share of manufactures in total exports rose sharply in all these countries except Tanzania. By 1990–1, manufactures' share of total exports had reached 33 per cent in Colombia (from 20 per cent in 1980), 44 per cent in Mexico and 68 per cent in Turkey (from 12 and 27 per cent, respectively, in 1980). In Chile, according to UNCTAD standardized trade classifications, this share in 1991 (13 per cent) was still only at about the Tanzanian level (12 per cent). Chile's own national data, however, include many more processed natural resource products within 'manufactures'. Using the Chilean data, shown in brackets in Table 1.2, manufactures had risen to 41 per cent of total exports by 1991.

Overall GDP growth rates fell in the 1980s in four of these countries, all except Chile; in all but Mexico and Tanzania, they were still, however, sufficient to generate significant increases in per capita GDP. Manufacturing value added also grew more slowly in the 1980s than in the 1970s in Colombia and Mexico; it actually fell in Tanzania. As implied by the export share data noted above, in the 1980s exports grew more rapidly than GDP, and manufactured exports more rapidly still, in all of the countries except Tanzania.

This disparate experience will be elaborated with country-level detail in the chapters that follow. At this point, it is worth noting that, in many respects, Chile and Tanzania are 'outliers' within our sample countries – Chile because of the relatively small role of its manufacturing sector in its recent export success, and Tanzania because of its relatively weak initial economic conditions, in manufacturing as well as in general.

Table 1.2 Key structural characteristics of sample countries[a]

	GDP per capita ($ 1991)	Manufacturing/GDP (%)			Total exports/GDP (%)			Manufactured exports/Total exports (%)			
		1970	1980	1991	1970	1980	1991	1970	1980	1991	
Colombia	1,260	21	22	20	14	17	21	8.0	19.6	33.3	
Chile	2,160	26	21	19	25	21	36	4.3	9.1	13.4	
								[11.6]	[37.2]	[41.2]b	(1990) (1989) (1990)
Mexico	3,030	22	22	22	6	14	16	32.5	11.9	44.1	
Tanzania	100	10	9	4	26	14	20	12.7	14.1	11.8	
Turkey	1,780	17	21	24	6	7	20	8.9	26.9	67.9	

a These data are from standardized international sources and may differ from the country-level data employed in subsequent chapters
b Bracketed figures show Chile's own data, using a different definition of 'manufactured'
Sources: World Bank 1982, 1993a; UNCTAD 1992; Meller, this volume (ch. 2)

Table 1.3 Key growth rates in sample countries[a]

	GDP		Manufacturing		Total exports		Volume of manufactured exports[b]	
	1970–80	1980–91	1970–80	1980–91	1970–80	1980–91	1970–80	1980–91
Colombia	5.4	3.7	5.8	3.4	1.9	12.0	9.1	7.9
Chile	1.4	3.6	-0.8	3.6	10.4	5.2	14.4	8.7
Mexico	6.3	1.2	7.0	1.8	13.5	3.5	4.5	17.6
Tanzania	3.0	2.9	3.7	-0.8	-7.5	-1.9	-2.0	-12.0
Turkey	5.9	5.0	6.1	7.2	4.3	7.2	7.0	24.6

a These data are from standardized international sources and may differ from the country-level data employed in subsequent chapters
b Dollar value deflated by index of unit value of exports of developed market economies
Sources: World Bank 1993a; UNCTAD 1992 (base data from which manufactured export growth was calculated)

ATTRIBUTES OF MANUFACTURED EXPORTS

Manufactured exports are valued for attributes that they are frequently believed to possess, beyond those of more traditional primary exports. Some of these attributes are also associated with other 'non-traditional' exports, and, particularly, with export diversification as a route toward greater stability of export earnings and the terms of trade. In some countries, notably Chile, policy has focused on the desirability of expanding 'non-traditional exports' rather than manufactured ones; in typical developing country circumstances, the former category is much larger than the latter.

Generally, both income elasticity and price elasticity of global demand are presumed higher for manufactures than for most traditional primary exports from developing countries. So is short-run supply elasticity. Apart from the stabilizing effects of diversification that they may bring, the earnings from manufactured exports are also themselves usually more amenable to stable growth than those from primary products. Nonetheless there remain important uncertainties emanating from protectionist measures in principal markets; and the terms of trade for developing countries' manufactures may deteriorate just as much as those for primary products (Sarkar and Singer 1991).

More important still to most developing countries is the prospect of 'dynamic' growth-stimulating effects from the activity of manufacturing for export that do not emanate to the same degree from more traditional activities. Learning effects, the realization of scale economies and the creation of positive externalities for the rest of the economy may derive from many kinds of economic activity; but these potential benefits are nowadays often particularly associated with manufacturing for export. The recent successful Chilean experience with non-traditional primary products, notably fruits, however, has stimulated debate as to whether some kinds of primary export may do just as well. Moreover, some types of manufactured exports are likely to generate greater dynamic effects than others; unskilled labour-intensive exports may be especially weak in this regard. While there is some econometric evidence for more dynamic effects from manufactured exports (Fosu 1990), there is also some evidence that manufactured exports may be the result rather than the cause of rapid growth (Bradford 1994).

In the context of the 1980s – a period characterized by debt crisis, recession and structural adjustment in much of the developing world – manufacturing for export took on added importance for its short-to medium-term macroeconomic attributes. Pressure to service debt and re-establish international creditworthiness, while typically simultaneously to introduce structural reforms that included import liberalization, required both severe domestic macroeconomic restraint and rapid export expansion. Depressed world markets for many traditional primary products, however, limited the range of export possibilities, necessitating resort to non-traditional exports. Manufactured exports provided output maintenance and growth for existing industries facing domestic recession while at the same time earning the desperately needed foreign exchange for the stabilization effort. The transition to manufacturing for export (and other non-traditional exporting) in the developing countries in the 1980s was therefore usually seen as a key element in recovery from macroeconomic crisis.

TYPES OF MANUFACTURED EXPORT

In all of the countries in this study manufactured exports have been categorized as 'non-traditional exports'. ('Non-traditional' exports include minor and/or new primary product exports as well.) Public policy often distinguishes 'traditional' from 'non-traditional' exports, and goes no further.

Manufactured exports can themselves be categorized, however, in different ways. For analytical and/or policy purposes, different kinds of manufactured exports may be important to distinguish; and the authors of the case studies in this volume often do so. The standard international trade or industrial classifications provide one means for doing so. In order to paint with a somewhat broader brush, however, the authors have also frequently made distinctions based upon factor-intensity characteristics in production: particularly in respect of natural-resource intensity, unskilled-labour intensity, capital intensity, and skill intensity. Whole theories of stages of industrial exporting have been built upon such factor-intensity distinctions (e.g. Balassa 1979; Blejer 1978). The Colombian study in this volume distinguishes, at one point, between 'traditional' and 'late' manufactured exports. The theory of comparative advantage, and its factor endowment complement, would lead one to expect that poor countries would begin industrial exporting via primary product processing and unskilled-labour-intensive activities, progressing to more capital-intensive and skill-intensive exports only when more development has been achieved. Equally, from product cycle theory and

theoretical approaches stressing international differences in technology, one would expect that industrial exports from developing
countries would draw upon 'mature', rather than 'frontier', technologies. The patterns of industrial exporting described in the case
studies that follow are broadly consistent with these theoretical
presumptions.

For instance, Colombian manufactured exports are intensive in the
use of natural resources, labour and skilled labour; skilled labour
inputs have been important in exports to regional, rather than
developed country, markets. In the export boom of the early 1990s,
however, unskilled labour (particularly female labour) and resource-
intensive exports to developed countries were dominant. Turkey's
manufactured exports have spanned a range of industries, but the
textiles and clothing sector has always dominated and its share rose
(from 35 per cent to 40 per cent) in the late 1980s. Chilean and
Tanzanian exports are still overwhelmingly based on natural resources, many of which are in processed form, constituting the bulk
of their so-called 'manufactured exports'.

Exports are also sometimes characterized according to the degree
to which they incorporate domestic value added, or 'retained value',
in their gross value. Manufacturing in import- and foreign-
investment-dependent export platforms, for instance, frequently
involves a remarkably small proportion of local value added (consisting mainly of the wage bill) in the total value of its exports.
(Similarly, in final-stage assembly import-substituting industries,
where the inputs are all imported, this proportion is often small.) In
the case of the processing of domestic raw material for export,
particular interest resides in the degree of value added, in the
manufacturing process, to the materials which could otherwise have
been exported in raw form. Such categorizations are also, in some
cases, deployed in the studies that follow. The importance of the
nature of forward and backward linkages from different kinds of
exports is undoubtedly great, and is particularly highlighted in the
study of Chile.

The studies in this volume do not specifically address the question
of the relative merits, in terms of development effects, of different
kinds of manufactured exports, although this is obviously a major
policy issue. The methodology for addressing such issues remains
undeveloped and the data requirements would be demanding. The
studies that follow are, in this respect as well as others, basically in
the nature of positive, rather than normative, analyses. In the main,

they seek to sharpen understanding of what has transpired rather than to prescribe. In any case, caution is appropriate in seeking to generalize from a sample of only five countries.

PRINCIPAL ISSUES

This summary account considers only some of the issues taken up in the individual country studies:

1 Did manufactured exports expand through the 'switching' of sales or through expanding capacity?
2 What role did exchange rate policies play in successful manufacturing for export?
3 What role did export subsidies play in this regard?
4 Did overall import liberalization or other changes in the import regime play an important part in the emergence of manufacturing for export?
5 What influence did external capital flows, and capital account liberalization, have upon the progress of manufacturing for export?
6 What were the characteristics of the firms that were most successful at manufacturing for export?

'Switching' or expanding capacity?

When manufactured exports expand rapidly, particularly when they do so for the first time in a nation's history, it is tempting to attribute such 'success' to the emergence of new export-oriented manufacturing capacity, either in existing industries (and firms) or in new ones. In the countries whose recent experience is analysed in this volume, however, the creation of new industrial capacity cannot, on the face of the evidence, explain much of the expansion in industrial exporting. Rather, manufactured exports are most frequently the product of the redirection of existing manufacturing production from domestic to external markets in response to altered domestic incentives and depressed domestic demand. Except in the case of the new resource-intensive exports from Chile, most of these exports originated from industries (and firms) that had previously substituted for imports and benefited from significant import protection. Many were foreign-owned firms (see also Blömstrom and Lipsey 1993). During the Turkish boom in manufactured exports in the 1980s, while some investment in export-oriented manufacturing did take place in sectors where initial utilization of capacity was high, the share of manufacturing in the total capital stock actually fell (see also Faini 1993). In Tanzania, there was a sharp slowdown in the growth of manufactured exports in 1990 and thereafter, once the potential for redirecting output away from the local market had been exhausted. Equally, in Mexico and Colombia, a pre-existing industrial base, nurtured by a supportive government at least in its earliest stages, was critical to the success of these countries' manufacturing for export in the past two decades. (In Colombia, see also Roberts and Tybout 1992.)

It follows that the maintenance of growth in manufactured exports from these countries will eventually require fresh investments for this purpose. Where investment demand remains constrained by high domestic real interest rates and/or uncertainty as to the sustainability of policies and incentive structures (including access to foreign markets), the booms in manufactured exports may sputter to a halt.

The role of the exchange rate

Increased incentives for exporting were critically important to the expansion of manufactured exports. Appropriate exchange rate policy played a major role in every export 'success' story studied in this volume. Real currency devaluation occurred in all of the sample countries, and it was invariably followed by increases in manufactured exports. Where the real devaluation was sustained, growth in manufactured exports continued or even, as in Chile, accelerated. Sharp nominal currency devaluations were typically accompanied by impressive macroeconomic restraint within stabilization programmes (e.g. in Chile in the mid-1970s, Mexico and Turkey in the early and mid-1980s, and Tanzania in the later 1980s). The Chilean, Mexican and Turkish cases also demonstrate the critical role of real wage restraint in the achievement of stabilization and expansion of manufactured exports; exchange rate policy was validated by appropriately consistent management of real wages. In all of these cases, a significant increase in the relative price of tradables was accompanied by significant real wage reduction and by slackened domestic demand pressure on existing productive capacity. Some of the latter was directly attributable to real currency devaluation as well as tightened fiscal and monetary policy. Together, these changes offered strong encouragement to industrial production for sale on export markets, and made it possible for industrial exports to expand rapidly without, as noted above, any immediate need for new investments for this purpose.

In Colombia, a 'crawling peg' was introduced for the first time as early as 1967, in an effort to stabilize the real exchange rate. The real value of the currency thereafter tended to 'track' the terms of trade, creating increased incentives for manufactured and other non-traditional exports whenever coffee exports faltered, and conversely when they boomed.

Appropriate exchange rate policy, to achieve a domestic relative price of tradables that creates incentives for exports and export-oriented investments, will undoubtedly continue to be critical to the future of manufacturing for export. Such exchange rate policy can only be sustained, however, if it is accompanied by fiscal, monetary and real wages policies that are fully consistent with it.

The role of export subsidies

While the real exchange rate dominated in the determination of the overall structure of incentives for manufactured exports, other export incentives also played a role, particularly in the earlier years before necessary exchange rate 'corrections' had been undertaken and, in later years, to offset real currency appreciations, as in Colombia in 1978 and 1982–4 (though not in 1990–2). Export subsidies were provided to compensate for the disincentives to industrial exporting implicit in industrial import protection and overvalued currencies. They took many forms – import duty rebates and other special tax provisions, subsidized credit, preferential exchange rates (including rights to retain foreign exchange) and direct subsidies – all of which reduced what would otherwise have been a heavy anti-export bias in the overall structure of industrial incentives. Direct export subsidies were important in the early phases of Turkey's export drive (in the early 1980s) and that of Colombia (much earlier, but to varying degrees right up to 1990).

Encouragements provided to manufactured exporters through the credit system were also often important; and they tended to remain, in some form, even when overall anti-export bias had been reduced. This form of support was typically tilted, if only implicitly, in favour of smaller firms. In other respects, however, export subsidy pro-grammes did not generally appear to be consciously targeting particular industries. Nor were the beneficiaries of such support generally required to meet performance standards in order to qualify for continued support.

Governmental support for the conscious building of particular competence and capacity in manufacturing for export did not seem to have been a feature of trade or industrial policy in these countries. As noted above, however, previous overall encouragement of industry (and, in the case of Chile, new areas of primary production like forestry and fruits) certainly did increase countries' eventual capacity to export.

Tighter GATT provisions inhibiting the use of direct or indirect export subsidies will reduce developing countries' resort to this instrument in the future and force greater reliance by governments seeking to encourage non-traditional exports on the exchange rate. Where the real exchange rate is driven, in the short to medium run, by influences other than the long-run 'economic fundamentals' (e.g. volatile capital flows or fluctuations in the terms of trade), the stability of returns to manufacturing for export will therefore presumably suffer. The reduced availability of this potentially stabilizing policy instrument may thus discourage some investment in non-traditional export capacity.

The role of the import regime

On purely theoretical grounds, it is common to associate export performance with the nature of the import regime as well as the export regime. In a general equilibrium analysis, taxes or barriers on imports are equivalent to taxes on exports, a proposition usually known as the 'Lerner symmetry' theorem (for its author). By raising the 'fundamental' (or equilibrium) value of the domestic currency, in such analysis, import barriers discourage exports just as surely as if exports had been taxed directly. Holding long-term capital flows constant, imports and exports must move broadly in parallel over the medium to longer run. Hence it is frequently argued that import liberalization, and the consequent reduction of anti-export bias, is a fundamental requirement for sustained export expansion and, in particular, that of manufactured exports.

There are some flaws, however, in the logic of this argument, and they are amply demonstrated in the case studies in this volume (and in the previous one, Helleiner 1994). First, as has been seen, anti-export bias can be reduced, and frequently has been, via the provision of export subsidies as well as by lowering import barriers. In deploying the symmetry argument, one must therefore begin by measuring the degree of protection (or anti-export bias) *net* of the effect of export subsidies; this may significantly reduce the 'required' degree of import liberalization and/or the effects of removing all trade policy interventions (on both imports and exports).

Second, movements in the real exchange rate – and hence in the price of tradables (exports and import substitutes) relative to non-tradables – can, and frequently do, swamp those in the anti-export bias within the tradables sector. Export expansion can therefore rest upon a high price of exportables relative to non-tradables, rather than a high price of exportables relative to importables. Equally, real currency appreciation can discourage exports even when imports have been fully liberalized.

Third, analysis of only one kind of export, manufactured exports, must employ a model that is more complex than the simple two (or three) sector version featured in the export–import symmetry argument; the determinants and effects of changes in non-manufactured exports will have to be considered separately and this analysis integrated with that of manufacturing for export.

Fourth, the symmetry argument rests on an assumption that there are no unemployed or underemployed resources. In developing country circumstances it may be possible to mobilize previously underutilized factors of production for expanding economic activity. Indeed, in general, the symmetry theorem abstracts from cyclical variation in demand and, for that matter, in balance of payments experience, which may be the prime motivation for the imposition of (short-term) barriers to imports.

Last, and even more fundamentally, the effects of the degree of dispersion of governmental 'wedges' between world and domestic prices for both importables and exportables needs to be analysed, not just the average size of such wedges; trade liberalization will have substantially different effects on the pattern of manufacturing, including that for export, depending upon whether previous governmental interventions had been relatively uniform or diverse from industry to industry.

For all of these reasons, it is easy to contemplate, on theoretical grounds, the possibility of significant expansion of manufactured exports without prior or simultaneous overall import liberalization. In fact, while 'liberal' treatment of the imports of those inputs used in manufactured exports was usually one of the concomitants of rapid expansion in manufacturing for export, the role of across-the-board import liberalization in such successes has generally been rather less clear.

A considerable degree of import liberalization actually took place during the period of study in all of the countries examined. Of the countries studied in this volume, Chile's import liberalization was the most dramatic. Chile began a rapid liberalization process in the mid-1970s, at roughly the same time as (actually shortly after) it undertook a major real currency devaluation, and ended with a low and virtually uniform industrial import tariff and the total elimination of non-tariff barriers by the early 1980s; exporters also received import tariff rebates. The currency devaluation initially buffered the import-substituting industrial sector against some of the effects of the import liberalization, but with subsequent real appreciation, there was considerable 'shakeout' in this sector. Non-traditional (i.e. non-copper) exports expanded extremely rapidly in the late 1970s in response to the new incentives, stagnated with the relatively appreciated currency in the early 1980s, then resumed rapid growth for the rest of the decade. In Chile's case the overall import liberalization sharply reduced incentives for many import-competing industrial activities and increased those for exports, particularly the primary products in which Chile has comparative advantage; for example, fruit, fish, forest products and minerals, and primary processing for export. Import liberalization in Chile thus significantly altered the overall structure of the economy (reducing the relative size of the manufacturing sector) and the structure of manufacturing, particularly encouraging new exports based on Chilean natural resources at the expense of protected import-substituting industry. Hopes for the expansion of manufactured exports and manufacturing more generally rest significantly on the prospects of new industries that are linked, either forward through processing or backward through the supply of inputs, to the rapidly expanding primary exports.

Turkey's import liberalization was more gradual and, in the end, less extreme. It followed the conventionally recommended sequence, beginning with the gradual reduction and removal of import quotas and licences and their replacement with tariffs over the course of the 1980s, followed by the lowering and simplification of tariffs in 1989–90 and thereafter. Accession to the European Free Trade Area and eventually, perhaps, to the European Union will require considerable further liberalization *vis-à-vis* other members and non-members. Manufactured exports, particularly of consumer goods (mainly textiles and clothing), rose very rapidly over the 1981–7 period, in response to the early real currency devaluation, the associated decline in real wages and tight control over domestic aggregate demand. This export success preceded much of the import liberalization. Indeed by the time that the import liberalization had reached more advanced stages in the 1989–93 period, growth in manufactured exports had already slowed dramatically in consequence of emerging macroeconomic imbalances.

The Mexican experience with import liberalization and manufacturing for export was, in some respects, similar to that of Turkey. Liberalization was initially, in the mid-1980s, fairly gradual and accompanied by real currency devaluation that, to some degree, preserved the profitability of import-competing industries. Rapid growth in manufactured exports was not obviously associated with overall import liberalization. (The Mexican study below also casts some doubt as to whether import liberalization improved manufacturing productivity to the degree that has previously been believed.) The most successful manufacturing for export resulted from special industry-specific regimes – in automobiles, computers and the *maquiladora* sector. By the time of the further import liberalizations from 1988 onwards, there had been considerable real appreciation of the currency and, although manufactured exports continued to grow, manufactured imports grew much more quickly. The NAFTA agreement implies a commitment to further import liberalization. Pressure on the import-competing sector, together with continued low investment and low overall productivity growth, threaten new macroeconomic imbalances and the sustainability of the Mexican recovery.

Colombia consciously pursued a 'mixed' policy of simultaneous export promotion and import substitution in the industrial sector from as early as the mid-1950s onwards. (Earlier, Colombia had been pursuing protectionist import substitution strategy for several decades.) As has been seen, exchange rate policy played a major role in this approach; as Colombia was among the first to introduce a 'crawling peg' (in 1967). Changes in the real exchange rate thereafter broadly reflected the economic 'fundamentals', particularly the fortunes of the coffee sector; these changes typically dominated commercial policy changes and, of course, left the incentives for exporting relative to local sales of manufactures broadly unaltered. Moderate efforts at import liberalization were made from time to time – gradually in the 1970s and more quickly in 1985 – but these were not significant in terms of altered manufactured export performance. A major liberalization initiated in 1991 sought to reduce the overall degree of anti-export bias, among other objectives, but its main rationales were overall economic liberalization, in line with the tenor of the times, and reduction of price inflation. The import regime was thus not an important element in Colombia's development of manufacturing for export.

Tanzania retained fairly tight import controls in its post-independence period. These were severely further tightened during the periods of sharp balance of payments shocks in the early 1970s and again from 1979 onwards, with an associated serious over-valuation of its currency. Tanzania began to liberalize imports in 1984. There followed a period of significant further decontrol accompanied by major real currency devaluation. The real depreciation of the currency generated significant changes in the domestic incentive structure and these 'led' (preceded) the further liberalization of the import regime. The unprecedented expansion of manufactured exports was thus, in Tanzania as elsewhere, associated with the former more than with the latter.

Changes in the overall nature of the import regime thus did not, of themselves, play a prominent role in the emergence of successful manufacturing for export in the countries under study. Other influences, notably the real exchange rate, were far more important. In some instances (Mexico and Turkey) import liberalization created macroeconomic imbalance that threatened to impede the process of steady adjustment and growth.

The role of the capital account

An emerging and unanticipated problem in many of the newer industrializing countries, as they strain to expand manufactured exports, is the effect of large changes in the size (and even the direction) of private international capital flow. This has particularly been a problem where, as in Mexico and Turkey in the late 1980s and in Chile a little earlier, international capital flow was liberalized along with other aspects of the economy.

Private capital flows often respond sharply to short-term influences – including interest rates and price/exchange rate expectations – that have little to do with the longer term economic 'fundamentals' or the requirements of successful longer term development strategy. They do so even when these flows are ostensibly subject to foreign exchange controls – through various evasions, leads and lags in foreign receipts and payments, and the like. When efforts to control capital flows, imperfect as they may be, are abandoned, the potential for volatile and disruptive changes in the real exchange rate, driven by private capital flows, is heightened.

Domestic financial liberalization often results in sharp increases in domestic nominal interest rates. When, at the same time that nominal interest rates are 'freed', stabilization achieves a reduction in inflation rates and a stabilization of exchange rates, domestic *real* interest rates can reach very high levels, generating strong incentives for capital inflow, much of it quite short term in its motivation. Such inflows create upward pressure on the value of the currency or domestic monetary expansion (and inflationary pressure) or both.

It has been noted above that the real exchange rate has exerted a major influence upon the performance of manufactured exports. It thus follows that private capital flows, through their effects on the real exchange rate (and potentially on real wages), can impact importantly on export performance, and on other aspects of longer term performance. In the late 1980s, in Mexico and in Turkey, as documented in the studies in this volume, such influences have been important – and probably, on balance, quite negative.

Mexico experienced a massive capital inflow in the late 1980s in response to its domestic stabilization and adjustment programme and its relatively favourable (above all, *vis-à-vis* the USA) interest rates. This capital inflow unfortunately failed, however, to stimulate domestic Mexican investment or associated productivity gains or growth itself. Rather, through its effect on the real exchange rate, it seems to have dampened ('crowded out') domestic savings, worsened the trade deficit and forced continued macroeconomic restraint. Despite real currency appreciation, Mexican manufactured exports continued to grow rapidly – but imports grew more rapidly still. Much of the continued good performance of manufactured exports (as well as the attractiveness of Mexico to foreign capital) depends on the continued restraint of domestic investment and consumption, which may, as in Turkey, prove politically difficult. Import liberalization, in the context of the real currency appreciation associated with capital inflow, it is argued in this volume, is unlikely to be sustainable.

Turkey liberalized domestic financial markets in 1980–1, then began to liberalize its external capital account from 1984 onwards, attaining full convertibility in 1989–90. Foreign capital poured into Turkey in 1989–90, in response to strong interest incentives, generating significant real currency appreciation, at the same time that import liberalization was completed. As in Mexico, imports consequently expanded rapidly. In Turkey, unlike Mexico, macroeconomic and wage restraint did not survive domestic political pressures. Added to the effects of currency appreciation at this time were increases in real wages, which had been severely repressed during the previous period of stabilization and adjustment, and rising fiscal deficits. Together, these developments *reduced* overall savings rates, generated a rising current account imbalance and, eventually, a reversal of the direction of capital flow, and a currency and macroeconomic crisis. The 1980s episode of adjustment, towards manufacturing for export among other objectives, had not been sustainable. Volatile private capital flows – first inward, then outward – had contributed to the breakdown of the adjustment programme.

Chile's capital account liberalization in the late 1970s and early 1980s, accompanying its trade and domestic financial liberalizations, also led to significant capital inflows and real currency appreciation. The heavy external shocks experienced by Chile in 1982 drove the country into a severe macroeconomic crisis, from which it emerged only through major real devaluation, the reintroduction (for a time) of more import protection, and determined subsequent measures to retain the devalued real exchange rate in the face of subsequent surges of capital inflow in the late 1980s and early 1990s (through monetary sterilization via the deployment of new reserve requirements on the banks). As has been seen, Chile's non-traditional exports continued to grow rapidly but, in the main, they were not manufactures (in the standard international meaning of the term).

External capital flows, particularly those engineered by the public sector, also played some role in macroeconomic experience in Colombia and Tanzania but, in both cases, they were much more stable. External shocks were concentrated in the current account.

Volatile flows of private capital can create grave macroeconomic management problems, and thus complicate the orderly processes of development, including manufacturing for export. The liberalization of the capital account has, in some instances, intensified such problems.

Characteristics of exporting firms

Systematic attempts to discover the characteristics of the firms that were most engaged in manufacturing for export were undertaken in some of the studies. Colombia and Chile have particularly rich micro-level data. In Colombia, firms that were exporting manufactures at all in the early 1990s were, on average, larger, less unskilled-labour intensive and less dependent on domestic raw materials than non-exporting firms in the same industries. On the other hand, firms with high export shares of their total sales were smaller, more labour intensive and more reliant on domestic material than those for which exports were less important. Within each industry, there were typically very few exporting firms.

In Chile, both large (100 employees or more) and small firms engaged in manufacturing for export, but large firms were much more prominent in the export than in the non-export manufacturing sector. Generally, whatever the size of firm, exporting firms had higher capital–labour ratios, higher labour productivity and lower value added as a proportion of gross value of production than other firms in the same manufacturing industry.

More empirical research on the micro-level characteristics of the manufacturing firms that move into exporting and, in particular, their investment activities, would help to shed light on the detailed nature of the economic transition that is under way. It could also assist policymakers as they seek to build industrial competitiveness into their overall development (Lall 1990).

AREAS NOT COVERED IN THIS VOLUME

The countries in this volume's sample do not include those that built their manufacturing for export primarily upon 'export platforms' – export processing zones, and the like (although Mexico's *maquiladora* sector played a prominent role in its exporting in an earlier period). Export platforms may have a useful role to play; in small countries the entire economy may constitute such a 'platform'. But, in most instances, such platforms stand outside the mainstream of the industrial sector and the economy, and thus raise issues that differ from those of the *general* economic transition which is the object of study in this volume.

Primary focus here is, rather, upon the *entire* industrial sector and indeed the entire economy. That is not to suggest that the only transition of interest involves the shift, in response to new overall incentives, from import substitution to exporting at the level of individual firms or industries; an effective macro transition involves the introduction of new export-oriented firms and industries as well as an altered orientation in those that already exist. Whether firms and industries that embark upon exporting, both old and new, learn and become more efficient, and whether they remain oriented toward exporting over the longer run, are empirical questions that deserve more research.

It is also important to note, at the outset, another area that this volume does not address. The continued success of manufacturing for export, as with any other kind of export, is clearly more likely with the maintenance and growth of external demand for the products to be sold. Pessimism on this score has been influential in earlier analysis and policy formation with respect to industrialization in developing countries. Apart from the already existing trade barriers against the industrial exports of developing countries in the industrialized countries, which are considerable (despite the still very low levels of overall developing country penetration of their markets), many fear the possible protectionist consequences of significantly accelerated efforts on the part of large numbers of developing countries to sell manufactures in world markets. Such efforts, which are generally recommended to them by economic advisors, may be vulnerable to the 'fallacy of composition'. If so, such effects have not yet manifested themselves in sharply increased protectionist practices. Those developing countries that have performed the best in terms of industrial exporting have so far done so, above all, via their capacities and policies on the supply side (assisted, of course, at the micro-level, by foreign investors and sourcers of imports). Without wishing to minimize the importance of demand-side considerations, and quite considerable risks in this respect in the future, this volume does not devote much attention to them – either at the country level or in the aggregate.

ACKNOWLEDGEMENTS

I am grateful for comments on an earlier draft to Albert Berry, Merih Celasun, Alberto Isgut, Patricio Meller, Benno Ndulu, Dani Rodrik, Hans Singer and Moshe Syrquin, none of whom carries any responsibility for the current version.

REFERENCES

Amsden, Alice, *et al.* (1994) 'Special Section: The World Bank's "East Asian Miracle: Economic Growth and Public Policy"', *World Development* 22, 4, April: 614–70.

Balassa, B. (1979) 'A Stages Approach to Comparative Advantage', in Irma Adelman (ed.) *Economic Growth and Resources, Volume 4, National and International Policies*, London: International Economic Association, Macmillan.

Blejer, M.I. (1978) 'Income Per Capita and the Structure of Industrial Exports: An Empirical Study', *Review of Economics and Statistics*, November.

Blömstrom, Magnus and Lipsey, Robert E. (1993) 'Foreign Firms and Structural Adjustment in Latin America, Lessons from the Debt Crisis', in Göte Hansson (ed.) *Trade, Growth and Development* (109–32), New York: Routledge.

Bradford, Colin I. Jr (1994) 'From Trade-Driven Growth to Growth-Driven Trade: Reappraising the East Asian Development Experience', Paris: OECD Development Centre, Documents.

Faini, Riccardo (1993) 'Export Supply, Capacity, and Relative Prices', Centro Studi Luca D'Agliano–Queen Elizabeth House Development Studies Working Papers, no. 66, October.

Fishlow, A., Gwin, C., Haggard, S., Rodrik, D. and Wade, R. (1994) *Miracle or Design? Lessons from the East Asian Experience*, Washington, DC: Overseas Development Council.

Fosu, A.K. (1990) 'Export Composition and the Impact of Export on Economic Growth of Developing Economies', *Economics Letters* 34: 67–71.

Helleiner, G.K. (ed.) (1994) *Trade Policy and Industrialization in Turbulent Times*, London: Routledge.

Lall, Sanjaya (1990) *Building Industrial Competitiveness in Developing Countries*, Paris: OECD Development Centre.

Roberts, Mark and Tybout, James (1992) 'Sunk Costs and the Decision to Export in Colombia', mimeo.

Sarkar, P. and Singer, H.W. (1991) 'Manufactured Exports of Developing Countries and Their Terms of Trade Since 1965', *World Development* 19, 4, April: 333–40.

UNCTAD (1992) *Handbook of International Trade and Development Statistics, 1992*, Geneva: UNCTAD.

Wade, Robert (1995) 'The East Asian Miracle: Why the Controversy Continues' in UNCTAD, *International Monetary and Financial Issues for the 1990s* (Research Papers for the Group of Twenty-Four), V, Geneva: UNCTAD.

World Bank (1982) *World Development Report 1982*, Washington, DC: World Bank.

World Bank (1993a) *World Development Report 1993*, Washington, DC: World Bank.

World Bank (1993b) *The East Asian Miracle, Economic Growth and Public Policy*, Oxford: Oxford University Press.

2

CHILEAN EXPORT GROWTH, 1970–90: AN ASSESSMENT

Patricio Meller

INTRODUCTION

In Latin America, Chilean economic reforms have been given the status of a standard of reference. The results of these reforms are said to include macroeconomic stability, a high rate of economic growth, and a rapid expansion of exports. Rapid export growth in particular is considered to be the consequence of the full complement of deep economic reforms such as market price liberalization, external opening of the economy, state reform, and privatization.

The profound Chilean structural economic reform process was not a smooth one; there were serious policy mistakes and many policy reversals. At the beginning of the 1980s social costs were heavy and the Chilean economy went through a deep internal and external crisis.[1] By contrast, at the beginning of the 1990s, the Chilean economy exhibited high growth, relatively low rates of price inflation and unemployment and increasing real wages. The successful expansion of Chilean exports is considered to be one of the key elements generating this good economic performance. The importance of structural economic reforms and the role of the exchange rate in promoting exports has been analysed elsewhere (Meller 1994). In this chapter we review some other factors contributing to Chilean export growth, and some issues associated with future export expansion.

The first of the four main sections of this chapter (pages 22–34) undertakes a decomposition of Chilean export expansion patterns during the 1970–90 period. This section suggests that, on the one hand, 30 per cent of the expansion of Chilean exports was due to the role played by Chilean public ownership of large-scale copper mining (LCM). On the other hand, products produced by private

21

entrepreneurs based on natural resources had quite high annual growth rates, representing more than 80 per cent of non-copper exports by 1990. Chile has a comparative advantage in the production of natural resources; however, special government measures have played a key role in the expansion of this type of export.

The second section (pages 34–40) examines Chile's comparative advantage by market destination (developed versus Latin American countries) in respect of three types of export goods: natural resources, industrial goods consisting of processed domestic natural resources, and other industrial products. Given the predominance of natural resources in the export basket – mining (mainly copper), fish, forestry, and fruit – this section also assesses the potential for a 'second export stage', emanating from forward and backward linkages in natural resource export production.

The third section (pages 40–6) provides a comparison of the performance of export and non-export manufacturing firms. This section concludes that, in general, export firms have higher productivity, higher wages, higher investment (in machinery) per worker, and lower value added than non-export firms of the same manufacturing industry. However, non-export firms broadly reveal an increasing trend in real wages with low fluctuations, while real wages in export firms have a highly fluctuating pattern.

The fourth section (pages 46–9) reviews Chilean trade strategy based on the assumption that it is a small country without a 'natural' trade partner. Given the free trade area (FTA) and regional trade bloc arrangements observed in Latin America, it is argued that a small country like Chile cannot remain isolated (i.e. outside specific trade arrangements) if it is to expand exports and investment. In this context, there is a short discussion on the benefits of establishing a Chile–USA FTA and/or the entry of Chile to MERCOSUR (Mercado Común del Sur, the trade bloc of South America's Southern Cone plus Brazil).

OVERVIEW OF THE EXPORT BOOM

Sources of the successful expansion of exports

Prior to 1970 the export mood was pessimistic. It was thought that Chile had to export mainly (or only) copper. Moreover, given the fact that large-scale copper mining (LCM) (representing around 80 per cent of total copper exports) was controlled by foreign firms

(Anaconda and Kennecott, both US companies), export expansion required foreign investment. The reluctance of the two US copper firms to expand their investment in Chile led first to government acquisition of 50 per cent of their shares in 1965–7, and later to complete nationalization in 1971.

Since 1970, however, exports have become a key sector in the economy, increasing from US$1.1 billion to US$8.3 billion in 1990. Three indicators reveal this development:

1 The export share of gross domestic product (GDP), at constant prices, increased from 14.2 per cent in 1970 to 30.2 per cent in 1990 (Table 2.1). Exports increased at 7.9 per cent per year while the GDP growth rate was 1.7 per cent during the 1970–90 period. (The data for subperiods are shown in Table 2.3.)
2 There was an important diversification of the export basket, with the share of copper in total exports reduced from almost 80 per cent in 1970 to less than 48 per cent in 1990 (Table 2.2).
3 The number of Chilean firms exporting more than one million dollars' worth of goods exceeded 500 by 1991.

Table 2.1 The export share of GDP (per cent), Chile 1960–90

Year[a]	Constant prices	Current prices
1960	13.5	16.3
1965	13.9	16.4
1970	14.2	20.2
1975	15.6	22.9
1980	23.0	23.0
1985	25.9	26.7
1990	30.2	37.2

[a] Figures shown are the average of the year shown and the previous year; however, the first figures are the average of the years 1960 and 1961
Source: Central Bank

The standard explanation of events claims that successful Chilean export development is due to the following:

1 Implementation of deep economic reforms – market price liberalization, external opening of the economy, state reform, and privatization; in short, reforms similar to IMF and World Bank policy packages widely recommended for stabilization and structural adjustment.

23

2 Implementation of a large (real) devaluation in 1973–5, and maintenance of a stable and undervalued currency during the 1980s (see
Meller 1994).

3 Neutral policies and neutral incentives, in other words, absence of
industrial policies or specific incentives to promote exports.

This is consistent with the view that elimination of the previous anti-
export bias of the import substitution industrialization strategy
would be a sufficient condition for expansion of exports.

In short, the expansion and diversification of exports in Chile is
being used as an example for Latin America of the successful
application of basic orthodox principles: getting the prices right (i.e.
using world prices), maintaining policy neutrality, and letting the
private sector be the main (and eventually, only) productive agent.
The argument is that the transformation of Chile's highly protected
economy into a new dynamic export economy was the outcome of
implementing the correct 'fundamental' policies.[2]

In this respect, discussion in many other Latin American countries
has focused on how to implement the basic (orthodox) stabilization
and structural reforms without incurring the high social costs
observed in the Chilean case.[3] Moreover, a key question has been,
'Is it possible to implement those reforms without a General
Pinochet?' In this chapter, we shall address a different issue: on
careful analysis of the characteristics of Chilean export growth, is it
true to say that no specific government measures were required? That
is, were private entrepreneurs and market prices the only elements
which contributed to Chile's successful export expansion?

Decomposition of the export expansion

As previously mentioned, copper has played an important role in the
Chilean export basket. Moreover, in spite of its diminishing share in
total exports, copper has still been a key product in the recent
expansion of exports. Of the US$7.2 billion increase in the total value
of exports between 1970 and 1990, 42 per cent was due to the
augmentation of copper exports. A breakdown by decades shows an
increasing share of copper in total export expansion: 31 per cent for
the 1970s and 53 per cent for the 1980s.

LCM generates, on average, more than 75 per cent of total copper
exports. LCM output prior to 1965 was either stagnating or falling,
with a growth rate for the 1960–5 period of –2.1 per cent.[4] During

Table 2.2 Importance of copper in exports, Chile 1960–90

Year	Share of copper in total exports[a] (%)	Volume of copper exports (tons)[a]		Value of copper exports (million US$)	Value of total exports (million US$)
		Large-scale mining	Total		
1960	67.1	469	532	314	470
1965	61.9	438	539	396	684
1970	77.2	514	663	883	1,112
1975	65.1	682	823	1,246	1,590
1980	47.2	865	1,028	2,007	4,705
1985	45.5	1,023	1,288	1,697	3,804
1990	47.8	1,150	1,556	3,908	8,310

[a] Figures shown are the average of two years, the year shown and the previous year; however, the first figures are the averages of the years 1960 and 1961
Source: Central Bank and COCHILCO

Table 2.3 Export growth rates, Chile 1960–90 (annual average, %)

Year	Large-scale copper mining	Copper exports	Non-copper exports	Total exports	GDP
1960–70	1.2[a]	2.7	5.9	3.6	4.2
1970–5	4.5	3.3	9.9	5.6	−2.2
1975–80	6.3	5.8	24.3	15.1	7.5
1980–5	4.2	5.3	−1.2	1.8	−0.4
1985–90	0.7	2.8	15.4	9.6	6.1

[a] A breakdown for 1960–5 and 1965–70 provides the following annual growth rates: −2.1% (1960–5) and 4.6% (1965–70)
Note: Total export growth rates have been calculated from National Accounts (1977 constant prices). Copper export growth rates have been calculated using exported copper tons. Non-copper export growth rates have been obtained as a residual using the average (first and final year of each respective period) of copper and non-copper shares of total exports
Source: Central Bank and COCHILCO

the 1965–85 period, however, with government intervention (public ownership) in LCM, annual output growth rates were higher than 4.2 per cent (Table 2.3). About 30 per cent of the expansion of Chilean exports in the 1970–90 period was due to the role played by public ownership of LCM.[5] Furthermore, a simple econometric regression shows a structural break in LCM output before and after full nationalization of LCM (see Figure 2.1).[6]

It seems strange that under a military dictatorship where orthodox monetarist economists were implementing deep reforms oriented towards the reduction of the role played by the state in the economy,

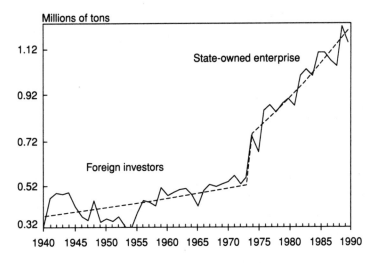

Figure 2.1 Large-scale copper mining (LCM), Chile 1940–90

there was a significant expansion of the output generated by a public enterprise (LCM). One simple explanation would be related to the importance of LCM in fiscal revenues. LCM generated 3.4 per cent of GDP per year as fiscal revenue during the 1980–90 period and 2.6 per cent of GDP per year during the 1960–90 period (Romaguera 1991). However, there is a more crucial element. In 1976 a special law was enacted (Ley Reservada del Cobre) which allocated 10 per cent of LCM export earnings (in US$) directly to the armed forces (as special resources for buying armaments).[7] Hence, the armed forces were a special interest group, directly interested in the expansion of LCM output.

Illustrating Chilean comparative advantage in copper production, the sharp increase of LCM output during the 1970–90 period augmented the Chilean world export copper share from 14 per cent (during the 1950s and 1960s) to almost 20 per cent (during the 1980s).[8] From 1985 on, private investment (especially foreign investment) helped to increase Chilean copper exports. The relative share of the public sector in total copper exports fell from around 85 per cent prior to 1985 to less than 75 per cent at the beginning of the 1990s.

Non-copper exports had uneven growth rates (Table 2.3); the high growth rates observed in the 1970s were from a small initial base. Non-copper exports amounted to US$272 million in 1970; they increased to US$2.5 billion in 1980 and to US$4.5 billion in 1990 (Table 2.4). In the 1985–90 period non-copper exports had a 15.4 per cent annual growth rate, constituting the main factor behind the recent high total export and GDP growth rates (9.6 per cent and 6.1 per cent respectively; see Table 2.3).

Let us look more closely at the composition of non-copper exports and its evolution through time (Table 2.4). Natural resources (NR) or products based on domestic NR represented more than 80 per cent of non-copper exports in 1990. Agriculture (mainly fruit), forestry, and fish exports, all of which were practically negligible in 1970, each reached figures around US$900 million by 1990. Non-copper mining also experienced a significant increase to a similar level of annual exports (US$795 million in 1990). Almost all of this export expansion was generated by private entrepreneurs.

Table 2.4 Composition of non-copper exports, Chile 1970–90
(million US$/% of total non-copper exports each year)

Year	Mining (non-copper)	Agricultural products	Fish and sea products	Forestry and wood products	Total non-copper exports
1970	111 (40.8)	30 (11.0)	1 (0.4)	10 (3.7)	272
1975	185 (27.9)	76 (11.5)	35 (5.3)	126 (19.0)	662
1980	619 (24.6)	281 (11.2)	291 (11.6)	591 (23.5)	2,518
1985	567 (27.5)	452 (21.9)	338 (16.4)	314 (15.2)	2,062
1990	795 (17.6)	962 (21.3)	915 (20.3)	870 (19.3)	4,515

Note: The difference between the values of Tables 2.4 and 2.3 is due to the fact that balance of payment figures are used in Table 2.3, while Customs Export Declarations are used in this table
Source: Central Bank, Customs Export Declarations

Table 2.5 provides a comparison of the export growth rates of the main Chilean NR non-copper (and non-mining) products with those of Latin America and the world for the 1970–90 period. Growth rates of Chilean grape and apple exports (18.5 per cent and 9.4 per cent respectively) were three times greater than world export growth rates. Chilean export growth rates of raw fish and fish meal (fluctuating between 13 per cent and 26 per cent per year) were much greater than the corresponding world growth rates. Chilean export growth rates of sawn wood and wood pulp (around 9 per cent per year) were two to three times greater than world growth rates. These seven products (shown in Table 2.5), each showing high growth rates, represent around 40 per cent of Chilean non-copper exports.

Table 2.5 Comparison of export growth rates between Chile, Latin America and the world, for specific fruit, fish and forestry products, 1970–90

Exports	Growth rates (1970–90[a]) (%)			Export level (1990) (million US$)		
	Chile	Latin America	World	Chile	Latin America	World
Grapes	18.5	16.5	6.0	379	405	1,661
Apples	9.4	2.3	3.4	131	210	2,067
Fish capture[b]	3.0	−4.9	−3.6	6.4[c]	17.9[c]	99.5[c]
Fish products[b]	13.3	3.9	7.1	896	3,447	32,787
Raw fish[b]	26.0	14.7	8.8	207	747	13,193
Fish meal[b]	13.4	0.0	0.5	515	958	1,640
Forestry products	9.3	7.0	4.4	750	2,743	94,470
Sawn wood	8.3	0.4	3.5	136	426	16,989
Wood pulp	9.6	14.0	3.5	326	962	15,817
Paper and cardboard	2.8	12.7	6.2	82	830	45,268

[a] Annual growth rates shown have been calculated using the current value of exports, transformed into constant US$ (1990) using the US wholesale price index
[b] Growth rates are for the period 1970–89 and the export level is for the year 1989
[c] Millions of tons
Source: CEPAL 1992

This NR export potential existed in Chile before 1970; what are the factors explaining its increase during the 1970s and the 1980s? Among the possible explanations are the deep structural economic reforms of the 1970s and 1980s which changed domestic relative prices, aligning them with international relative prices; the removal of tariff and non-tariff barriers and the elimination of other industrial policies, reducing the pro-industry bias in the incentive structure; and the maintenance of a high real exchange rate.[9] There were also, however, special government measures and incentives which helped non-copper NR export expansion directly. It is to these latter measures that we now turn.

Government measures encouraging export expansion

We examine three types of measures: sector-specific taxes and subsidies, broad government policies related to a specific sector, and general subsidies to exporters.

Forestry has been subject to specific sectoral tax treatment for a long time. A special law of 1931 (Ley de Bosques) made forestry an income-tax-free activity for thirty years after a tree was planted. This law was replaced in 1974 by a new one (Decree 701). Decree 701 established two types of benefits exclusively for forestry (these benefits do not extend to wood-processing activities):

1 A direct subsidy of 75 per cent of costs.
2 A special 50 per cent tax credit on income generated by forestry.

However, the 1974 law envisaged the complete elimination of forestry tax benefits by 1996. Hence, during the 1974–96 period, forestry benefited from two special elements of tax treatment; however, the 75 per cent financing of the costs of activity had the most significant impact on the sector.

Newly forested area increased from 329,000 acres in 1970 to 1.9 million acres in 1980 and 3.9 million acres in 1990.[10] Chile has around 7.4 million acres of privately owned land which have been appropriated for forestry and wood production. It is now claimed that Chilean land has a comparative advantage in forestry, but this land has always been there and in private hands. Private entrepreneurs apparently required the special government credit and tax benefit treatment in order to exploit their NR comparative advantage. The fiscal cost of the special tax and subsidy treatment of forestry has been estimated to be around US$20 to 30 million per year (Bitrán and Fierro 1988). This figure is about 3 per cent of current forest and wood products exports, which is a sharp reduction from an almost 10 per cent estimate for 1985.

Chile has become an important world fruit exporter. Grape and apple exports had annual growth rates of 18.5 per cent and 9.4 per cent respectively during the 1970–90 period (Table 2.5). The shares of Chilean exports in world exports of grapes and apples increased from 2.5 per cent and 1.0 per cent in 1970 to 22.8 per cent and 6.4 per cent in 1990 (CEPAL 1992). Chile has a comparative advantage in the production of temperate fruit; moreover, given its opposite season schedule, temperate Chilean fruit production is available in the main developed countries' markets during their winter season.

Private sector technological achievements (improvements in orchard management and post-harvest techniques) played an important role in the spectacular increase of fruit exports. (For details, see Jarvis 1991 and CEPAL 1990.)

Why were private entrepreneurs able to introduce modern technology and innovations in the fruit production sector? At least part of the answer involves broad public sector measures taken in the 1960s, which played an important role in the Chilean fruit exports of the 1980s.[11] In 1964 a semi-autonomous agricultural technological research institute (INIA) was created, hiring highly paid professionals, which had a broad mandate for doing research. In 1965 a ten-year Chile–University of California programme was established which assigned high priority to graduate training of agricultural economists (at Davis). California and a large part of Chile have similar temperate climates, and during the 1960s it was thought that it could be useful for Chile to learn about California fruit production. The result of the INIA and the Chile–California universities relationship was to enable Chile to 'acquire frontier knowledge about modern fruit science and its applications' and update Chilean universities' agricultural economics curricula. Moreover, an academic relationship was established which became an important mechanism for later technology transfer (Jarvis 1991: 6).

This new sector-specific human capital and knowledge was critical to the identification and planting of new fruit varieties which fit foreign consumption patterns, and also contributed to orchard improvement and better harvest management. The private sector accessed this expertise by paying much higher wages than universities and public research institutes, thereby attracting skilled personnel. After 1974, and related to the deep economic reforms, there was a sharp diminution of fruit research at INIA and universities. The basic rationale for this was that since the private fruit export sector was the main one benefiting from such research, it should pay for it, and scarce public resources should not be devoted to it.

Public institutions and universities[12] also contributed directly to the introduction, adaptation, and innovation of modern fruit technologies (Jarvis 1991). In particular:

1 To avoid grapes rotting during long transport trips, SO_2 pads were developed by CORFO (Corporación de Fomento) at the end of the 1960s, and were later introduced and further developed by private fruit exporters.

2 The substitution of existing Chilean seeded grapes by seedless varieties was pursued via a joint research venture between university researchers and private producers.

3 Grape fumigation in the cooling process to overcome insect pests was also designed through a joint research project between a public research institute, fruit exporters, and US officials.

In each of these technological developments the existing Californian technology was the starting point; Chilean officials identified the California technological solution to a given problem, and then tested its application and adapted it to the specific Chilean fruit situation.

In short, government programmes and measures introduced in the 1960s, like specific human capital training, the development of technological research institutes, and the link with a comparable developed area (California), were key complementary factors in fruit export expansion; as will be seen, private entrepreneurs were the key agents in the implementation of modern technology processes. Jarvis (1991) has pointed out that with the dismantling of Chilean fruit research capacity, while existing human capital is sufficient to adapt available technology and to help in its diffusion, there did not thereafter exist human capital able to develop new technology or to face new problems. Given the important role acquired by Chile in the world fruit export market, this may constitute a bottleneck in the future.

One of the special incentives provided to the export sector was a mechanism for the reimbursement of tariffs paid on imported inputs. In order to qualify, exporters had to provide all the documentation related to the importation of inputs and the effective payment of the tariff duties. This process turned out to be quite cumbersome for exporters. Therefore, a simplified tariff reimbursement process was established for small exporters.

The special benefits (simplified tariff reimbursements) for small exporters changed over time. When the mechanism was established in 1985, in order to qualify as a small exporter the annual average level of a given disaggregated category of export goods had to be smaller than US$2.5 million (in 1983–4). These small exporters would then be entered on a special small exporters list, to receive automatically a reimbursement of 10 per cent of their total exports, the assumed tariffs paid for the imported inputs used in the export production process.[13] This type of reimbursement benefit was to be received by small exporters only until the level of the disaggregated category of exports reached US$7.5 million, at which point the automatic reimbursement disappeared. In 1987, to overcome this discontinuity, a new reimbursement rate of 5 per cent was established for goods with an export level above the previous maximum, up to a new ceiling of US$11.25 million. The 'trigger' export levels were also indexed, reaching the level of US$10 million (for the previous US$7.5 million level) and US$15 million (for the previous US$11.25 million level) by 1990. In 1992, a third reimbursement rate of 3 per cent was established for export goods categories in the US$15 million to US$18 million range.

In 1992 Chilean small exporters exporting less than US$10 million of a particular category had a simplified imported inputs tariff reimbursement rate of 10 per cent; small exporters in the US$10 million to US$15 million range had a tariff reimbursement rate of 5 per cent; and small exporters in the US$15 million to US$18 million range had a tariff reimbursement rate of 3 per cent. The total amount of reimbursements to small exporters through the use of this mechanism increased from US$25 million in 1986 to US$96 million in 1991 (Table 2.6). The total value of exports benefiting from the broader export subsidy mechanism increased from US$246 million in 1986 to over US$900 million in 1991.

There was an implicit subsidy to small exporters in the use of this automatic imported inputs tariff reimbursement mechanism. Calculations done for two years (1988 and 1989) indicate that effective tariff payments of small exporters would have been equal to only 60 per cent of the automatic reimbursement received (Table 2.7); i.e. of the US$96 million of simplified tariff reimbursement received by small exporters during 1991, around US$38 million was subsidy, which is equivalent to 4 per cent of the total level of minor exports

Table 2.6 Imported inputs tariff reimbursement to small exporters, Chile 1986–91 (million US$)

Year	Amount of reimbursement	Total value of exports benefiting from reimbursement
1986	25	246
1987	37	368
1988	54	571
1989	66	738
1990	71	786
1991	96	908

Source: Central Bank

Table 2.7 Implicit subsidy to small exporters, Chile 1988–9 (millions US$)

| | 1988 | | | | 1989 | | | |
	Industry	Agriculture	Mining	Total	Industry	Agriculture	Mining	Total
Simplified tariff reimbursement	37	12	1	50	42	15	1	58
Tariff payment	26	2	1	29	33	2	1	36
Implicit subsidy	11	10	0	21	9	13	0	22

Source: Central Bank and calculations using 1986 input–output matrix

benefiting from this mechanism. Whereas this subsidy system, based on category-specific maxima, established upper bounds on the level of subsidies, it also stimulated the export of new types of goods.

This general simplified imported inputs tariff reimbursement mechanism provided a subsidy that was discriminatory among small exporters (Table 2.7). Small exporters in agriculture received the largest implicit subsidy because their production process is least intensive in imported inputs. Their subsidy corresponded to around 9 percentage points of the 10 per cent reimbursement rate (Table 2.7). Small mining exporters were at the other extreme. They did not receive any implicit subsidy, since they have a high share of imported goods in total inputs. Small industrial exporters received a subsidy equivalent to 2.5 percentage points of the 10 per cent automatic reimbursement rate (Table 2.7).

To summarize, the three export promotion measures used in Chile and their rationales were as follows:

1 Implicit subsidies were offered to small exporters, to help to reduce barriers to entry in new export goods markets; this can be considered an infant export subsidy which is bounded in dollar terms at a given export category level.
2 Specific tax incentives were offered to forestry production, to offset the high time discount rate prevailing among entrepreneurs in this very long gestation-period sector; in the forestry sector, subsidy measures were more effective when they were provided at the beginning of the productive process rather than at the end (witness the effects of the 1931 and 1974 Chilean laws upon forestation).

3 Public investment was undertaken in specific human capital training, research and technology in the fruit sector, to capture positive externalities in technology transfer. The California link shows the importance of having a specific concrete technological model which can be imitated; moreover, in this case, it provided the required external expertise for solving specific domestic technological problems.

CHILE'S COMPARATIVE ADVANTAGE

Revealed comparative advantage

To examine Chile's revealed comparative advantage, we consider a breakdown of the structure of Chilean exports (in 1991) according to the following two dimensions:[14] type of export good, comprising natural resources (NR), industrial goods based on further processing of NR exports (PNR),[15] and other industrial products (OIP);[16] and market destination, including the United States, the European Economic Community (EEC), Japan, and the Latin American (LA) markets. More than 80 per cent of Chilean exports go to these four markets (Table 2.8).

Exports destined for developed country markets are highly intensive in NR. In 1991 NR exports constituted more than 61 per cent of exports going to the USA and Japan and almost 70 per cent of exports to the EEC. PNR exports constitute the second category of importance in exports to developed countries, making up about 30 per cent of total exports to each of these developed country markets. Finally, the OIP export category represents only slightly more than 10 per cent of exports to the US market; this percentage is only 5 per cent and 1 per cent in the cases of the EEC and Japan, respectively. In the case of exports to Latin America, there is a more even composition for the three categories: PNR (38 per cent), NR (35 per cent), and OIP (27 per cent).

The EEC and Japan markets make up 26.6 per cent and 21 per cent, respectively, of total exports of PNR industrial goods; the USA and LA absorb around 16 per cent respectively. LA represents the main market for OIP exports, with a 38 per cent share of the total; the EEC and the USA constitute 18 per cent and 15 per cent of total OIP exports, while Japan accounts for less than 3 per cent.

There is considerable similarity in the structure of Chilean exports to the developed countries; NR and PNR make up more than

Table 2.8 Sectoral distribution of exports according to market destination, Chile 1991 (%)

Sector	USA	EEC	Japan	Latin America	Rest	Total (%)	Total (mill. US$)
Natural resources (NR)							
Mining[a]	9.7	38.5	24.5	8.5	18.8	100.0	4,037
Fruit and vegetable	48.2	35.7	0.7	7.2	8.3	100.0	1,081
Cattle	8.5	49.9	1.1	30.0	10.5	100.0	22
Fish	57.3	31.8	8.4	0.8	1.7	100.0	111
Forestry	0.7	6.3	30.1	1.3	61.6	100.0	67
Subtotal	18.4	37.4	19.3	8.1	16.8	100.0	5,319
Processed natural resources (PNR)							
Mining	39.3	31.4	6.2	13.2	10.0	100.0	451
Fruit and vegetable	25.6	16.9	9.3	33.3	15.0	100.0	505
Cattle	0.1	17.1	19.7	51.8	11.3	100.0	43
Fish	8.5	34.7	25.4	2.4	29.0	100.0	977
Forestry	8.0	21.0	30.5	22.5	18.0	100.0	872
Subtotal	16.1	26.6	21.0	16.5	19.9	100.0	2,849
Other industrial products (OIP)							
Chemical	15.5	18.0	4.2	29.0	33.2	100.0	507
Textiles	35.5	14.4	0.1	40.9	9.0	100.0	148
Basic metals	11.3	10.3	0.1	68.7	9.6	100.0	181
Other	20.2	5.3	0.1	12.5	61.9	100.0	45
Subtotal	18.2	15.2	2.5	38.3	25.8	100.0	881
Total	17.6	31.8	18.2	13.7	18.7	100.0	9,049

[a] This sector includes refined copper
Source: Campero and Escobar 1992

90 per cent of total exports going to those markets. However, there are some differences in the type of NR and PNR exported to each of these markets. Exports of mining NR go mainly to the EEC and Japan, while exports of mining PNR go to the USA and the EEC. In the case of NR exports of fruits and vegetables and fish, the USA and the EEC are the main markets. PNR exports of fish and forestry go mainly to the EEC and Japan. In the OIP category, LA and the USA are the most important markets for basic metals and textile products.

Examining the evolution of exports to developed countries in the 1986–91 period, Campero and Escobar (1992) found a negative association between NR exports and the corresponding industrial PNR exports to the same market destination; for example, forestry exports to the USA fell while processed forestry exports increased; a similar situation was observed in the cases of fish and cattle. This finding would suggest that there is substitution in the Chilean export market between NR and the corresponding PNR for a given market destination.

The present structure of Chilean exports suggests that Chile's comparative advantage with respect to developed countries is in NR; the observed increase of Chilean industrial exports to these markets would seem to be related to the expansion of PNR. In relation to Latin America, Chile's comparative advantage, in addition to traditional NR, seems to be in PNR and in some specific OIP (basic metals, chemicals, textiles). Chile's textile exports to the USA and to LA suggest that there is further potential for OIP exports.

The conclusions can be complemented by data on the composition of planned real investment by economic sector (Table 2.9). If investment projects in infrastructure (including transportation) and non-tradables (energy, telecommunications) are excluded, mining and industries related to PNR accounted for around 90 per cent of the total amount of investment in 1990–5.

The second export stage

The recent Chilean export boom has been mainly based on exports of NR. There are several possible drawbacks to a development strategy based on NR exports. First, NR have low price and income elasticities of demand; therefore, the rate of expansion of NR exports will eventually fall to low levels. Moreover, the long-run terms of trade tend to move against NR. These were the basic arguments used to promote the implementation of the earlier import substituting

Table 2.9 Investment projects by economic sector, Chile 1990–5 (million US$)

Mining	5,373
Industry[a]	5,199
Energy	4,921
Telecommunications	1,517
Infrastructure	1,067
Transport	1,035
Tourism	401
Total[b]	19,691

[a] 70 per cent to 80 per cent of these industrial projects are related to processing of Chilean natural resources
[b] This figure includes other minor investments
Source: Aninat 1990. This table is based on a survey of 442 investment projects of the private and public sectors

strategy. Second, most NR exports go to the developed countries. Given the low growth rates lately observed in those countries, this generates a further constraint on the demand for NR. This is an argument for export diversification of not only goods but also market destinations. Third, the 'enclave' nature of mining has been seen as a problem throughout Chilean history, notably in the cases of nitrate mining at the end of the nineteenth century (Chile was the largest world nitrate exporter prior to World War I) and of copper during the 1930–70 period. An extreme version of this perception posits that Chile has benefited very little from enclave mineral exports (especially when it was conducted by foreign investment): 'after the total exploitation of the mine, the only things left are ghost towns and big holes'. Finally, the new theories of international trade and growth stress the importance of using and developing modern technology. Exports of NR are generally thought to use a low level of technology so that the overall economy does not enjoy any technological externalities from them. This is an argument for promoting exports of industrial goods which require the use of modern technology.

These arguments have been used to suggest the need to move to a second export stage. The discussion of the second export stage focuses on the achievement of more value added to current NR exports, through processing. In other words, this second export stage is based on the idea of promoting NR forward linkages; for example, by exporting apple juice, wine, and canned fruit (instead of fresh grapes and apples), wood furniture and paper (instead of sawn wood), manufactured copper products, etc. The implicit assumption is that PNR goods will introduce and disseminate modern technology, generating therefore greater domestic externality effects.

There are several different issues in the promotion of a second export stage strategy. As previously observed, there seems to be a natural sequence in the evolution of exports, so that it may be that no special promotion measures would be required. Exports of some PNR could be expected to increase naturally in markets to which raw NR are already being exported. Table 2.10 shows the recent export evolution (1970–90) of three products included in the PNR category. The main export expansion of these types of PNR export took place in the final part of the 1980s. It is possible that specific incentives could have sped this process, and, also, could have increased the number of products included in the PNR export category. One of the key issues is the rationale for promoting the specific export of PNR in preference to other types of exports. The goals of export diversification and use of modern technology, for example, have been achieved by exports of fruit. Let us look at these issues in more detail.

Table 2.10 Evolution of processed natural resource exports, Chile 1970–90 (million US$)

	1970	1980	1985	1990
Fish meal	16	203	282	515
Wine	2	19	11	52
Paper and cardboard	15	49	66	82

Source: CEPAL 1992

Even though grapes and apples constitute the main fruit exports (see Tables 2.5 and 2.11), Chile has achieved a considerable diversification in its fruit export basket. During the 1990s fruit exports include (besides grapes and apples) pears, peaches, plums, kiwis, avocados, nectarines, apricots, cherries, berries and lemons. (See Table 2.11 for the evolution of exports of some of these fruits during the 1970–90 period.) Again, most of this export expansion was concentrated at the end of the 1980s.

Overall figures related to Chilean fruit production and export show the following (Jarvis 1991):

1 Area planted increased at 8.1 per cent per year during the 1980s.
2 Fruit production had a 10.9 per cent annual growth rate during the

whole decade of the 1980s, and a 12.0 per cent growth rate in the second half of the 1980s.

3 Fruit export volume increased at 16.9 per cent per year during the 1980s.

4 At the end of the 1980s fruit exports represented 43.3 per cent of total fruit production.

In short, Chile has become the main Latin American fruit exporting country (see Tables 2.5 and 2.11). Given its relatively small share of world exports, and the advantage of its inverse season with respect to the developed countries, there is still the possibility of further expansion of Chilean fruit exports. However, it is not expected that the 1980s fruit export expansion will be repeated during the 1990s.

Table 2.11 Evolution of new types of fruit exports, Chile 1970–90 (million US$)

	1970	1980	1985	1990	Chilean export share – 1990 Latin America (%)	World (%)
Pears	1	11	13	45	41.3	6.5
Peaches	1	7	22	55	97.2	6.9
Plums	–	3	11	40	94.1	16.6
Kiwi	0	0	0	28	100.0	4.5
Avocado	0	0	1	26	61.7	14.2

Source: CEPAL 1992

The case of fruit exports provides a different perspective as to how to proceed in a second export stage strategy. While the strategy of expansion of PNR exports stresses forward linkages as the mechanism for the introduction of modern technology, fruit exports show that the exploitation of backward linkages can also have an important effect upon domestic use of modern technology. Exporting fresh fruit is a highly complex process requiring careful coordination and surveillance of the whole production, distribution, wholesale, and retail trade chain (for a deeper discussion see CEPAL 1990; Jarvis 1991). The preservation of fresh quality requires the establishment of a cooling system that keeps constant temperatures in the different stages of production and wholesale trade. This cooling system involves the use of controlled temperature storage sites and containers, refrigerated trucks and refrigerated ships. High technology equipment and specialized human capital are required to handle large volumes of fruit which have to be preserved in fresh condition. Moreover, Chilean ports have had to upgrade operation systems, install special isolated temperature control storage places, and speed up ship loading systems. To avoid rotting and pests in the many different stages, fumigation must be incorporated into the cooling system, and special modern packaging is required. Also, modern technology is used to produce a standard-sized high quality fruit product fitting developed country consumers' tastes. Furthermore, with rapid expansion of fruit exports, more land has been planted, in some cases on hillsides or in the northern part of Chile where water is scarce. This has required the introduction of a variety of new technologies, such as sophisticated drip irrigation systems. Some of this technology was imported together with human capital skills, but some was also developed locally using domestic human capital.

Backward linkages induced by fruit exports have therefore required the introduction of technological innovations. It would be very difficult to specify which type of technology has the largest beneficial externality effect in the overall economy: the technology used in the forward processing of NR exports or the technology used in the backward linkages related to fruit exports. Mining is another NR export sector which could have backward linkage technological effects similar to those observed in fruit exports. However, in spite of the level of Chilean mining exports, not much seems so far to have happened in this regard; and there are no studies examining this issue.

Finally, the Asian manufactured export pattern shows the possibility of moving into higher export processing stages in product lines totally unrelated to the domestic availability of NR. There are only a few export goods of this nature in the Chilean export basket (Table 2.8). A key issue in the second export stage discussion is whether a specific industrial policy is required. Should there be specific promotion of particular types of exports? If so, what should be the criteria for their selection? What incentives should be used?

A COMPARISON OF EXPORT AND NON-EXPORT MANUFACTURING FIRMS

A sample of Chilean manufacturing export and non-export firms in five ISIC industries was used to compare relative labour productivity (value added per worker), wages, investment per worker, and value added/gross value of production (Y/V). A firm was considered an exporter if at least 30 per cent of its production was destined for foreign markets. A firm was considered 'non-export' if 100 per cent of its production was destined for the domestic market. Firms were separated by size; small firms have less than 100 workers, while large firms have 100 or more workers. The information for each firm was obtained annually for a four-year period (1986–9). The information provided in Tables 2.12 to 2.16 shows median values.[17] The sample has 138 export firms (38 small and 100 large) and 436 non-export firms (364 small and 72 large).

A comparison of average labour productivity (value added per worker) of export and non-export firms at the industry level provides the following results (Table 2.12):

1 Small export firms have higher labour productivity than small non-export firms; the labour productivity differential is around 30 to 40 per cent for wine (313) and wood products (331), and higher than 100 per cent for food (311), chemical (35) and basic metal products (37).

2 Large export firms have higher labour productivity in general than large non-export firms; in three industries – food (311), wine (313), and wood (331) – the differential is around 100 per cent. However, in chemicals (35), large non-export firms show 10 per cent higher labour productivity than export firms.

3 Considering only exporters, large firms show a labour productivity differential greater than 100 per cent in three industries – wine, wood products, and basic metals – and a 12 per cent differential in the food industry. On the other hand, small chemical firms have a higher than 200 per cent labour productivity differential with respect to large chemical firms.

4 Considering only non-exporters, large firms show systematically higher labour productivity than small firms; the magnitude of the labour productivity differential fluctuates between 15 per cent and 42 per cent.

Table 2.13 provides the results of non-parametric and parametric tests of (average) labour productivity differentials between all export and non-export firms. The results show that both in small and large firms, there are significant differences in the level of (average) labour productivity between export and non-export firms. Moreover, the negative sign of the Wilcoxon Z statistics indicates that workers in export firms have consistently higher productivity levels than those of non-export firms, in both small and large firms. The parametric

Table 2.12 Average labour productivity for export and non-export manufacturing firms, Chile (1989 dollars per worker)

ISIC	Industry	Export firms				Non-export firms			
		Small firms	No. of firms	Large firms	No. of firms	Small firms	No. of firms	Large firms	No. of firms
311	Food	12,090	(16)	13,495	(72)	5,264	(44)	6,082	(20)
313	Wine	9,848	(4)	20,707	(4)	7,769	(20)	10,983	(4)
331	Wood products	7,397	(6)	16,082	(14)	5,090	(150)	6,611	(16)
35	Chemicals	40,659	(10)	12,017	(4)	9,200	(144)	13,362	(32)
37	Basic metals	19,661	(2)	58,039	(6)	6,911	(6)	–	(0)

Small firm = less than 100 persons
Large firm = 100 or more persons

Table 2.13 Tests for productivity differentials among export and non-export firms, Chile

Type of firm	Non-parametric tests		Parametric test
	Sign	Wilcoxon[a]	mean differences[b]
Small	−4.26	4.72	
	(0.000)	(0.000)	(0.000)
Large	−3.06	4.03	
	(0.012)	(0.002)	(0.001)

Small firm = less than 100 persons
Large firm = 100 or more persons
[a] Z statistics of Wilcoxon test
[b] t statistics
Note: Numbers in parentheses indicate the probability of error by rejecting the null hypothesis of equal means

test of mean differences supports this result; the null hypothesis of equal means (for labour productivity levels) among export and non-export firms (for small and large firms separately) is rejected at the 1 per cent level of significance.

Labour productivity differentials should generate wage differentials. A comparison of wage differentials among exporting and non-exporting firms at the industry level shows the following (Table 2.14):

1 Small export firms pay higher wages than small non-export firms; wage differentials correspond to the previous labour productivity differentials at (each) industry level. However, wage differentials are in general higher than labour productivity differentials.
2 Large export firms pay higher wages than large non-export firms; in this case, wage differentials are smaller than labour productivity differentials.
3 Considering only exporting firms, large firms in general pay higher wages than small firms; the opposite is the situation in the basic metals industry.
4 Considering only non-exporting firms, large firms pay higher wages than small firms; the magnitude of the wage differentials is greater than the labour productivity differentials.
5 Interestingly, there has been a different evolution of real wages in export and non-export firms. Non-export firms (both small and large) show, in general (real) wages not only with an increasing trend but also with low fluctuation. On the other hand (real) wages in export firms (small and large) have a high degree of fluctuation.

The same non-parametric and parametric tests as those shown in Table 2.13 for labour productivity differentials among export and non-export firms were undertaken for wage differentials; the results obtained were similar to those shown in Table 2.13:

1 The null hypothesis of equal means for wage levels among export and non-export firms (for small and large firms separately) is rejected at the 1 per cent level of significance.

2 Workers of export firms have consistently higher wages than those from non-export firms. (For more details see Meller and Repetto 1994.)

Labour productivity differentials should be generated by differences in investment. The comparison of differences in investment in machinery among export and non-export firms at the industry level shows the following (Table 2.15):

1 Small export firms have invested in machinery per worker between three and ten times more than small non-export firms in four industries (food, wine, wood products, basic metal products).

2 Large export firms show investment in machinery per worker which is between 20 per cent and 50 per cent higher than in large non-export firms in two industries (food and wine); these figures increase to 180 and 280 per cent for wood products and chemicals, respectively.

3 Large export firms in general show higher investment (in machinery) per worker than small export firms.

Again, the same non-parametric and parametric tests as before were applied for investment (in machinery) per worker differentials among export and non-export firms, and similar results as before were obtained. (For more details, see Meller and Repetto 1994.)

Comparing the Y/V (value added/gross value of production) of export and non-export firms at the industry level it is observed (Table 2.16) that:

1 Small export firms in general have smaller Y/V coefficients than small non-export firms in four industries: food, wine, chemical, and basic metal products; the opposite is observed in the wood products industry.

2 Large export firms have smaller Y/V coeffients than large non-export firms in only two industries: wine and chemical; there are no clear differences in the other two industries, food and wood products. A relatively smaller Y/V coefficient suggests that in the

Table 2.14 Average annual wages for export and non-export manufacturing firms, Chile (1989 dollars per worker)

ISIC	Industry	No. of Firms	Small firms				No. of firms	Large firms			
			1986	1987	1988	1989		1986	1987	1988	1989
Export firms											
311	Food	(16)	2,178	2,548	2,319	2,753	(72)	2,744	2,803	2,686	3,416
313	Wine	(4)	2,731	3,263	2,695	2,846	(4)	2,813	2,878	3,489	4,355
331	Wood products	(6)	1,525	1,641	1,680	1,788	(14)	2,204	1,784	2,376	3,305
35	Chemical	(10)	5,199	4,800	4,668	5,050	(4)	3,738	6,409	6,522	6,481
37	Basic metal	(2)	9,006	9,125	6,882	7,314	(6)	8,397	6,401	6,998	6,718
Non-export firms											
311	Food	(44)	1,239	1,168	1,115	1,301	(20)	1,572	1,506	2,087	2,251
313	Wine	(20)	1,313	1,247	1,271	1,285	(4)	1,734	1,755	1,994	2,357
331	Wood products	(150)	1,186	1,186	1,325	1,433	(16)	1,546	1,813	2,042	2,396
35	Chemical	(144)	2,079	2,115	2,093	2,379	(32)	3,060	3,516	3,600	3,691
37	Basic metal	(6)	2,002	2,136	2,480	2,007	(0)	–	–	–	–

Small firm = less than 100 persons
Large firm = 100 or more persons
Note: Wage figures indicate the median value of small and large firms of the respective ISIC industry

Table 2.15 Investment in machinery per person for export and non-export manufacturing firms, Chile (1989 dollars per worker)

ISIC	Industry	Export firms		Non-export firms	
		Small firms	Large firms	Small firms	Large firms
311	Food	3,130	6,132	969	5,058
313	Wine	4,151	1,360	494	895
331	Wood products	2,847	4,744	555	1,702
35	Chemical	4,731	10,700	3,006	2,809
37	Basic metal	2,933	16,334	196	–

Small firm = less than 100 persons
Large firm = 100 or more persons

export firms, imported inputs are important, though nothing like the extreme case of the *maquiladoras*.

Thus, there do seem to be differences in the characteristics and performance of manufacturing export and non-export firms. Export firms in general have higher labour productivity, pay higher wages, show higher investment (in machinery) per worker and have lower value added/gross value of production than non-export firms of the same manufacturing industry.

TRADE STRATEGY

Recent Chilean trade strategy up to 1992 had two main elements:

- unilateral trade liberalization;
- export market diversification.

The present trade regime consists of a flat 11 per cent tariff structure, and there are no non-tariff barriers. Because of the export success of this trade strategy, it has been argued that it should be maintained. However, given the present relatively low level of tariffs, not much can be expected by way of further reductions. Further reductions would, in any case, be relatively insignificant when annual real exchange rate fluctuations can be close to 10 per cent. Furthermore, special trade arrangements, like the bilateral FTAs (free trade areas) and regional trade bloc (NAFTA, MERCOSUR, the Andean Pact) have acquired a special importance. A small country like Chile cannot remain isolated; membership in an FTA or a regional trade bloc helps to increase trade and investment. Chile has to evaluate the advantages of two alternative FTAs, which are not necessarily mutually exclusive – an FTA with the USA and admission to MERCOSUR.

Table 2.16 Value added/gross value of production for export and non-export manufacturing firms, Chile (%)

ISIC	Industry	Small firms				Large firms			
		1986	1987	1988	1989	1986	1987	1988	1989
Export firms									
311	Food	24.3	34.3	31.2	31.1	36.7	43.7	48.4	39.8
313	Wine	46.0	42.9	29.2	30.4	56.6	45.6	36.6	56.5
331	Wood products	52.7	41.7	45.8	49.3	48.2	43.7	53.6	44.4
35	Chemical	24.9	39.0	30.6	43.5	34.1	34.8	30.3	37.0
37	Basic metal	27.9	18.5	52.5	53.3	31.7	31.2	45.7	45.0
Non-export firms									
311	Food	35.9	37.3	41.1	38.7	37.8	35.9	40.2	43.0
313	Wine	40.2	30.6	37.8	39.8	56.4	64.8	72.6	78.4
331	Wood products	36.9	37.2	36.4	35.7	51.1	47.2	41.6	46.8
35	Chemical	43.2	42.5	40.3	45.7	46.7	45.9	45.3	47.2
37	Basic metal	41.2	42.4	58.6	54.8	–	–	–	–

Small firm = less than 100 persons
Large firm = 100 or more persons
Note: Value added/gross of production figures are the median value of small and large firms of the respective ISIC industry

The USA has historically been Chile's main trade partner. The US government has stated that Chile will be the next country to sign an FTA with the USA after Mexico. This eventual FTA with the USA has been perceived as a positive possibility for the economy. However, an FTA with the USA will not have a spectacular effect upon Chilean exports, since these exports now face, on average, only 1.8 per cent tariffs and most Chilean exports are not affected by non-tariff barriers.[18]

Then why is there such a positive enthusiasm in Chile for establishing an FTA with the USA? There are several reasons for this:[19]

1 An FTA with the USA is perceived as a positive sum game where the smaller Latin American countries will gain relatively more by having preferential access to the large US market.
2 An FTA will provide long-run stable rules of access to the US market, at a time when there are prospects of increasing protectionist domestic forces there. The FTA could help to reduce tariff and non-tariff barriers for potential exports of the PNR type.
3 An FTA with the USA, or alternatively admission to NAFTA, will eventually become a seal of approval for economic reforms and development policies, equivalent to the IMF seal of approval for macroeconomic management. A Chile–USA FTA will, then, constitute a positive signal both to attract foreign investment and to stimulate domestic investors.

The new Southern Cone trade arrangement, MERCOSUR, between Argentina, Brazil, Paraguay and Uruguay, constitutes a natural geographic trade alternative for Chile. Brazil and Argentina already represent 60 per cent of total Latin American–Chilean trade. However, the Chilean government has been reluctant to pursue admission to MERCOSUR. There are several reasons for this:

1 The Brazilian macroeconomy is unstable, and the same is potentially true of Argentina. An enlarged trade relationship with those economies will increase Chilean vulnerability to Brazilian and Argentinean macroeconomic instability, which could generate important real exchange rate variation, sectoral trade disequilibria and increased uncertainty for Chilean domestic producers.
2 The MERCOSUR countries are still discussing the structure of their common external tariff. Given the Brazilian trade regime, that common external tariff could have a widely differentiated

structure with an average higher than 11 per cent, which is the present flat level of the Chilean tariff structure. Chile has already incurred heavy social costs in its trade reform. Therefore, there is not much interest in generating a new change of relative prices which would constitute a reversal of previous reforms.

There are some benefits, however, that MERCOSUR offers to Chile. Given its relatively high protective structure, preferential access to MERCOSUR could open quite profitable market opportunities for Chile. Moreover, Chilean membership in MERCOSUR could attract foreign investment that is oriented to the MERCOSUR market. This argument is more valid in the MERCOSUR case than in the NAFTA case, due to the fact that Mexico will probably attract most of the new foreign investment going to Latin American NAFTA members (since Mexico has the closer geographic advantage for US firms and will benefit from being the first Latin American country to be a member of NAFTA). Furthermore, increasing trade integration with MERCOSUR will allow the expansion of types of Chilean export different from those exported to developed country markets, in particular, manufactured goods. This would contribute to an important diversification of the export basket.

In short, the Chilean government could sensibly try to develop a trade proposal which allows domestic exporters to benefit from trade preferences in MERCOSUR, while at the same time trying to avoid the macro and micro problems pointed out above. One such possibility could be the establishment of a Chilean FTA with MERCOSUR. MERCOSUR countries may not be interested in this type of arrangement, but Argentina has already shown great interest in Chilean incorporation into MERCOSUR in order to increase its bargaining power for a lower level of the external common tariff, which is facing strong Brazilian opposition. In the long run, a trade arrangement with MERCOSUR could be highly beneficial for Chile once all member countries achieve domestic macroeconomic stability.

FINAL REMARKS

Discussion in Chile as to which has been the key economic policy generating the recent export boom is sometimes polarized. This chapter contends that this is not a useful discussion. Rather, Chilean export experience suggests that the various policies on which debate centres are only necessary conditions, and none of them, by itself, is a sufficient one. The present smooth and successful functioning of the Chilean economy is not the result of a grand master scheme, nor of a programmed complementarity between private and public sector actions. The purpose of this chapter has been to specify ex post the measures which have contributed to the final positive outcome.

The Chilean export boom has been mainly based on NR exports. Should other developing countries copy this strategy? Can they copy it? We answer in the affirmative. In addition to traditional arguments related to comparative advantage, and to the fact that foreign exchange generated by NR exports is required to break a structural bottleneck and that such foreign exchange has the same value in that respect as that generated by other types of exports, we stress the investment in know-how and in human capital. NR exports have facilitated learning by many Chilean entrepreneurs as to how to compete in the world economy, information about foreign markets, and new types of business possibilities. In short, there has been an important upgrading in the managerial capability of domestic entrepreneurs.

The satisfactory performance of NR exports has opened up discussion as to how to proceed into a second export stage which would include more manufactured exports. Many issues will have to be resolved in future research relating to strategies directed at the achievement of such a second stage. For example, should these manufactured exports be related to the type of NR products which are now being exported? If the answer is positive, should forward (PNR) or backward linkages be stressed? In many circles there prevails the idea that for the implementation of a strategy based on the export of relatively complex manufactured goods, an industrial policy is required. However, it is also often observed that in a developing country there does not typically exist the human capital and ability in the public sector to develop and run one. The Chilean fruit export experience shows that in the 1960s a sort of industrial policy was implemented where human capital professional training and research and development technology institutes had a specific sectoral orientation. Structural reforms in the 1970s introduced clear and stable market incentives, allowing private entrepreneurs to take full advantage of the existing stock of specific technology and human capital. While the public sector has the ability and the potential to make big mistakes, in Chile it has also demonstrated that it sometimes can help to achieve a positive outcome.

ACKNOWLEDGEMENTS

The author is grateful to Andrea Repetto for efficient research assistance. WIDER Conference participants Gerry Helleiner, Rob Davies, Sanjaya Lall, Carlos Paredes, David Kaplan and Chilean colleagues Pablo González, Cristián Morán, Gabriel Palma and Raúl E. Sáez provided helpful comments to earlier drafts. The usual caveats are valid.

NOTES

1 For a review of these issues, see Meller 1994, and further references provided there.
2 Public sector reform, about which there should be no controversy, was also important: the de-bureaucratization or reduction of public sector administrative red-tape procedures. This step enormously facilitated private sector export (and non-export) productive activities. Import procedures which used to take more than sixty days were reduced to two days during the 1970s.
3 On the social and distributive costs of Chilean economic reforms, see Meller 1992.
4 LCM copper production under 100 per cent foreign investment control increased at a rate of less than 2 per cent per year during the period 1945–65.
5 The 30 per cent figure has been obtained using LCM shares in the total value of copper exports (US$) in the years 1970 and 1990. This increase in LCM exports (US$) is then related to the US$7.2 billion of total export expansion.
6 A semi-logarithmic LCM output regression with a dummy variable, d, with values 0 and 1 for a two-period breakdown, 1940–70 (d = 0) and 1971–90 (d = 1), estimated by the Cochrane–Orcutt method, provides the following results (figures in parentheses show t values):

$$\text{Ln } Q = \ \ 5.95 - 0.47d + 0.008t + 0.0232dt \quad R^2 = 0.78$$
$$\qquad\quad (73.8) \ \ (1.27) \ \ (2.02) \ \ (2.40) \qquad F = 57.5$$

The dummy variable, d, tests the existence of a change in the slope of the estimated regression line. If the t statistic is significant, i.e. larger than 2.0, then there exists a change in the slope and the numerical value of the estimator corresponds to the increment of the slope.
7 To avoid the effects of world copper price fluctuations, a floor was put to the level of resources that the armed forces were getting. If 10 per cent of the value of LCM exports fell below that floor, the Treasury had to fill in the gap. There was, however, no ceiling. Moreover, in 1987, the floor level amount (expressed in US$) was fixed to the US wholesale price index.
8 These figures exclude copper exports by the previously centrally planned countries.

9 When foreign investment controlled LCM, an overvalued (low) real exchange rate was used as a tax mechanism. After the nationalization of LCM, the exchange rate was used as a resource allocation mechanism.

10 One hectare (10,000 m²) equals 2.471 acres.

11 For a much deeper review and analysis of this subject, see Jarvis 1991.

12 The main Chilean universities (University of Chile and Catholic University) have always had important financial support from the government.

13 It was assumed that the share in inputs of imported goods used in the export production process was 50 per cent; the level of tariffs was 20 per cent in 1985.

14 For a more extensive discussion of this subject see Campero and Escobar 1992.

15 There is a correspondence between industrial goods included in PNR and the primary products included in NR; PNR are those NR goods exported by Chile where there has been domestic value added. The NR selected are copper, fruit and vegetables, cattle, fish, and forestry.

16 The sum of the three categories (NR + PNR + OIP) represents around 95 per cent of total exports.

17 The use of weighted (by employment) or simple means introduces minor changes in the figures.

18 The present low level of US tariffs and non-tariff barriers on Chilean exports is related to the present basket of exports; the situation could be different for future Chilean potential exports.

19 For a deeper discussion, see Butelmann and Meller 1992.

REFERENCES

Aninat, E. (1990) 'Investment Opportunities in Chile: Results from a Survey of Projects 1990–5', mimeo, Comité de Inversiones Extranjeras.

Bitran, E. and Fierro, G. (1988) 'Racionalización Tributaria en los Sectores Agropecuario, Forestal y Pesquero', mimeo, Departamento de Ingeniería Industrial, Santiago: Universidad de Chile, November.

Butelmann, A. and Meller, P. (eds) (1992) *Estrategia Comercial Chilena para la Década del 90. Elementos para el Debate*, Santiago: Ediciones CIEPLAN.

Campero, M.P. and Escobar, B. (1992) 'Evolución y Composición de las Exportaciones Chilenas, 1986–1991' in A. Butelmann and P. Meller (eds) (1992): 113–42.

CEPAL (1990) 'La Cadena de Distribución y la Competitividad de las Exportaciones Latinoamericanas: La Fruta de Chile', Santiago: Naciones Unidas, July.

—— (1992) 'La Exportación de Productos Básicos no Tradicionales de América Latina', Santiago: Naciones Unidas, August.

Jarvis, L. (1991) 'The Role of Markets and Public Intervention in Chilean Fruit Development since the 1960s: Lessons for Technological Policy', mimeo, Santiago: University of California (Davis) and CIEPLAN.

Meller, P. (1992) *Adjustment and Equity in Chile*, Paris: OECD.

Meller, P. (1994) 'The Chilean Trade Liberalization and Export Expansion Process 1974–90' in G. K. Helleiner (ed.) *Trade Policy and Industrialization in Turbulent Times* (96–131), London: Routledge.

Meller, P. and Repetto, A. (1994) 'Empleo y Remuneraciones en el Sector Exportador Chileno', mimeo, Santiago, CIEPLAN, May.

Romaguera, P. (1991) 'Las Fluctuaciones del Precio del Cobre y su Impacto en la Economía Chilena', *Notas Técnicas* 143, Santiago: CIEPLAN, October.

3

COLOMBIAN MANUFACTURED EXPORTS, 1967–91

José Antonio Ocampo and Leonardo Villar

INTRODUCTION

As many other Latin American countries, Colombia initiated in 1991 a major trade policy reform which eliminated a century-long protectionist tradition, and adopted a very liberal, though not strictly neutral, trade regime. The reform was defended on the grounds that protectionism was generating strong anti-export biases and curbing productivity and economic growth. However, the nature of the association between the trade regime, exports and productivity growth has been the subject of an extensive debate in recent years and conclusions regarding the effects of protectionism have been mixed.

Although there remain important controversies in the area, conceptual differences have narrowed to the following. First, although it is generally recognized that there is a positive association between exports and overall economic growth, there are growing doubts as to the direction of causation and, particularly, as to whether the association is related to specific policies (Prichett 1991; World Bank 1991: ch. 5; Harrison 1991; Helleiner 1993, 1994). Second, there is now a consensus that there is no simple link between trade orientation and policies and productivity performance (Pack 1988; Rodrik 1992; Tybout 1992; Helleiner 1994). Third, it is recognized that traditional structural adjustment packages, particularly those implemented since the mid-1980s, give rise to poor supply responses under conditions characterized by the underdevelopment of government institutions and infrastructure, shortages of entrepreneurial and managerial abilities and of trained labour, and poorly developed input supply lines – conditions which are typical of many low-income and even some middle-income countries (Thomas *et al.* 1990; Thomas and Nash 1991: ch. 3; Helleiner 1992).

With respect to trade policies, it is also recognized by some World Bank analysts that 'a reduction in export restrictions has a clearer association with GDP growth than does a reduction in import restrictions' (Thomas and Nash 1991: 53). This prescription comes very close to UNCTAD's conclusions on the subject. It suggests that many developing countries have been able to develop an important export base while maintaining traditional protectionist instruments by using a variable mix of activist exchange rate policies, export subsidies, duty-free access of exporters to imported inputs and free trade zones (Agosin 1991; UNCTAD 1992, part III: ch. 1). Although such a mix may be interpreted in some cases as a sign of overall 'neutral' policies, it is difficult to see the prototypical liberal non-interventionist trade regime in these highly interventionist protectionism cum export promotion policies.

As shown in a previous paper (Ocampo 1994), Colombian trade policies evolved early on into such a 'mixed' regime, with favourable effects on exports and productivity growth. Indeed, the more liberal trade regime adopted in 1991 inherited from the previous much criticized model of development a strong export base with a fairly diversified mix of agricultural, mining and industrial goods. This inheritance may, in fact, be the clue to its likely success over the next few years. The simultaneous opening up of other Latin American economies (if sustained) and preferential treatment granted by developed countries as a counterpart to Colombia's drug war, will also be crucial to the success of the new, outward-oriented model, whereas the potential 'Dutch disease' effects of the upcoming oil boom constitute the most important threat to such success.

This chapter explores the determinants of the evolution and structure of manufactured exports in Colombia. It is divided into five sections. The next (second) section briefly reviews industrial and trade policies over the past decades (pages 55–61). The third section (pages 61–75) summarizes the evolution of export incentives and performance since 1967. The fourth (pages 76–9) presents a series of econometric exercises on the time-determinants of manufacturing exports. Finally, the fifth section considers the structural determinants of such exports in 1990 (pages 79–94).

AN OVERVIEW OF TRADE AND INDUSTRIAL POLICIES[1]

Although the origins of import substitution industrialization (ISI) can be traced back in Colombia to the late nineteenth century, the process only took off in the 1930s. Starting in that decade, the share of manufacturing in GDP grew rapidly for half a century as the industrial sector underwent a rapid structural transformation (Table 3.1).

Structural change had three major determinants: the growing integration of the domestic market, backward linkages generated by industrial growth, and real exchange rate fluctuations. Since the 1920s the latter had a cyclical pattern opposite to that of the (mainly coffee-determined) terms of trade. Real depreciation provided a signal to deepen import substitution when coffee prices collapsed (the 1930s, the second half of the 1950s, and the 1960s). In the intermediate periods of high coffee prices, appreciation played an alternative role: it provided relatively cheap foreign exchange to accelerate capital accumulation.

The traditional instruments of state promotion of industrialization were designed in the 1930s, but most of them came to play an important role only in the mid-1950s. This turning-point can be traced back to the very stringent balance of payments conditions generated by the collapse of coffee prices which took place at the time. As a response to those conditions, foreign exchange controls, tariffs and quantitative restrictions (QRs) were all used on a much broader scale. Furthermore, the incentives generated by protectionism were reinforced in this period by moderate public sector investments in manufacturing and by the design of appropriate instruments to finance the industrial sector.

The intensive use of both tariffs and QRs induced by the collapse of coffee prices in the mid-1950s also led the government to introduce a complete set of policies to promote the diversification of exports (see pages 61–5). Thus, the anti-export bias generated by intensive protectionism was eased by devaluation and aggressive export promotion policies from the mid-1950s onwards. The policy package followed since then can be characterized as a 'mixed' strategy of import substitution cum export promotion, which included aggressive exchange rate policies as a central element during periods of low coffee prices. Since the late 1950s rapid import substitution was in fact accompanied by rapid export diversification (Table 3.1).

This mixed strategy was incorporated into a coherent framework in the major foreign exchange and trade reform of 1967, the principal ingredient of which was the adoption of the crawling exchange rate peg. In 1969 the Cartagena Agreement, which created the Andean Group, added a new element to the strategy: ISI in a regional context.

Table 3.1 Structural transformation of Colombian manufacturing and exports (%)

	Share of manufacturing in GDP (1975 prices)	Composition of manufacturing value added[a]			Foreign trade (share of GDP, 1975 prices)		Composition of exports (current dollars)		
		Early[b]	Intermediate[c]	Late[d]	Exports	Imports	Coffee	Mining[e]	Non-traditional
1925–9	7.8	77.4	13.7	8.9	24.0	24.1	67.7	17.9	14.3
1930–4	7.6	76.2	16.7	7.1	24.4	13.1	60.5	27.7	11.7
1935–9	10.2	60.8	30.5	8.7	24.0	15.9	53.6	36.1	10.3
1940–4	15.7	55.6	35.3	9.0	20.4	11.2	60.7	31.7	7.7
1945–9	14.9	51.5	37.9	10.6	21.0	14.4	72.1	20.2	7.7
1950–4	17.6	48.4	38.4	13.2	18.4	18.4	78.7	16.3	5.0
1955–9	19.5	43.0	36.9	20.1	17.2	15.9	76.2	16.8	7.0
1960–4	20.7	39.9	37.0	23.1	16.0	14.1	68.9	18.9	12.2
1965–9	21.2	40.4	35.5	24.1	15.6	14.1	61.0	15.2	23.7
1970–4	22.5	34.1	36.2	29.7	14.9	16.9	50.5	8.7	40.8
1975–9	22.9	32.7	35.7	31.6	15.1	16.0	57.9	6.6	35.4
1980–4	21.3	34.1	34.3	31.6	14.1	19.3	48.7	13.0	38.3
1985–9	21.2	32.5	34.8	32.7	17.5	15.6	35.6	31.0	33.5
1990–1[f]	21.4	32.9	34.0	33.1	21.6	14.8	19.0	37.6	43.3

a Excludes wood, paper and their products up to 1935–9
b Foodstuffs, tobacco, wood and furniture
c Beverages, textiles, apparel, leather and products, oil derivatives, non-metallic minerals and miscellaneous manufactures
d Paper and printing, chemicals and rubber, basic metals, metal products, machinery and equipment
e Oil, fuel oil, coal, nickel and gold
f 1990 for composition of industrial value added

Sources: Estimates based on National Accounts of ECLAC (1925–50); Banco de la Republica (1950–65); DANE (1965–91); Foreign Trade Yearbooks and Banco de la Republica balance of payments estimates

However, dissatisfaction with ISI soon spread in Colombia, and the mechanisms adopted by the Andean Group proved inoperative. Thus, from the early 1970s, ISI became a villain, as the succeeding development plans reflect. This did not lead, however, to a dismantling of the protectionist mechanisms established in previous decades but rather to a disregard for new IS initiatives.

From 1967 on, but particularly from the early 1970s to 1990, exchange rate and trade policies followed a sharp cyclical pattern associated with macroeconomic conditions. From 1967 to 1974 Colombia experienced its 'golden age': GDP grew at an average of 6.3 per cent per year, with manufacturing reaching an impressive growth rate of 9.6 per cent a year. Aggressive devaluation policy and high export subsidies led to a boom in non-traditional exports (see pages 65–75). Import controls were gradually eased throughout this process, though almost exclusively for non-competing goods as 'water' in the tariff was reduced, but protection for domestic goods was kept at fairly high levels.

The 1967–74 expansion came to an end as a result of the contractionary fiscal and monetary policies adopted by the Lopez Administration – inaugurated in August 1974 – to reduce the high inflation rates experienced at the end of the boom. When the stabilization programme was just starting to bear some fruit in terms of reduced inflation, the Colombian economy was faced with a large and persistent coffee price boom. The major preoccupation of the economic authorities then was how to manage five consecutive years of current account surpluses. A harsh monetary and fiscal policy was adopted, together with strong controls on external indebtedness and moderate import liberalization. Although the authorities initially tried to avoid the real exchange rate effects of the boom, the attempt was finally abandoned in 1977.

The inauguration of the Turbay Administration in 1978 led to a radically different strategy: an expansionary fiscal policy, accompanied by a contractionary monetary policy and a more ambitious import liberalization. A corollary of fiscal expansion was massive borrowing abroad by the public sector. Simultaneously, controls on private capital flows were lifted. The country thus experienced a debt boom – sufficiently late, however, to avoid the devastating effects which a similar process had in other Latin American countries. Foreign borrowing maintained the excess supply of foreign exchange and real exchange rate appreciation after the coffee boom came to an end in 1980 and the economy started to run record current account deficits.

Since the mid-1970s the share of manufacturing in GDP stagnated, industrial factor productivity and export coefficients levelled off, and structural change ceased (Table 3.1). The half-century-long industrial boom thus came to an end. This turning-point may be regarded as resulting from the joint effects of the abandonment of the IS component of the mixed model and the 'Dutch disease' effects of booms in international coffee prices and foreign indebtedness. Starting in 1980, conditions faced by the manufacturing sector further deteriorated as the Colombian economy entered the worst recession of the post-war period.

The deterioration of economic conditions led the Betancur Administration, inaugurated in 1982, to a sharp turnaround in trade policy. The new administration rapidly reversed more than a decade of gradual import liberalization by both increasing tariffs and QRs. Export subsidies were also increased as the crawl of the peso accelerated. The global package thus had many similarities to the 'mixed' strategy which the country had followed up to 1974. The package was successful in generating an important recovery of industrial production and simultaneously reducing current account imbalances. However, the attempt to devalue the currency in real terms was checked by continued revaluation of the dollar. Together with a severe loss of foreign exchange reserves and increasing difficulties faced by the authorities in negotiating new international loans, this led to a radical change in economic policy in the second half of 1984. In 1985 restrictive aggregate demand policies and a rapid crawl of the peso replaced the role which had been assigned since 1982 to QRs as the mechanism for balance of payments adjustment.

Devaluation was extremely successful in generating a strong effect on relative prices. It thus facilitated the moderate liberalization of the trade regime agreed with the World Bank in 1985. However, the moderate liberalization of QRs, mostly for non-competitive goods, was accompanied by higher import duties, generating a net protectionist effect. Export subsidies were also moderately reduced, but exchange rate devaluation induced a massive increase in export incentives. Thus, by 1986, the effective exchange rate for both exports and imports had amply surpassed their historical peaks.

Under the favourable conditions created by the 1986 coffee boom, the economy returned to a more steady growth path. More generally, the return to the central features of the mixed model was reflected in the renewed dynamism of the industrial sector, as reflected in productivity growth and, particularly, rapid manufactured export expansion. Nonetheless, frustration with the inability to return to rapid ('golden age') rates of growth with price stability, the meagre results of the import substitution elements of the mixed model, and the radical change in external conditions facing the country, generated a perception on the part of the authorities that trade policy required a radical change towards an explicitly outward-oriented strategy.

As a result, a series of decisions taken after February 1990 by the Barco Administration, and by the Gaviria Administration which was inaugurated in August of that year, led to a rapid turnaround in trade policy, particularly import policy. By November QRs had been virtually eliminated. In December the government announced a tariff reduction schedule, which would bring the consolidated tariff and surcharges to an average slightly under 15 per cent by 1994.[2] As a result of strong inflationary pressures, the government decided, between June and August 1991, in two steps, to speed up the reductions planned for 1992-4. Tariffs were further reduced in March 1992, when a common Colombian–Venezuelan tariff was adopted. This meant that import duties were cut by three-fourths in two years – from an unweighted average of 43.7 per cent to 11.7 per cent – at the same time as QRs were eliminated.

Simultaneously, a series of meetings of the Andean Presidents, starting in December 1989, led to a major turnaround of the Andean Group, which finally created a free trade area among four of the five members of the Group in 1992 (with the exception of Peru). Negotiations towards free trade agreements with Mexico and Chile were also initiated. In late 1990 the EEC granted Andean countries preferential market access for a four-year period, and in December 1991 the US Congress approved the Andean Trade Preference Act, intended to be in place for a decade, which offers treatment similar to that previously provided in the Caribbean Basin Initiative.

To pave the way for import liberalization, the crawl of the peso was accelerated in mid-1989, generating by 1990 an additional real devaluation. However, acceleration of inflation, which many analysts have associated with undervaluation of the peso, led to a new stabilization programme in 1991 which included a moderate real appreciation of the domestic currency and, as we have seen, the acceleration of tariff reductions programmed for 1992-4. The combined effect of exchange rate revaluation, QR liberalization, and tariff reduction has been a massive revaluation of the real import exchange rate and a more moderate appreciation of the exchange rate applicable to non-traditional exports.

MANUFACTURED EXPORT INCENTIVES AND PERFORMANCE

Incentives

Preferential exchange rates for non-traditional exports were granted for the first time in 1948. As part of the policies adopted in the mid-1950s to face the collapse in coffee prices, a whole set of new export promotion policies was adopted. Preferential exchange rates were then complemented by tariff exemptions for imports used in the production of non-traditional exports, known in Colombia as the Vallejo Plan (1957), by tax incentives (1960), and special credit facilities, including, in particular, access to external commercial credit free of exchange rate risks. Up to 1967 such incentives were very high (an average of 35 per cent in 1953–66) but unstable (Diaz-Alejandro 1976: ch. 2).

The 1967 foreign exchange and trade reform rationalized the existing system of export promotion, establishing four major mechanisms:

1 A tax rebate certificate; this mechanism replaced the exchange rate and tax incentives typical of the 1960s.
2 Tariff exemptions for imports used in the production of non-traditional exports (a revised Vallejo Plan).
3 The prefinancing of exports free of exchange rate risks.
4 Export financing by the new Export Promotion Fund, PROEXPO.

As Table 3.2 indicates, from 1967 to 1974 the subsidy component of these incentives fluctuated between 19 per cent and 27 per cent of the value of the relevant exports. The global incentive was smaller than that typical of the two decades prior to 1967, but considerably more stable. It was dominated by tax rebates, but prefinancing also played an important role in some years. More importantly, high direct incentives were mixed with real exchange rate devaluation, generating a significant stimulus to diversify the export base.

As part of the stabilization package of 1974, the Lopez Administration reduced the average tax certificate received by exporters, effective the following year. The attempt to compensate for this

Table 3.2 Non-traditional export policy, Colombia 1967–91

	Total subsidy (%)					Weighted real exchange rate*	Real effective export exchange rate*
	Avg tax certificate	Vallejo Plan	Anticipated reimbursement	PROEXPO credit	Total		
1967	15.2	1.9	6.0	–	23.1	76.1	82.9
1968	15.1	2.2	3.9	–	21.2	84.0	90.1
1969	16.5	1.3	1.4	–	19.1	85.7	90.3
1970	15.7	2.5	1.6	–	19.8	90.3	95.7
1971	16.3	1.9	4.3	–	22.6	95.8	103.9
1972	18.4	2.0	6.0	0.5	26.8	99.2	111.3
1973	21.5	2.2	1.9	1.1	26.6	97.5	109.2
1974	19.9	2.3	0.0	1.3	23.5	95.7	104.6
1975	7.4	1.7	1.9	2.0	13.0	100.0	100.0
1976	5.8	1.8	0.8	1.8	10.2	95.4	93.0
1977	4.4	2.2	–	3.4	9.9	85.7	83.4
1978	6.3	2.1	–	5.7	14.1	85.5	86.3
1979	7.2	1.9	–	5.0	14.1	81.7	82.5
1980	6.9	2.4	–	5.7	15.1	83.5	85.0
1981	7.6	2.0	–	6.8	16.4	81.6	84.0
1982	8.8	1.8	–	8.2	18.8	75.6	79.5
1983	11.9	1.4	–	10.3	23.7	73.6	80.5
1984	15.8	2.1	–	9.2	27.0	79.9	89.8
1985	18.2	2.8	–	5.4	26.4	91.4	102.2
1986	11.6	3.7	–	3.1	18.4	108.5	113.6
1987	8.6	3.9	–	3.1	15.6	111.2	113.7
1988	8.0	4.5	–	1.6	14.1	111.3	112.3
1989	8.3	4.4	–	2.1	14.8	113.5	115.3
1990	8.2	3.0	–	1.5	12.8	127.4	127.2
1991	7.8	2.1	–	0.7	10.6	123.7	121.1
1992	6.2	0.7	–	1.1	7.9	117.5	112.2

*1975 = 100
Source: Authors' estimates based on information from Banco de la Republica, INCOMEX, PROEXPO and DANE

reduction and the temporary suspension of export prefinancing with a temporary acceleration of the crawl of the peso and with increased credit from PROEXPO was only partly successful, and a real appreciation of the exchange rate applicable to non-traditional exports thus ensued. Export prefinancing was briefly revived but finally eliminated in 1976. Global incentives further weakened as the real value of the peso appreciated during the coffee boom. To offset the adverse effects of the real peso appreciation on non-traditional exports, tax and credit subsidies were increased in 1978. However, once again, rising direct incentives were insufficient to compensate for the further real appreciation of the peso during the years of high capital inflows from foreign borrowing.

In the face of the balance of payments crisis, tax rebates were massively increased in 1983–4. Simultaneously, credit subsidies peaked as a result of high interest rate differentials and growing coverage of PROEXPO credit. By 1984 global export subsidies were back to the peak levels of 1973–4 though their composition was significantly altered: tax incentives were less important, whereas credit subsidies – now channelled through PROEXPO rather than the more traditional prefinancing mechanisms – had greater weight. Increased incentives led the initial turnaround of the real effective exchange rate.

Acceleration of the crawl of the peso allowed overall export incentives to remain high in the second half of the 1980s, despite falling tax and credit subsidies. Indeed, the real effective value of the peso in 1986–91 fell below the historical low of the early 1970s. Whereas falling tax incentives were the result of explicit policy decisions, credit subsidies decreased as a reflection of both a gradual increase in the interest rate charged to exporters and the inadequate growth of PROEXPO funds in the face of a new boom in non-traditional exports. As part of the reforms adopted in 1985, the Vallejo Plan was broadened, to allow the importation of intermediate and capital goods for non-traditional export activities, even if these goods were domestically produced. As compensation, 'indirect' exporters were also allowed access to the system. Thus, after that year, exporters had access to imported inputs free of any restriction.

During the recent liberalization direct export incentives were further reduced. Credit subsidies, which had been gradually adjusted since the mid-1980s, were virtually eliminated in October 1990. The tax rebate was reduced in May 1991 and April 1992. Currently, its average level (though not its structure) does not differ significantly from the incidence of indirect taxes. As a result, overall export subsidies are now relatively small. Indeed, to the extent that the average tax rebate is not very different from indirect tax incidence, and the Vallejo Plan has greater relative weight than in the past, the real subsidy is now relatively even smaller. More importantly, however, the reduction of direct incentives coincided in 1991 and 1992 with a real appreciation of the peso. The extraordinary global price incentives typical of the second half of 1990 were thus eroded, but the real effective exchange rate for exports remains at levels not unlike those of the early 1970s.

Overall, the real effective exchange rate has followed a well-defined cycle. It increased in the late 1960s and early 1970s, declined in the second half of the latter decade and in the early 1980s, sharply increased in the mid-1980s and remained relatively high up to 1992, even after the reversal of the additional real peso devaluation attempted in the first stages of the recent trade liberalization. Direct export incentives have fluctuated significantly over the period, sometimes reinforcing and sometimes compensating real exchange rate fluctuations. Nonetheless, the latter have clearly dominated the evolution of the real effective exchange rate for exports (Figure 3.1a).

The relative domestic price of manufactured exports followed broadly the same cycle. Nonetheless, international prices clearly

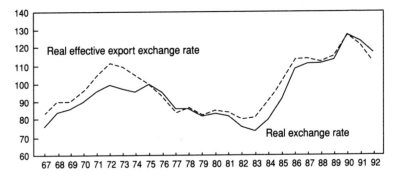

(a) Real exchange rate and real effective export exchange rate

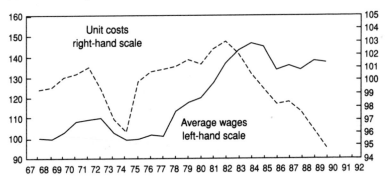

(b) Real average wages and unit costs of production in manufactured exports

Figure 3.1 Indexes of the real exchange rate, relative prices and costs of manufactured exports, Columbia 1967–92 (1975 = 100)

both reinforced the boom of the early 1970s and constituted an additional adverse factor in the difficult first half of the 1980s. As a result of continuously low international prices, the real peso devaluation of the mid-1980s was not fully reflected in the relative domestic price of manufactured exports.

To compensate for this fact, average unit costs in manufacturing fell significantly over the past decade (Figure 3.1b). This may have been, in part, a reflection of the effect of real devaluation on the relative price of non-tradables, but was also a result of other factors which more directly affected real wages. Real wages also fell in 1973 and 1974 in the face of rapidly rising inflation rates, generating a sharp but temporary reduction in unit manufacturing costs. Finally, as a previous study has shown (Ocampo 1994) total factor productivity in manufacturing increased in 1967–74 and in 1982–9, but stagnated in between. Given the evolution of real wages, productivity increases were fully reflected in falling unit costs over the 1980s.

Overall, price incentives for exports came primarily from the real effective export exchange rate in 1967–74, but were reinforced by high international prices and falling real wages at the end of the boom. The deterioration of such incentives from the mid-1970s to the early 1980s came primarily from the real effective export exchange rate, but were reinforced by falling international prices in the early 1980s. Finally, since the mid-1980s, aggressive exchange rate policy and falling unit costs have amply compensated for the adverse effects of continuously depressed international prices.

Performance

A cursory look at Figure 3.2a shows the close association between the evolution of relative prices and the performance of manufactured exports, measured by the ratio of such exports to potential sectoral GDP (the ratio of exports to GDP adjusted by capacity utilization).[3] This ratio shows a sharp increase in the late 1960s and the first half of the 1970s, followed by stagnation in the second half of the 1970s and collapse in the early 1980s. From 1985 onwards, exports experienced a spectacular boom, which accelerated in 1990 and 1991. Quarterly estimates indicate that non-traditional exports peaked in the second quarter of 1991 and fell thereafter. However, after adjusting the data for fictitious exports,[4] there was still moderate growth in 1992 (5 per cent in current dollars).[5]

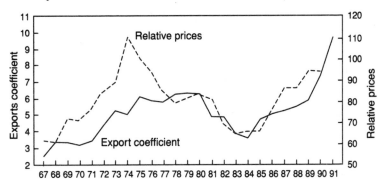

(a) Manufactured exports coefficient and relative price of manufactured exports

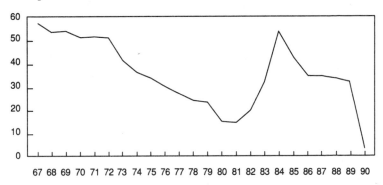

(b) Quantitative restrictions (tariff equivalent)

Figure 3.2 Manufactured exports coefficient and its determinants, Colombia 1967–91

In quantum terms, manufactured exports increased at an annual rate of some 10 per cent over the last quarter-century. The growth rate was very high in 1967–74, at 16.4 per cent, but slowed down considerably in 1974–9, to 9.1 per cent, still above the growth rate for concurrent actual and potential industrial production (Table 3.3). In 1979–83 manufactured exports experienced a dramatic contraction, but rapid growth resumed in 1983–9, at an annual rate of 12.0 per cent (not very different from that achieved in 1985–9 alone). In 1990 and 1991 it accelerated to 29.5 per cent. For the 1983–91 period, the annual growth rate of manufactured exports was 16 per cent, very similar to that for 1967–74.

Table 3.3 Growth of manufactured exports, Colombia 1967–91 (%)

	Foodstuffs	Beverages	Tobacco	Textiles, apparel and leather	Wood and furniture	Paper and printing	Chemicals	Non-metallic minerals	Metal and products	Machinery	Transport equipment	Total
Annual growth												
1967–74	4.00	—	—	24.74	19.26	-2.40	28.60	17.96	16.47	27.21	74.36	16.37
1974–9	13.12	-10.59	28.99	7.17	-1.74	22.86	8.56	10.70	-1.78	16.58	16.24	9.14
1979–83	0.62	41.42	-20.47	-16.95	-23.81	-3.42	-1.99	-21.90	-18.51	-18.44	-16.59	-9.94
1983–9	3.78	16.98	18.00	20.19	1.70	10.92	13.22	14.95	4.69	13.04	-3.89	11.96
1989–91	27.62	65.45	147.18	22.62	51.29	30.58	31.17	43.16	32.40	51.04	66.32	29.49
1983–91	9.29	27.57	41.96	20.80	12.32	15.54	17.46	21.43	11.02	21.54	10.23	16.11
Share of exports												
1967	37.96	0.00	0.00	21.02	5.24	10.37	7.54	7.74	7.28	2.41	0.07	100.00
1974	17.29	0.05	0.05	34.19	6.22	3.03	15.18	8.51	7.32	4.50	1.12	100.00
1979	20.67	0.02	0.12	31.22	3.68	5.47	14.78	9.13	4.32	6.25	1.53	100.00
1983	32.21	0.12	0.07	22.57	1.88	7.24	20.73	5.17	2.90	4.21	1.12	100.00
1989	20.44	0.15	0.10	34.56	1.06	6.84	22.17	6.05	1.94	4.46	0.45	100.00
1991	19.64	0.26	0.38	31.58	1.43	7.06	22.92	7.42	2.16	6.39	0.76	100.00
Exports/gross production												
1967	5.80	0.00	0.00	3.57	6.39	6.59	1.77	7.07	3.44	2.98	0.12	3.70
1974	5.18	0.04	0.14	10.19	15.47	2.48	4.34	12.94	5.11	5.67	1.57	5.75
1979	7.35	0.02	0.60	12.43	14.33	5.48	5.59	16.65	4.05	9.63	2.37	7.31
1983	6.98	0.06	0.23	7.29	5.24	4.67	5.09	5.88	1.96	4.96	1.41	4.95
1989	7.11	0.14	0.64	16.87	3.91	6.20	7.91	9.40	2.16	7.25	0.80	7.54
1991	11.41	0.37	3.34	23.78	9.02	9.09	12.47	17.92	3.74	16.91	2.81	12.08

Sources: Estimates based on DANE National Accounts; 1991 data are based on preliminary estimates of FEDESARROLLO; the gross value of production includes commercial margins

Viewed as a whole, the quarter-century under study was characterized by a long-run upward trend of manufactured exports, relative to both concurrent actual and potential industrial production. The trend slowed, however, during the coffee boom years of the 1970s and was sharply but temporarily reversed in the early 1980s. Aside from the price incentives analysed in the previous section (including unit costs) other factors were certainly relevant to this experience. First, the evolution of the global export coefficient shows clear inertia, as the tests presented indicate (pages 76–9). This behaviour was particularly important in the second half of the 1970s where, despite significant reductions in price incentives, manufactured exports continued to expand. Second, the strong contraction typical of the early 1980s had additional determinants, aside from the reduction of relative price incentives. Probably the most important additional factor was world recession, including the collapse of intra-regional trade in Latin America. International recession was also associated with the slowdown of the mid-1970s, but not so in recent years.

An additional factor which may have played a role in export performance was the anti-export bias generated by the import regime. As tariffs were consistently high up to the 1991 liberalization, major changes in protection throughout the period were associated with fluctuations in import QRs. Figure 3.2b shows the evolution of an estimate of the tariff equivalent of QRs.[6] It shows a gradual but important liberalization from 1972 to 1981, followed by a sharp turnaround in 1982–4, and a liberalization thereafter including the elimination of most QRs in 1990. To the extent that this variable has influenced the evolution of manufactured exports, it helped support export expansion in the second half of the 1970s and added a further element to the cycle of the 1980s. It must have added, in particular, to the 1990–1 boom. Nonetheless, the interpretation of this association is unclear, as we will see below (pages 76–9).

The sectoral disaggregation used in Table 3.3 indicates that manufactured exports have been dominated by foodstuffs, textiles (including apparel and leather products) and chemicals. This indicates the complex factor characteristics of Colombian manufactured exports (see pages 79–94). Overall, these three sectors made up two-thirds of industrial exports from 1967 to 1979 and three-fourths in the 1980s. Exports of foodstuffs have been the most stable but the least dynamic. Their share in total manufactured exports, measured at constant prices, has, thus, been anti-cyclical: it has tended to increase when the aggregate export coefficient declined, indicating that these exports are less sensitive to shifts in domestic policies and international demand. Textiles display, on the contrary, an upward trend and strong pro-cyclical performance. Finally, chemicals exhibit a strong upward trend and a less marked pro-cyclical pattern.

Although less important in the global picture, three other sectors also have relatively high export coefficients: paper and printing (particularly the latter), non-metallic minerals, and machinery. By 1991, the latter two sectors exported 18 per cent and 17 per cent of gross production respectively, the highest export coefficients next to the textiles sector. Overall, these three sectors have made up between 16 per cent and 21 per cent of manufactured exports. All three show a strong cyclical pattern. Among them, machinery exports have been the most dynamic. Other sectors – beverages, tobacco, wood and furniture, basic metals and metallic products, and transport equipment – do not contribute significantly to the global export picture.

Table 3.4 explores in greater detail the evolution of manufactured exports in 1980–92, and their destination. Information is expressed here in current dollars. Original data at the three-digit ISIC have been classified according to their factor intensity in four groups, using information from the domestic manufacturing surveys:

1 Natural resource-intensive manufactures (foodstuffs, leather and leather manufactures, and wood).
2 Unskilled labour-intensive goods (apparel, shoes, printing, manufactures from plastic, pottery, and miscellaneous manufactures, primarily jewellery).
3 Capital-intensive manufactures (beverages, textiles, glass, cement and non-ferrous metals).
4 Skilled labour- or technology-intensive goods (industrial chemicals, rubber, basic ferrous metals, metal and metalmechanic products).

An alternative sub-classification in Table 3.4 divides exports only into 'traditional' and 'late'. The latter includes ˚capital-intensive manufactures, except textiles, and the whole group of skilled labour- and technology-intensive goods. The first group broadly includes those industries considered 'early' and 'intermediate' in Table 3.1.

This classification is not unlike that used in comparative international studies. There are, however, important differences, particularly with respect to the third group (capital intensive manufactures), which includes manufactures which in other studies are considered either unskilled labour-intensive (textiles) or natural

Table 3.4 Manufactured exports, Colombia: trade matrices, 1980–92 (million US$)

Year/ factor intensity	Developed countries			Latin America[b]		Rest of the world	Total	
	USA[a]	Europe	Japan	Andean	Rest			%
1980								
Natural resources	184,696	27,428	13,413	59,714	59,929	8,523	353,704	35.77
Unskilled labour								
Apparel, shoes	14,986	4,343	310	70,565	4,236	1	94,441	9.55
Other	14,381	10,442	54	32,848	18,340	1,333	77,398	7.83
Capital								
Textiles	30,717	56,109	0	19,218	14,396	573	121,013	12.24
Other	12,357	15,446	0	39,184	30,016	1,845	98,847	10.00
Skilled labour and technology								
Chemicals	12,573	2,267	15	57,638	26,180	1,190	99,864	10.10
Metal products	21,220	4,237	255	84,194	32,630	1,154	143,689	14.53
Total	290,929	120,272	14,047	363,361	185,728	14,618	988,955	100.00
Traditional (%)[c]	37.86	15.21	2.13	28.20	14.99	1.61	100.00	
Late (%)[d]	13.48	6.41	0.08	52.87	25.94	1.22	100.00	
Total (%)	29.42	12.16	1.42	36.74	18.78	1.48	100.00	
1985								
Natural resources	101,805	35,156	19,582	35,378	15,047	5,600	212,567	31.09
Unskilled labour								
Apparel, shoes	31,736	3,278	78	20,719	1,296	23	57,131	8.36
Other	27,881	5,413	340	27,940	10,451	1,090	73,114	10.69
Capital								
Textiles	35,974	17,483	583	10,146	10,060	991	75,236	11.00

Other	29,061	7,714	900	9,796	14,892	745	63,108	9.23
Skilled labour and technology								
Chemicals	30,474	3,877	144	54,370	42,320	557	131,742	19.27
Metal products	11,730	1,159	15	34,985	22,662	254	70,806	10.36
Total	268,661	74,080	21,641	193,335	116,728	9,260	683,704	100.00
Traditional (%)c	47.22	14.67	4.92	22.53	8.82	1.84	100.00	
Late (%)d	26.83	4.80	0.40	37.32	30.07	0.59	100.00	
Total (%)	39.29	10.84	3.17	28.28	17.07	1.35	100.00	
1989								
Natural resources	234,563	61,579	32,620	38,877	29,180	5,629	402,447	31.57
Unskilled labour								
Apparel, shoes	112,827	14,319	361	40,954	4,856	85	173,402	13.60
Other	67,948	10,702	575	27,315	28,567	820	135,926	10.66
Capital								
Textiles	75,432	28,850	324	14,192	18,126	3,005	139,929	10.98
Other	29,485	396	101	11,882	27,717	74	69,654	5.46
Skilled labour and technology								
Chemicals	32,466	5,736	254	100,507	79,268	12,349	230,581	18.09
Metal products	15,217	9,792	96	37,343	59,178	1,281	122,908	9.64
Total	567,937	131,375	34,330	271,069	246,893	23,243	1,274,847	100.00
Traditional (%)c	57.62	13.56	3.98	14.25	9.48	1.12	100.00	
Late (%)d	18.24	3.76	0.11	35.39	39.27	3.24	100.00	
Total (%)	44.55	10.31	2.69	21.26	19.37	1.82	100.00	

Table 3.4 continued

Year/factor intensity	Developed countries			Latin America[b]		Rest of the world	Total	
	USA[a]	Europe	Japan	Andean	Rest			%
1991								
Natural resources	238,485	144,666	35,996	131,057	50,469	42,036	642,708	27.36
Unskilled labour								
Apparel, shoes	204,743	43,865	770	45,918	53,975	1,851	351,121	14.95
Other	95,754	9,246	1,476	77,504	81,201	3,238	268,418	11.43
Capital								
Textiles	108,946	76,749	5	37,712	33,122	3,343	259,876	11.06
Other	50,928	3,505	158	36,429	32,760	1,555	125,334	5.33
Skilled labour and technology								
Chemicals	31,126	19,053	75	165,336	143,620	20,338	379,549	16.16
Metal products	62,194	54,406	1,234	112,613	85,896	6,032	322,374	13.72
Total	792,175	351,489	39,714	606,568	481,043	78,392	2,349,380	100.00
Traditional (%)[c]	42.57	18.04	2.51	19.20	14.37	3.32	100.00	
Late (%)[d]	17.44	9.30	0.18	38.00	31.70	3.38	100.00	
Total (%)	33.72	14.96	1.69	25.82	20.48	3.34	100.00	
1992								
Natural resources	193,401	166,651	30,877	164,228	42,676	56,188	654,022	25.94
Unskilled labour								
Apparel, shoes	258,256	41,810	671	61,874	35,929	1,271	399,811	15.86

Other	58,082	12,759	1,345	71,087	72,204	1,626	217,104	8.61
Capital								
Textiles	115,697	52,529	111	79,054	35,792	4,328	287,511	11.40
Other	33,247	3,815	63	68,358	54,891	1,453	161,827	6.42
Skilled labour and technology								
Chemicals	36,265	15,085	33	201,182	165,980	13,615	432,159	17.14
Metal products	71,045	20,929	590	164,824	91,815	19,811	369,015	14.64
Total	765,993	313,579	33,690	810,608	499,288	98,291	2,521,448	100.00
Traditional (%)c	40.13	17.57	2.12	24.14	11.97	4.07	100.00	
Late (%)d	14.60	4.14	0.07	45.11	32.47	3.62	100.00	
Total (%)	30.38	12.44	1.34	32.15	19.80	3.90	100.00	

Memo: Late, as % of exports to each destination

1980	15.86	18.25	1.92	49.82	47.83	28.65	34.62
1985	26.53	17.21	4.89	51.28	68.43	16.80	38.86
1989	13.59	12.12	1.31	55.24	67.30	58.96	33.19
1991	18.21	21.90	3.69	51.83	54.52	35.62	35.21
1992	18.35	12.70	2.04	53.58	62.63	35.48	38.19

a USA, Canada and Puerto Rico
b Includes Caribbean
c Natural resource and unskilled labour intensive, and textiles
d Capital intensive, except textiles, skilled labour and technology intensive
Source: Authors' estimates based on original data of DANE

resource intensive. Indeed, this group includes in our classification mostly standard intermediates which are, in fact, both somewhat resource intensive (including even textiles, the comparative advantage of which, in the case of Colombia, is based on the processing of domestic cotton) and capital intensive by developing country standards. However, the global picture drawn is not very different from that which comes out from alternative classifications.

Several observations can be derived from a careful analysis of Table 3.4. First, it is clear that the reduction of manufactured exports in the early 1980s was mostly associated with the collapse of intra-regional trade in Latin America. Since exports to the rest of Latin America made up 55.5 per cent of total Colombian manufactured exports in 1980, the effect of this contraction was severe. It explains fully 78 per cent of the reduction in the value of exports in 1980–5. The rest is explained principally by falling international prices. The 1980 level of exports to Latin America as a whole was only recovered one decade later – somewhat earlier in non-Andean Latin American markets, as there has been a diversification of exports to the area. In the intermediate period, growth was concentrated almost exclusively in exports to the US market. During the recent boom, however, there has also been a significant diversification towards European markets, which may be associated with the four-year preferences granted in late 1990. Indeed, one of the major features of the 1989–92 boom was the considerable diversification of markets.

Second, late manufactures are mostly exported to regional markets. The proportion was 78.8 per cent in 1980, fell to 67.4 per cent in 1985, but then increased again to 74.7 per cent in 1989 and 77.6 per cent in 1992. On the other hand, traditional manufactures, with the partial exception of labour-intensive manufactures other than apparel and shoes (printing, in particular), are mostly exported to developed countries. This pattern was less marked, however, in 1980 (when 43.2 per cent of traditional manufactures were also exported to Latin America) than it was afterwards, and may have also struck a minimum in 1989. With respect to trade with developed countries, the composition of manufactured exports has been diversified slightly more in trade with the USA, much less with Europe, and remains absolutely traditional with respect to Japan (where overall exports are also extremely low).

Due to the combination of the aforementioned factors, there was no increase in the share of non-traditional (late) Colombian exports over the past decade. Indeed, the adverse effect on late manufactures generated by collapsing regional markets was roughly compensated for by a marginal diversification of exports towards the developed countries and particularly the US market. As a result, late manufactures have made up slightly over one-third of manufactured exports throughout the period of analysis. However, at a more disaggregated level there have been important changes. Among traditional manufactures, unskilled labour-intensive products have gained ground, whereas the opposite is true of natural resource-intensive goods. Among late manufactures, chemicals have gained at the expense of capital-intensive exports, not including textiles. Metalmechanic exports, after collapsing during the early part of the 1980s, gained ground considerably and, in fact, rapidly increased their share in overall exports during the recent export boom.

These various influences during the period covered by Table 3.4 gave rise to important changes in the trade matrix. In 1980–5, the major element, as mentioned, was the collapse of exports to Latin America, particularly of traditional exports. The only expansionary element during this period was the growth of non-resource-intensive exports to the USA. In 1985–9 there was a boom in exports of traditional manufactures to the USA combined with a recovery in the exports of late manufactures to Latin America. During the recent boom, all markets and exports have grown but Latin American and European markets and metalmechanic exports have done best.

This analysis indicates that Colombian manufactured exports did not follow any simple overall factor intensity pattern but that a pattern is clearer when the destination of different exports is taken into account. If regional markets continue to expand in response to stable trade liberalization processes, the outlook for Colombian manufacturing development, including renewed structural diversification, looks rather good. The strong comparative advantage accumulated in traditional manufactures in developed countries' markets is an additional strength, although its contribution to a dynamic diversification of domestic manufacturing production is less obvious. If this is so, trade liberalization came at a fairly good time: it follows on the development of an extremely solid export base; it does not have to create it. Thus, the transition is likely to be fairly smooth, except for the macroeconomic dimensions which can be associated with domestic policy mistakes. In the medium term, new 'Dutch disease' influences associated with recent oil discoveries are also a possibility, but they are not explored in this chapter.

THE TIME DETERMINANTS OF
MANUFACTURED EXPORTS

The econometric literature on the determinants of non-traditional exports in Colombia is now quite rich.[7] The strongest common conclusion which emerges from existing studies is the sensitivity of such exports to relative prices, a fact which confirms the inference one can draw from simple observation of Figure 3.2a. The relative price variable used by these studies is not uniform: some authors used the real effective exchange rate whereas others utilized a more direct measure which includes the effects of changing international prices. Despite this fact and regardless of differences in methods of estimation, other variables included, and the period covered in the statistical exercise, most estimates of the elasticity of non-traditional exports to relative prices lie in the 0.5–1.5 range. According to existing studies, the elasticity is generally lower for primary goods. Manufactures generally come in the higher part of the range (above it in some sectors).

Several studies indicate that exchange rate stability is also important.[8] A few studies have also tried to measure the effect of direct export incentives (Lora 1985; Alonso 1992). They conclude that this instrument is generally less effective than devaluation, due to the uncertainty regarding its sustainability. The method of estimation which divides the relative price faced by exporters into the real exchange rate and the subsidy component may be inadequate, however, particularly if subsidies are used to compensate for real exchange rate movements. Few studies have also included costs as a determinant of non-traditional exports. Those which have included real wages as an additional determinant (Botero and Meisel 1988; Villar 1992) have found them to exercise a statistically significant negative effect on non-traditional exports.

There are important differences among the estimated models in the treatment of external demand. The conceptual difference relates to the interpretation of the undoubted fact that Colombia is a very small country in most, if not all, non-traditional exports. The usual interpretation is to assume that Colombia faces an infinitely elastic foreign demand, which implies that only an export supply function has to be estimated. This supply function should include domestic productive capacity, or simply domestic production, as an argument. This is the procedure used by many authors. The basic assumption which they make is that external demand only affects exports through the incentives generated by the relevant international prices.

This procedure is probably adequate for many primary goods, but it ignores an important observation regarding 'small producers' in imperfect markets, such as are typical in manufacturing: the fact that producers lack market power, in the sense of having no effect on international prices, does *not* imply that producers face an infinitely elastic foreign demand. This is due to the fact that there are many forms of market segmentation associated with transactions costs and, particularly, with information problems: producers must make themselves known to demanders and make a reputation as reliable suppliers. In other words, they have to create their clientèle, no matter how small they are. To the extent that manufactures are highly diversified, they have also to accumulate knowledge regarding quality levels which are acceptable to specific customers. Both factors generate effects which may be classed as forms of dynamic economies of scale, associated with either marketing or production.

This conceptual observation cannot be adequately grasped in simultaneous supply–demand models, as such models do not make sense if small producers have no effect on international prices.[9] It may be better grasped by introducing variables which capture the costs of penetrating international markets, and the knowledge or experience acquired in servicing them. The rationale for including external demand in supply functions may, thus, be that it is a proxy for the costs of penetrating markets (i.e. it is easier to penetrate them when external demand is expanding), as Villar (1984a) has argued. It may also reflect the fact that the returns to a given stock of 'information' accumulated by the firm depend on the dynamism of external markets: if the traditional buyers are in good shape, such information is very valuable, but if the contrary is true, the clientèle network of the firm may be of little value. The accumulated effects of knowledge of external markets or the network of buyers which the firm has built up could be captured by either a measure of 'experience', as Ocampo (1994) has suggested, or alternatively by the non-stationary dynamics of exports (see below).

Empirically, many studies have included external demand as an argument of the supply function and find it to exercise a strong effect, with the elasticity depending on the specific index of demand and the specification used.[10] Earlier studies also used the share of Latin American Free Trade/Integration Association (LAFTA/LAIA) or the Andean Group in exports as an argument of the export function.[11]

More recent studies have used weighted indexes of external demand in which regional trading partners are given shares proportional to their relevance to Colombia's non-traditional exports.[12]

The recent attempts to include aggregate domestic demand, to capture the 'crowding out' effect which it may have on exports, for a given productive capacity have so far yielded poor results.[13] Ocampo (1994) and Villar (1992) have also tried to test the direct 'anti-export' bias of protection by including it explicitly in the export supply function. The results have confirmed that variations in the levels of protection – mainly QRs – do exercise an effect on non-traditional exports. The interpretation of this result is subject to some practical difficulties. As Colombia has extensively used QRs over the past decades as a balance of payments tool, it is unclear what the causal link is: does it reflect the theoretical effects of anti-export bias on exports, or does it reflect the fact that when exports have performed poorly, QRs have been strengthened?

Table 3.5 presents additional empirical evidence on the short-term determinants of manufactured exports. The dependent variable is in all cases sectoral exports relative to sectoral capacity output. This assumes that exports have unit elasticity with respect to productive capacity. Two price variables are included: the price of sectoral exports relative to the overall manufacturing price deflator (the real effective export exchange rate in some cases) and unit domestic costs. In some cases, the ratio of these two prices (i.e. export prices relative to costs) was tried as the only relevant price variable, but this procedure did not in general give good results, probably due to the different lags involved in the effect of each price variable.

Given the fragmentation typical of markets for manufactured goods, an index of world income is also included as an independent variable in the regressions.[14] The dynamic economies of scale emphasized by new trade theories are captured by an index of 'export experience', which is defined as accumulated exports since 1951 assuming a 10 per cent annual depreciation of 'experience'. Both variables are measured relative to productive capacity in each sector. Finally, to capture the 'anti-export bias' generated by import policies, the tariff equivalent of QRs is also included as an explanatory variable.[15]

The results for the manufacturing sector as a whole confirm the explanatory power of all these variables. The strongest influence is that exercised by relative prices, as the standardized coefficients indicate. If only one price variable is used, the elasticity is 0.7; when the two variables are used, the elasticity of unit costs is much stronger than that of the traditional relative price variable. As unit costs have generally fallen over the 1980s, this indicates that they have had the strongest influence in recent years. Next, according to the size of the standardized coefficients, comes the effect of export experience. QRs and world income come last in the list, with the relative weight of each depending on the regression. The coefficient of the last of these variables is unstable according to the estimation procedure, but overall it indicates that the elasticity of Colombian manufacturing exports to world income is at least unitary.

The relative weight of these variables depends strongly on the sector. Among the three most important export sectors, only food-stuffs does not seem very sensitive to these variables. This indicates that the best description of the export behaviour of this sector is inertia around a constant share of exports in production. Textiles are mostly affected by relative prices, with an elasticity which is twice the manufacturing average. Chemicals are subject to very strong dynamic economies, but relative prices are also important.

Among the second group of export sectors, paper and printing is also subject to strong dynamic economies; machinery is sensitive to world demand; and non-metallic minerals to both effects. None of these sectors seems particularly sensitive to relative prices. The least important export sectors – wood and furniture, basic metals and transport equipment – are more sensitive to price variables, but also to world income (wood) and experience (metals).

The anti-export bias of high QRs is strongest for machinery and transport equipment. This result is consistent with previous analysis, which indicates that variations in QRs exercised the strongest effect on production in 1977–87 in these sectors (see Ocampo 1990b). The results for non-metallic minerals are not comprehensible in these terms and may thus be interpreted in terms of the possibility of reverse causality, mentioned above. This is also the case in respect of the weaker effects of this variable on the exports of foodstuffs and basic metals.

THE STRUCTURAL DETERMINANTS OF EXPORTS IN 1990

Contrary to the rich literature on the short-term determinants of non-traditional exports, there are rather few analyses of their structural determinants. One of the earliest and most comprehensive studies on

Table 3.5 Determinants of total export coefficients relative to potential output, Colombia 1967–90 (log of all variables; t-statistic in parentheses, standardized coefficient in brackets)

Sector[a]	Constant	Relative prices (lagged)[b]	Effective real export exch. rate	Unit costs	Tariff equiv. of QRs	World income	Export experience	First order auto-correlation	Adjusted R²	DW
Foodstuffs (−3.01) [0.315]	−2.89 (−6.51)	0.022 (0.11) [0.008]		−0.970 (−0.70) [−0.061]	−0.959 (−1.49)* [−0.137]				23.55	1.99
Textiles, apparel and leather [0.509]	−2.78 (−9.07)	1.386 (4.24)** [0.250]		−1.494 (−1.11) [−0.059]		0.899 (1.43)* [0.108]		0.681 (4.10)**	88.76	1.96
Wood and furniture (−2.688) [0.508]	−2.44 (−20.10)		1.025 (1.43)* [0.142]	−2.902[d] (−5.41)** [0.197]		2.797 (4.17)** [1.107]			61.45	1.87
Paper and printing (−3.269) [0.556]	−2.21 (−2.06)	0.604 (0.92) [0.078]		−0.737 (−0.18) [−0.018]		0.222 (0.13) [0.009]	0.707 (2.35)** [0.606]	0.581 (4.08)**	66.00	1.56
Chemicals (−3.251) [0.479]	−1.79 (−7.44)	0.722 (2.04)** [0.093]		−2.006 (−1.41)* [0.050]			0.870 (6.72)** [0.746]		78.59	1.63
	−1.76 (8.78)	0.854[c] (2.65)** [0.155]					0.749 (8.41)** [0.524]		81.57	1.85

Industry	Mean [a]	Constant	(1)	(2)	(3)	(4)	(5)	(6)	R²	DW
Non-metallic minerals	(-2.338) [0.356]	-1.90 (-3.03)	0.509 (0.75) [0.070]	-2.650 (-1.36)* [-0.078]	-1.366 (-2.69)** [-0.195]	1.747 (4.50)** [0.430]	0.719 (1.72)** [0.299]	0.554 (2.42)**	79.65	1.84
Metals and products	(-3.610) [0.356]	-2.02 (-4.15)	0.121 (0.32) [0.017]	-1.795^d (-3.21)** [-0.321]	-0.844 (-1.42)* [-0.121]	1.361 (1.57)* [0.181]	0.609 (2.29)** [0.219]		55.04	2.43
Machinery	(-3.227) [0.568]	-2.34 (-3.07)	1.048 (1.07) [0.086]	-0.681 (-0.29) [-0.022]	-1.722 (-2.77)** [-0.246]	1.467 (1.78)* [0.195]		0.817 (7.23)**	80.42	2.22
		2.11 (-1.99)	1.133 (1.04) [0.093]	-0.790 (-0.31) [-0.026]	-1.809 (-2.56)** [-0.259]	1.196 (1.27) [0.159]	0.247 (0.43) [0.166]	0.725 (2.35)**	79.23	2.14
Transport equipment	(-5.074) [1.135]	-2.97 (-3.85)	3.871 (1.94)** [0.534]		-5.831 (-3.47)** [-0.834]		0.009 (0.041) [0.010]	0.368 (2.96)**	46.63	2.12
Non-oil manufacturing	(-3.045) [0.280]	-2.80 (-14.60)	0.566 (3.46)** [0.095]	-3.857 (-3.68)** [-0.081]	-0.753 (-3.19)** [-0.108]	1.687 (3.21)** [0.113]	0.414 (4.54)** [0.177]		89.28	1.87
		2.27 (-19.03)	0.713^c (5.21)** [0.235]		-0.818 (-3.65)** [-0.117]	1.019 (1.98)** [0.069]	0.325 (3.38)** [0.139]		86.85	1.98

* Significantly different from zero at 90% confidence level
** Significantly different from zero at 95% confidence level
a Mean value of dependent variable in parentheses; standard deviation in brackets
b Price of exports relative to GDP deflator unless otherwise indicated
c Price of exports relative to unit cost
d Average wage per worker

this subject was that of Thoumi (1979). This author used data from the 1970 Manufacturing Census to classify four-digit ISIC sectors into four groups: export industries, import substitution sectors, import substitution sectors with low shares of domestic demand, and non-tradables. Using the ratio of employment to value added as the basic index of labour intensity, he found export industries to be more labour intensive than import substitution sectors. He also found that those industries which shifted from the import substitution to the export groups during the 1970–3 export boom were more labour intensive on average. Finally, he found that Colombian exports to developed countries were more labour intensive than those directed towards regional markets.

Using regression analysis on cross-section data at the three- and four-digit level for 1979 and 1980, Villar (1984b) found that the share of exports in total output was positively correlated with natural resource, labour and female labour intensity. The same variables were also positively correlated with the share of developed countries in the total exports of each sector. He also found labour-intensive sectors to be those which experienced larger average growth rates between 1960 and 1980. The high labour intensity characteristic of Colombian non-traditional exports was also confirmed by Crane (1991). Using input–output tables at the three-digit level, she correlated the direct and indirect content of wages in the gross value of production with export coefficients in 1981, and found a high positive correlation.

In apparent contradiction to the aforementioned studies, Echavarría and Perry (1981) found that the labour intensity of exporting firms was lower than that of non-exporting firms in 1974. This result coincides with the characterization of Colombian manufactured exports by Diaz-Alejandro (1975), who claimed that such exports are concentrated in large firms, which use capital, skilled labour and imported inputs in higher proportions than the industry average and are similar to those characteristic of import substitution firms. This apparent paradox can be explained, as Villar (1984b) indicated, by the fact that exporting firms are indeed less labour intensive than non-exporting firms but they tend to be concentrated in labour-intensive sectors.

To analyse the characteristics of both export sectors and exporting firms, we have used recent data from the 1990 Manufacturing Survey.[16] The analysis below uses both cross-section information at the four-digit ISIC level (sometimes three-digit) and data for some

1,000 exporting firms. Several measures of factor intensity are used. Natural resource intensity is measured by the direct and indirect content of agricultural and mineral products in the value of output.[17] A complementary measure of the share of domestic raw materials in the value of output explores whether backward linkages are important for export activities (alternatively, whether assembly is a source of competitiveness). Labour intensity is measured by the ratio of total employment to value added. The ratio of female to total employment is included as an additional explanatory variable. Skilled labour intensity is measured by the ratio of technical employees to overall employment. Although this last measure may also be taken as a measure of technology intensity, the ratio of royalties to total sales is directly used for such a purpose.

Table 3.6 classifies exporting firms according to the share of exports in total sales. Part I includes all sectors. Part II excludes natural resource-intensive activities.[18] Although 14.9 per cent of manufacturing firms are involved in the export business, the share of exports in total sales is rather low for most of them. Only 318 firms, equivalent to 4.6 per cent of total firms, have shares of exports in total sales greater than 20 per cent.

Table 3.6 confirms that exporting firms are larger, more capital-intensive, skilled labour- and technology-intensive, and less dependent on domestic raw materials than non-exporting firms. However, this traditional characterization is particularly appropriate for firms which have low shares of exports to total sales. Firms which have high shares are smaller and more labour- (and, particularly, female labour-) intensive, less skilled labour- and technology-intensive, and more dependent on domestic raw materials than firms which have low shares of exports to total sales. Those with more than 50 per cent of sales abroad are larger and more skilled labour-intensive, but also more labour and domestic raw material, and less technology-intensive, than non-exporting firms. These associations continue to hold when resource-intensive sectors are excluded from the analysis. They also apply at a more disaggregated level for nearly all four-digit ISIC sectors.

Table 3.7 corroborates the larger size characteristic of exporting firms. It also shows information regarding industrial concentration. The unweighted average four-firm concentration ratio in manufacturing – measured with respect to apparent consumption rather than domestic output – is 60 per cent. The weighted averages are slightly lower but still over 50 per cent, indicating that larger sectors

Table 3.6 Characteristics of manufacturing establishments according to share of exports in total sales, Colombia

	Non-exporting establishments	Exporting establishments					Total
		Shares of exports in total sales				Sub-total	
		0.1–10%	10–20%	20–50%	50–100%		
All manufacturing sectors							
Number of establishments	5,922	547	168	196	122	1,033	6,955
Average size of firm							
No. of employees	46	201	167	172	142	183	66
Total sales (US$ thousands)	1,244	9,625	7,944	6,842	3,743	8,129	2,267
Labour intensity (%)							
Employees/value added[a]	8.43	4.50	3.64	6.32	11.47	4.85	6.47
Female labour (%)							
Female workers/total workers	30.69	26.54	25.26	31.56	60.55	30.98	30.81
Skilled labour (%)							
Technical employees/total employees	2.86	5.49	4.60	4.20	4.21	5.01	3.74
Technology (%)							
Royalties/total sales	0.52	1.15	2.40	0.99	0.40	1.28	0.93
Domestic raw materials integration							
Domestic raw materials consumed/gross production	39.26	30.45	23.80	35.70	44.39	30.92	34.84

Non-natural resource intensive sectors

Number of establishments	4,849	500	156	167	89	912	5,761
Average size of firm							
No. of employees	46	196	168	142	148	176	66
Total sales (US$ thousands)	1,098	9,071	7,574	4,739	3,523	7,480	2,108
Labour intensity (%)							
Employees/value added[a]	8.33	4.85	3.67	7.66	11.51	5.10	6.58
Female labour (%)							
Female workers/total workers	32.24	27.14	25.68	39.34	66.03	32.58	32.38
Skilled labour (%)							
Technical employees/total employees	2.98	5.74	4.53	4.12	5.01	5.24	3.93
Technology (%)							
Royalties/total sales	0.72	1.34	2.71	1.68	0.23	1.56	1.19
Domestic raw materials integration							
Domestic raw materials consumed/gross production	31.43	28.87	19.45	27.08	36.03	27.34	29.17

[a] Value added in US$ thousands

Source: Authors' estimates based on original data of DANE

Table 3.7 Characteristics of export establishments versus all manufacturing establishments, Colombia

	Overall manufactur-ing industry average	Averages of four-digit ISIC sector indicators		
		Arithmetic average	Average weighted by sector exports	Average weighted by sector output
Export shares in total sales (%)				
Exporting establishments	13.24			
All establishments	7.05			
Number of employees by establishment				
Exporting establishments	183	210	349	273
All establishments	66	85	156	131
Average sales by establishment (US$ thousands)				
Exporting establishments	4,083	5,821	11,313	8,867
All establishments	1,139	1,883	4,588	3,846
Four-firm ratio in apparent consumption (%)		60.92	52.68	50.79
Concentration indexes (inverse of Herfindahl Index)				
Output of all firms in sector		0.192	0.117	0.108
Output of all exporting firms		0.349	0.198	0.255
Exports		0.404	0.253	0.284
Labour intensity (%) (employees/value added)				
Exporting establishments	4.85	7.73	6.62	
All establishments	6.47	10.41	7.91	
Female labour intensity (%) (female factory workers/ total factory workers)				
Exporting establishments	30.98	22.33	23.43	
All establishments	30.81	21.59	24.40	
Skilled labour intensity (%) (technical employees/total employees)				
Exporting establishments	5.01	5.19	6.01	
All establishments	3.74	4.32	5.16	
Technology intensity (royalties/total sales, thousandths)				
Exporting establishments	1.28	1.26	0.99	
All establishments	0.93	0.78	0.86	

Source: Authors' estimates based on original data of DANE

(measured by either output or exports) are somewhat less concentrated. The inverse of the Herfindahl Index also confirms this result. According to a common interpretation of this index, an average Colombian four-digit sector can be characterized as an oligopoly of some five firms (eight firms if weighted by size). What is more interesting, production of exporting firms is significantly more concentrated than overall output, and exports are even more concentrated. According to the average estimated index, on average, exports are concentrated in two firms (3.5 if weighted by size). Equally interesting, the high concentration typical of the output of exporting firms, and the even higher concentration of exports, is characteristic of most sectors.

Tables 3.8 to 3.10 present the results of regression analysis exploring the sources of revealed comparative advantage of Colombian manufacturing. Table 3.8 is based on analysis of aggregate four-digit ISIC data. The dependent variable is the ratio of exports to total sales, estimated for the sector as a whole (Panel A) and for exporting firms alone (Panel B), respectively. The method used for the regressions is weighted least squares, with the weights given by the shares of each sector in total manufactured exports. Given the large differences between exporting and non-exporting firms, the factor intensity characteristics of the former are used as explanatory variables. Industrial concentration is included as an additional explanatory variable, as well as the average rate of export subsidies, tariffs and QRs in each sector (available only at the three-digit level).

These regressions confirm the complex factor-intensity characteristics of Colombian manufactured exports. Natural resources, labour and skilled labour are all sources of comparative advantage. Capital intensity is a source of comparative disadvantage. However, the effect of technology is not statistically significant, possibly because it is measured in a very partial manner. Similarly, backward linkages, measured by the degree of use of domestic raw materials, do not show any significant effect. Female labour intensity was tried, but the results were not satisfactory and the relevant regressions are not shown in Table 3.8.

According to the regressions presented in Table 3.8, export subsidies do not have any significant effect on sectoral export ratios. However there is some evidence on the anti-export biases of import protection, particularly of QRs, as they have negative effects on sectoral export ratios (Panel A), though not on the export ratios of the exporting firms (Panel B). In Panel A, the effects of skilled labour-

Table 3.8 Determinants of export shares in total sector sales and in total sales of the exporting firms of the sector, Colombia (four-digit ISIC sectors; standardized coefficients; t-statistics in parentheses)

Independent variables	Determinants of export shares in total sector sales				Determinants of export shares in total sales of exporting firms of the sector			
	Regr. 1	Regr. 2	Regr. 3	Regr. 4	Regr. 1	Regr. 2	Regr. 3	Regr. 4
Natural resource intensity (direct and indirect content of natural resources in output)	0.014 (5.42)**	0.013 (7.23)**	0.005 (9.77)**	0.015 (8.20)**	0.011 (3.23)**	0.011 (4.45)**	0.012 (4.30)**	0.012 (4.64)**
Labour intensity (employees/value added in exporting establishments)	0.008 (4.66)**	0.007 (5.38)**	0.009 (7.65)**	0.009 (7.40)**	0.012 (6.23)**	0.012 (7.80)**	0.013 (7.63)**	0.013 (8.56)**
Skilled labour intensity (technical employees/total employees in exporting establishments)	0.004 (3.01)**	0.004 (2.88)**	0.001 (1.11)	0.005 (3.81)**	0.003 (2.00)**	0.003 (1.93)**	0.004 (1.82)**	0.004 (2.33)**
Technology intensity (royalties/total sales)	0.001 (0.75)				−0.001 (−0.59)			
Domestic raw materials integration (domestic raw materials consumption/total output of exporting establ.)	−0.002 (−0.82)				−0.001 (−0.37)			

	(1)	(2)	(3)	(4)	(5)	(6)	(7)	(8)
Industrial concentration Inverse of Herfindahl Index			0.005 (5.19)**	0.005 (4.71)**			0.004 (2.64)**	0.004 (2.72)**
Export subsidies (ISIC three-digit export subsidy average)			0.001 (0.59)				0.001 (0.54)	
Import restrictions Quantitative restrictions (ISIC three-digit share of items with prior licence requirements)			−0.006 (−4.21)**				−0.001 (−0.29)	
Constant of the regression	−0.033	−0.034	0.022	−0.104	0.021	0.008	−0.067	−0.046
Mean of dependent variable	0.165	0.165	0.165	0.165	0.231	0.231	0.231	0.231
R-squared	0.496	0.486	0.687	0.605	0.513	0.510	0.556	0.554
Adjusted R-squared	0.461	0.466	0.661	0.583	0.479	0.490	0.519	0.530
F value	14.36	23.67	26.36	28.31	15.35	25.97	15.02	22.99
Prob > F	0.0001	0.0001	0.0001	0.0001	0.0001	0.0001	0.0001	0.0001
Number of observations	78	78	78	78	78	78	78	78

** Significantly different from zero at 95% confidence level

Note: ISIC sectors 3111, 3114 and 3116 (slightly processed food); 3530 and 3540 (oil and coal derivatives), and 3710 (basic steel industries) are excluded

Table 3.9 Determinants of export shares in total sales of exporting firms, Colombia (standardized coefficients; t-statistics in parentheses)

Independent variables	Regression 1		Regression 2	
	Sector average of independent variable	Variable of firm, normalized by sector avg	Sector average of independent variable	Variable of firm, normalized by sector avg
Size of establishment (Total sales of establishment)	−0.0009 (−2.82)**	−0.0013 (−5.52)**	−0.0002 (−0.68)	−0.0014 (−5.80)**
Natural resource intensity (direct and indirect content of natural resources in output)	0.0007 (1.58)*		0.0018 (3.89)**	
Labour intensity (employees/value added in exporting establishments)	0.0028 (6.87)**	0.0003 (1.45)*	0.0019 (4.77)**	0.0003 (1.37)*
Female labour intensity (female/total factory workers in exporting establishments)	−0.0003 (−0.83)	0.0004 (5.00)**	0.0004 (0.98)	0.0003 (4.87)**
Skilled labour intensity (technical employees/total employees in exporting establ.)	0.0018 (5.90)**	0.0007 (2.87)**	0.0020 (5.93)**	0.0007 (3.30)**

	(1)	(2)	(3)	(4)
Domestic raw materials integration (domestic raw mat. consumption/ total output of exporting establ.)	0.0011 (2.72)**	0.0002 (0.75)	0.0014 (3.17)**	−0.0001 (−0.22)
Industrial concentration Inverse of Herfindahl Index			0.0004** (1.60)	
Export subsidies (ISIC three-digit export subsidy avg)			0.0014 (4.95)**	
Import restrictions Tariff protection (ISIC three-digit tariff avg, items with dom. prod.)			−0.0034 (−6.15)**	
Quantitative restrictions (ISIC three-digit share, items subject to prior licence)			0.0015 (3.10)**	
Officially owned firms ('Dummy' variable)				−0.0006 (−2.50)**
Constant of regression	0.1537		−0.0218	
R-squared	0.2781		0.3310	
Adjusted R-squared	0.2700		0.3210	
F value	34.32		30.15	
Prob > F	0.0001		0.0001	
Number of observations	991		991	

* Significantly different from zero at 90% confidence level

** Significantly different from zero at 95% confidence level

Note: ISIC sectors 3111, 3114 and 3116 (slightly processed food); 3530 and 3540 (oil and coal derivatives), and 3710 (basic steel industries) are excluded

intensity become statistically insignificant when export subsidies and protection rates are included in the regression. This may be interpreted as a sign that the previous system of protection-cum-export promotion had biases in favour of sectors with such factor intensity characteristics.

Finally, there is in Table 3.8 evidence that high industrial concentration is associated with larger export ratios of the exporting firms (Panel B) and of the sectors as a whole (Panel A), which confirms the results mentioned earlier.

Table 3.9 conducts the analysis at the level of individual exporting firms.[19] Factor-intensity characteristics included in the regressions refer to both the sectors and the specific firm, relative, in the latter case, to sectoral averages. The results confirm the role that natural resource, labour and skilled labour intensity have in determining Colombia's comparative advantage in manufacturing. In Table 3.9, female labour intensity, particularly at the firm level, also comes out as a strong determinant of exports. Similarly, domestic backward integration is a statistically important factor, with positive effects on export ratios at the sectoral level. When controlling for other factors, large average size is a disadvantage, which confirms the negative association between size and export shares found in Table 3.6.

Aside from the factor-intensity characteristics of the sectors and the individual firms, some additional variables show statistically significant effects on export ratios, according to Table 3.9. Public sector firms – which are actually not very important in Colombia – have low export shares, after controlling for the characteristics of the sectors in which they are established. Contrary to the results in Table 3.8, export subsidies are statistically significant, with positive effects on export ratios. The effects of QRs are again negative, but the sign for tariff protection is positive.

Finally, Table 3.10 reports on the relationship between the factor-intensity characteristics (in 1990) and the proportion of each sector's exports destined for developed countries. Variables are defined here at a three-digit ISIC level. Technology intensity, as measured by royalty payments, did not register as an important explanatory variable and it is, thus, excluded from the table. The results presented indicate that there have been important changes during the period of analysis in the determinants of exports, particularly in very recent years. Indeed, the stability of the dependent variable throughout the 1980s seems to have been interrupted during the 1989–92 export

Table 3.10 Factor determinants of shares of developed countries in manufactured exports of Colombia (three-digit ISIC sectors)

	1980	1985	1989	1991	1992
Constant	0.225	0.461	0.528	0.236	0.162
Natural resource intensity	0.696**	0.423	0.400	0.900**	0.964**
	(1.73)	(1.22)	(1.08)	(3.61)	(4.08)
Labour intensity	3.861	1.612	6.985*	5.930*	7.210**
	(0.76)	(0.36)	(1.49)	(1.47)	(2.40)
Skilled labour intensity	−0.008	−0.021*	−0.043**		−0.004
	(−0.413)	(−1.34)	(−2.49)		(−0.39)
Memo: Correlation with share of developed countries in other years					
1980	0.711	0.687	0.298	0.302	
1985		0.864	0.472	0.453	
1989			0.426	0.477	
1991				0.854	

* Significantly different from zero at a 90% confidence level
** Significantly different from zero at a 95% confidence level
Note: Excludes oil derivatives and exports of textiles, apparel, and leather to Panama and the Dutch Antilles

boom, when the destination of exports experienced significant changes (see the correlations at the bottom of the table).

Natural resource intensity generates strong dependence on developed countries' markets. However, the correlation was not strong in 1985 and has actually become stronger only in recent years. The most surprising result is that, contrary to previous evidence, labour intensity was not an important determinant of the destination of manufactured exports in 1980 and 1985, but has become so in recent years. There was a strong negative association between skilled-labour intensity and dependence on developed countries' markets (or, rather, a positive association between such factor-intensity characteristics and dependence on regional markets) in the 1980s. However, and equally surprising, this association became statistically insignificant in 1991 and 1992.

Together with the results presented in pages 65–75, the foregoing analysis confirms the very important role played by natural resources and unskilled (particularly female) labour as sources of comparative advantage in exports to developed countries. Firms that achieved large ratios of exports to total sales also have these characteristics.

Skilled labour intensity is also an important factor in some cases, both as a general source of comparative advantage and as a particular determinant of exports to regional markets. The latter characteristic may have disappeared during the recent export boom.

Despite these sectoral determinants of manufactured exports, exporting firms are larger and more capital, skilled labour and technology intensive than non-exporting firms in almost all sectors. High concentration is also a special feature of exporting activities, even when compared to the extremely high concentration ratios typical of Colombian manufacturing. Direct export incentives also exercise a significant effect on export performance in cross-section analysis. Finally, the evidence from such analysis confirms the negative effects of QRs on exports obtained in time-series estimations. However, as in those estimations, this may arise from a different causal link, namely, that sectors with lower degrees of competitiveness and lower export ratios receive more protection through QRs.

ACKNOWLEDGEMENTS

We are grateful to Carlos Alberto Arango, Guillermo Bonilla, Jesus Alberto Cantillo and Luz Marina Monroy for very helpful assistance.

NOTES

1 This section summarizes previous research on the subject, particularly Ocampo 1991 and 1994.
2 For further analysis of the recent import liberalization, see Garay 1991: ch. 1; Ocampo 1990a, 1992; Hallberg and Takacs 1992; Ocampo and Villar 1992.
3 The definition of manufacturing in this study follows the ISIC. However, when using National Accounts data, it excludes meat processing (to adjust for the fact that shrimp exports show as industrial goods according to traditional classifications) and oil derivatives. See Ocampo 1994 for information on how such data were processed and mixed with that from the DANE Annual Manufacturing surveys and the FEDESARROLLO opinion surveys. If direct export data are used, only oil derivatives and cut emeralds are excluded.
4 Particularly textiles and leather products exported to Panama and the Dutch Antilles, where several calculations indicated that fictitious exports were considerable in the late 1980s. With falling tax rebates, such exports have almost disappeared since mid-1991.
5 For a further discussion of recent trends, see Villar 1992.
6 This indicator is constructed on the basis of the proportion of items

subject to prior licensing and the proportion of requests rejected, using a methodology similar to that suggested in Ocampo 1994.

7 Early studies include Sheahan and Clark 1972; Teijeiro and Elson 1973; Diaz-Alejandro 1976: ch. 2; Cardona 1977. For studies written in the 1980s, see Echavarría 1980; Carrizosa 1980; Villar 1984a; Lora 1985; Edwards 1986; and Botero and Meisel 1988. Recent studies include Crane 1991; Alonso 1992; Aldana 1992; Villar 1992; and Ocampo 1994.

8 See, in particular, Diaz-Alejandro 1976: ch. 2; Echavarría 1980; and Alonso 1992.

9 Models of this sort have been estimated with variable success (Carrizosa 1980; Villar 1984a; and Reyes *et al.* 1978). Villar (1984a) compares them with models in which external demand enters the supply function, and finds the latter to be superior.

10 See, for example, Carrizosa 1980; Echavarría 1980; Villar 1984a; Lora 1985; Reyes 1985; Edwards 1986; Villar 1992; and Ocampo 1994.

11 Teijeiro and Elson 1973; Diaz-Alejandro 1976; Cardona 1977; and Echavarría 1980.

12 Villar 1992 and Ocampo 1994. This is also the method used in this paper.

13 See, for example, Crane 1991 and Aldana 1992.

14 The index used is an average of the GDP of the USA, the rest of the OECD, Venezuela and the rest of Latin America, weighted by the share of each country or region in non-traditional exports during the previous year.

15 Capacity utilization and average tariffs collected were also tried in the regressions, but no statistically significant effects were found for any sector.

16 The original data used below refer to establishments rather than firms, as the tables also make clear. For simplicity, however, we will refer to them as 'firms'. Data from the DANE 1990 Annual Manufacturing Survey was adjusted so that it excludes ISIC sectors 3111, 3114 and 3116 (slightly processed food); 3530 and 3540 (oil and coal derivatives) and 3710 (basic steel industries, for which exports consist mainly of ferro-nickel).

17 The data on this variable refer to 1980, and are estimated from input–output tables calculated by Leon and Centenaro 1986.

18 In addition to those ISIC sectors generally excluded (see note 16), this excludes the ISIC three-digit sectors with more than 30 per cent direct and indirect content of agricultural and mineral products in the value of output. They are ISIC 311–312 (food), 314 (tobacco), 323 (leather products) and 331 (wood products, except furniture).

19 As in Table 3.8, the method of weighted least squares is used in Table 3.9. In this case, weights are taken from the shares of each firm's exports in total manufactured exports.

REFERENCES

Agosin, Manuel (1991) 'Trade Policy Reforms and Economic Performance: A Review of the Issues and Some Preliminary Evidence', UNCTAD, Discussion Paper 41, August, Geneva: UNCTAD.

Aldana, Santiago (1992) 'Determinantes de las Exportaciones Menores Colombianas', mimeo, Bogotá: Banco de Comercio Exterior de Colombia, July.

Alonso, Gloria A. (1992) 'Determinantes de la Oferta de Exportaciones Menores en Colombia, 1970–90', mimeo, Bogotá: Banco de la República, May.

Botero, Carmen Helena and Meisel, Adolfo (1988) 'Funciones de Oferta de las Exportaciones Menores Colombianas', *Ensayos sobre Política Económica* 13, June.

Cardona, Martha Helena (1977) 'El Crecimiento de las Exportaciones y el Sistema de Fomento de las Exportaciones en Colombia', *Revista de Planeación y Desarrollo* 9, 2: April–September.

Carrizosa, Mauricio (1980) 'La Balanza Comercial en la Década de los Ochenta', in *La Economía Colombiana en la década de los Ochenta*, Bogotá: FEDESARROLLO.

Crane, Catalina (1991) 'Las Exportaciones Menores: Recorriendo Nuevamente el Camino', *Coyuntura Económica* XXI, 2: July.

Diaz-Alejandro, Carlos F. (1975) 'Efectos de las Exportaciones no Tradicionales sobre la Distribución del Ingreso: El Caso Colombiano', mimeo, Santiago de Chile: CIEPLAN.

—— (1976) *Foreign Trade Regimes and Economic Development: Colombia*, New York: Columbia University Press.

Echavarría, Juan José (1980) 'La Evolución de las Exportaciones Menores y sus Determinantes: Un Análisis Empírico', *Revista Mensual del Banco de la República*, August.

Echavarría, Juan José and Perry, Guillermo (1981) 'Aranceles y Subsidios a las Exportaciones: Análisis de su estructura Sectorial y de su Impacto sobre la Apertura de la Industria Colombiana', *Coyuntura Económica* XI, 2: June.

Edwards, Sebastián (1986) 'El Tipo de Cambio y las Exportaciones Menores', in Vinod Thomas, *Macroeconomía y Política Agropecuaria*, Bogotá: Banco de la República.

Garay, Luis Jorge (1991) *Apertura y protección: Evaluación de la política de importaciones*, Bogotá: Tercer Mundo-Universidad Nacional.

Hallberg, Kristin and Takacs, Wendy (1992) 'Trade Reform in Colombia, 1990', in Alvin Cohen and Frank Gunter (eds) *The Colombian Economy: Issues of Debt, Trade and Development*, Boulder: Westview.

Harrison, Anne (1991) 'Openness and Growth: A Time Series, Cross-Country Analysis for Developing Countries', Working Paper WPS809, November, Washington, DC: World Bank.

Helleiner, Gerald K. (1992) 'Structural Adjustment and Long-Term Development in Sub-Saharan Africa', in Frances Stewart, Sanjaya Lall and Samuel Wangwe (eds) *Alternative Development Strategies in Sub-Saharan Africa* (48–78), London: Macmillan.

—— (1993) 'Trade and Trade Policy for Very Low-Income Developing Countries', in M. Nissanke and A. Hewitt (eds) *Economic Crisis in Developing Countries: New Perspectives on Commodities, Trade and Finance; Essays in Honour of Alfred Maizels* (121–34), London and New York: Pinter Publishers.

—— (1994) 'Introduction', in G.K. Helleiner (ed.) *Trade Policy and Industrialization in Turbulent Times* (ch. 1), London: Routledge.

Leon, Alejandro and Centenero, Jorge (1986) *Relacions Intersectoriales de Producción y Empleo para Análisis de Políticas de Demanda*, Bogotá: SENALDE.

Lora, Eduardo (1985) 'Los Sistemas de Incentivos, el Financiamiento y el Comportamiento de las Exportaciones Menores', mimeo, Bogotá: FEDESARROLLO.

Ocampo, José Antonio (1990a) 'La Apertura Externa en Perspectiva', in Florángela Gomez (ed.) *Apertura Económica y Sistema Financiero*, Bogotá: Asociación Bancaria de Colombia.

—— (1990b) 'Import Controls, Prices and Economic Activity in Colombia', *Journal of Development Economics* 32, 2: April.

—— (1991) 'The Transition from Primary Exports to Industrial Development in Colombia', in Magnus Blomstrom and Patricio Meller (eds), *Diverging Paths: Comparing a Century of Scandinavian and Latin American Economic Development*, Washington, DC: Inter-American Development Bank.

—— (1992) 'La Internacionalización de la Economía Colombiana', mimeo, Bogotá: FEDESARROLLO, November.

—— (1994) 'Trade Policy and Industrialization in Colombia, 1967–91', in G.K. Helleiner (ed.) *Trade Policy and Industrialization in Turbulent Times* (ch. 5), London: Routledge.

Ocampo, José Antonio and Villar, Leonardo (1992) 'Trayectoria y Vicisitudes de la Apertura Económica Colombiana', *Pensamiento Iberoamericano: Revista de Economía Política* 21: January–June.

Pack, Howard (1988) 'Industrialization and Trade', in Hollis B. Chenery and T. N. Srinivasan (eds) *Handbook of Development Economics*, Amsterdam: North-Holland.

Pritchett, Lant (1991) 'Measuring Outward Orientation in Developing Countries: Can it Be Done?', Working Paper WPS 566, January, Washington, DC: World Bank.

Reyes, Alvaro (1985) 'Políticas Económicas, Niveles de Actividad y Empleo: Un Modelo Estructural para Colombia', *Coyuntura Económica* XV, 1: April.

Reyes, Alvaro, Kugler, Bernardo, Sarmiento, Eduardo and Rubio, Mauricio (1978) 'Un Modelo de Corto Plazo para la Economía Colombiana', *Revista de Planeación y Desarrollo* X, 2: May–August.

Rodrik, Dani (1992) 'Closing the Productivity Gap: Does Trade Liberalization Really Help?', in G.K. Helleiner (ed.) *Trade Policy, Industrialization and Development: New Perspectives*, Oxford: Clarendon Press.

Sheahan, John and Clark, Sara (1972) 'La Respuesta de las Exportaciones Colombianas a Variaciones en la Tasa Efectiva de Cambio', mimeo, Bogotá: FEDESARROLLO.

Teijeiro, J.D. and Elson, R.A. (1973) 'El Crecimiento de las Exportaciones Menores y el Sistema de Fomento de las Exportaciones en Colombia', *Revista Mensual del Banco de la República*, June.

Thomas, Vinod, Martin, Kasi and Nash, John (1990) *Lessons in Trade Policy Reform*, Policy and Research Series, No. 10, Washington, DC: World Bank.

Thomas, Vinod and Nash, John (1991) *Best Practices in Trade Policy Reform* (ch. 3), New York: Oxford University Press.

Thoumi, Francisco Elías (1979) 'Estrategias de Industrialización, Empleo y Distribución del Empleo en Colombia', *Coyuntura Económica* IX, 1: April.

Tybout, James (1992) 'Linking Trade and Productivity: New Research Directions', *World Bank Economic Review* 6, 2: May.

UNCTAD (1992) *Trade and Development Report*, Geneva: UNCTAD.

Villar, Leonardo (1984a) 'Determinantes de la Evolución de las Exportaciones Menores en Colombia, 1960–81', *Coyuntura Económica* XIV, 3: October.

—— (1984b) 'Características de las Exportaciones Colombianas de Manufacturas: Un Análisis Empírico sobre su Intensidad en Mano de Obra', *Cambio y Progreso* I, 2, DANE: May–August.

—— (1992) 'Política Cambiaria y Estrategia Exportadora', in Astrid Martínez (ed.) *Apertura: Dos Años Después*, Bogotá: Asociación Bancaria de Colombia.

World Bank (1991) *World Development Report, 1991*, New York: Oxford University Press.

4

TRADE LIBERALIZATION WITH REAL APPRECIATION AND SLOW GROWTH

Sustainability issues in Mexico's trade policy reform

Jaime Ros

The second half of the 1980s witnessed a complete revamping of Mexico's trade policy regime. Policy reforms included the removal of quantitative import restrictions, on intermediate and capital goods in July 1985, and on most consumer goods in December 1987. They also included a gradual reduction of tariffs to a maximum of 20 per cent and an average of 10 per cent after the late 1987 reforms, compared to an average tariff of 16.4 per cent and a maximum of 100 per cent in the early 1980s. Other policy changes were the elimination of export subsidies and the relaxation of export restrictions as well as of regulatory measures (such as domestic content requirements) previously included in industrial promotion programmes. These reforms were undertaken in the midst of harsh macroeconomic adjustments, first to the 1982 debt crisis and later to the 1986 collapse of oil prices affecting Mexico's major export product.

In its initial phase, the transition towards a liberalized trade regime turned out to be strikingly smooth. The high real exchange rate (i.e. low real value of the peso) that prevailed up to 1987–8 – which had been forced upon macroeconomic policy by the adjustment to the debt crisis and declining terms of trade throughout the decade – greatly softened the 'initial shock' of import liberalization and contributed to policy sustainability in a number of ways. First, in the absence of compensating capital movements, trade liberalization had to be accompanied by real depreciation of the domestic currency to maintain the precarious external and internal balance. Second, the high real exchange rate eased adjustment costs and facilitated the adaptation of industrial firms to a more open economy by providing 'implicit' protection to producers for the domestic market and increasing exporters' benefits. Third, to the extent that the losers from a currency depreciation are less organized than the losers from trade liberalization, the real depreciation acted as a deterrent to the formation of coalitions opposed to trade liberalization.[1]

The Mexican experience after 1988 has, by contrast, been one of (further) trade liberalization with real appreciation of the peso. As the real exchange rate has fallen (i.e. the peso has appreciated) to earlier levels, the macroeconomic adjustment costs of trade liberalization have been reappearing, as evidenced by declining competitiveness of Mexican industries and an accelerated process of import penetration in the domestic market. While the preservation of internal and external balance, as well as policy sustainability, have been made possible by massive capital inflows since 1989, the potential re-emergence of foreign exchange constraints in the future raises serious concerns about the overall effects of these changes on medium-term economic growth.

At the same time, trade liberalization is expected to bring about a significant improvement over past productivity and export perform- ance. The longer term impact and sustainability of trade liberal- ization is then related to two main issues. First, can the turnaround of the capital account since 1989 sustain an investment-led recovery, which would otherwise be prevented by the recent rapid deteri- oration of the current account balance? Second, will the initially dominant effects of trade liberalization on imports be gradually offset by a spurt of productivity growth and a change in the structure of investment and productive capacity toward exportable goods?

This chapter addresses these issues. Section one (pages 101–3) puts recent trends in the balance of payments and growth performance in a long-term perspective, and presents a framework for their analysis. Section two (pages 104–12) traces the origin of current trends to the loss of growth potential that the economy suffered during the 1980s, and discusses the role played by trade policy reform. Section three (pages 112–26) examines the evidence on productivity and employ- ment trends in manufacturing and the whole economy. A concluding section summarizes the chapter's main findings (pages 126–7).

THE SHIFT IN THE GROWTH–EXTERNAL BALANCE TRADE-OFF

Perhaps the most striking feature of the post-trade liberalization period is the extent to which the economy's current account balance has deteriorated despite the rather moderate pace of economic recovery since 1988. While the current account deficit had reached 6 per cent of GDP by 1992, well above the average (4.3 per cent) of the previous period of economic expansion (the oil boom from 1978 to 1981), GDP growth at 3 per cent on average since 1988 (2.7 per cent for 1992) is two-thirds below the pace of the previous expansion (9.2 per cent) and less than half the historical growth rate of the 1940–80 period (around 6.5 per cent per year). Similarly, current rates of capital formation, of the order of 21 per cent of GDP, remain 5 points below the average of the oil boom. Projections for 1993 show no signs of improvement: the current account deficit is expected to increase further to around 7 per cent of GDP, with economic growth remaining in the 2.5–3 per cent range.

Figure 4.1 puts recent trends in a long-term perspective by presenting the historical relationship between the current account deficit (as percentage of GDP) and the GDP growth rate (expressed as a two-year moving average). As suggested by the figure, from the mid-1960s to around 1987 there had been a fairly stable trade-off between the GDP growth rate and the current account balance. This trade-off was clearly influenced by factors such as abnormally low levels of the real exchange rate or terms of trade shocks, which explain some of the outlier observations (in particular, 1975, 1981 and 1986). These factors, however, cannot account for the apparent deterioration since 1988 in the traditional growth–balance of payments trade-off.[2] While a current account deficit of the order of 4.2 per cent of GDP (the average since 1989) would have normally been associated with growth rates of 8 per cent per year, recent GDP growth has been proceeding at rates of the order of 3 per cent.

Why has the pace of economic growth in recent years been so much slower than expected on the basis of past trends? To explore this question, we derive a relationship between the rate of output growth and the current account deficit from the following macro-economic model:

(1) $$i = s_g + s_p + s_f$$

(2) $$s_g = z_o + z_1 \cdot u + (x_o^* - j^*) \cdot e$$

(3) $$s_p = \partial_o + \partial_1 \cdot u$$

(4) $$s_f = m + j^* \cdot e - x_o^* \cdot e - x_{no}$$

(5) $$m = m_1 \cdot u + v \cdot i$$

(6) $$x_{no} = \varepsilon_o + \varepsilon_1 \cdot e$$

(7) $$g = g_o + k \cdot i$$

i = gross investment
0u = capacity utilization
s_g = public savings
s_p = private savings
s_f = foreign savings (current account deficit)
x_o^* = oil export revenues (in foreign currency)
x_{no} = non-oil exports
m = imports
j^* = interest on foreign debt (in foreign currency)
e = real exchange rate
g = growth rate of potential output

All flow variables are expressed as nominal values divided by nominal potential output.[3] Key exogenous variables are oil exports and interest on external debt, respectively revenue and expenditure items, in both the fiscal and external accounts, and the real exchange rate.

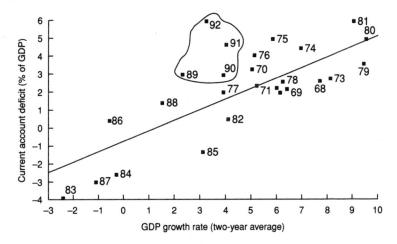

Figure 4.1 Current account deficit and GDP growth rate, Mexico
Sources: INEGI 1990; Banco de México, *Indicadores Ecónomicos*

Substituting the domestic savings functions (equations (2) and (3)) into the savings–investment identity (1) yields:

(8)
$$i = s_0 + s_1 \cdot u + (x_0^* - j^*) \cdot e + s_f$$

$$s_0 = z_0 + \partial_0$$

$$s_1 = z_1 + \partial_1$$

Substituting the import and export functions [equations (5) and (6)] into the foreign savings identity (4) yields:

(9)
$$i = 1/v \, (\varepsilon_0 + \varepsilon_1 \cdot e - m_1 \cdot u + (x_0^* - j^*) \cdot e + s_f)$$

Finally, eliminating u from (8) and (9) and substituting the result into the growth equation (7) yields the rate of output growth as a function of the rate of foreign savings:

(10)
$$g = \alpha + \beta \, s_f$$

where

$$\alpha = \Delta(s_0 m_1/s_1 + \varepsilon_0 + e(\varepsilon_1 + [1 + m_1/s_1][x_0^* - j^*]) + g_0$$

$$\Delta = \frac{k}{v + m_1/s_1} \quad \text{and} \quad \beta = \Delta(I + m_1/s_1)$$

Equation (10) – which in (s_f, g) space can be seen as the equation of the curve presented in Figure 4.1 – depicts a positive relationship between the output growth rate and the current account deficit. Higher growth rates (higher investment rates) yield larger current account deficits on account of both the larger levels of net imports and overall savings that are necessary to match the investment rate.

The rate of growth that the economy can achieve for a given current account deficit depends on the parameters of the domestic savings functions (s_0 and s_1); external public savings ($x_0^* - j^*$); and the non-oil trade balance measured at full capacity. In addition, the growth rate associated with a given current account can be affected by the real exchange rate (operating through both the non-oil trade balance and external public savings) as well as by the efficiency of investment (k) and the autonomous growth rate (g_0) reflecting employment and productivity trends. The rest of the chapter will explore the effects of each of these factors.

JAIME ROS

SAVINGS AND FOREIGN EXCHANGE CONSTRAINTS

The fall in domestic savings

Table 4.1 presents the evolution throughout the 1980s of the national savings rate and each of its components. Private and public savings are shown in their 'operational' definition, which excludes from private savings (and includes in public savings) the nominal component of interest payments representing compensation for the erosion by inflation of the value of existing public non-monetary debt. In this definition, private savings (s_p) as a fraction of GDP can be expressed as:

$$s_p = (1 - c)yd_p + ct_i$$

where yd_p is private disposable income (operational definition), t_i is the inflation tax, and c is the average propensity to consume out of real private disposable income (excluding the inflation tax from the operational definition of disposable income). Each of these elements affecting private savings is also shown in Table 4.1.

Public saving is divided into its domestic and external components, the latter being the public sector foreign exchange balance measured at current exchange rates – or, more precisely, the difference between oil export revenues (the main source of government foreign exchange revenues) and interest payments on public external debt. Because the latter have usually been offset by substantial oil revenues, even after the 1986 oil price collapse, the foreign exchange balance has been in surplus most of the time since the mid-1970s.

Each of the different components of the national savings rate underwent significant changes during the period – in 1982–4 following the debt crisis, in 1986–7 during the oil shock, and in 1988–90, the stabilization years. During the adjustment to the debt crisis, the private savings rate recorded a small decline, largely as a result of a contraction of private income (2.9 percentage points of GDP between 1980–1 and 1982–4) and a moderate increase in the propensity to consume (from 0.81 to 0.82). Their joint effect was almost offset, however, by the impact of the increase in the inflation tax (of the order of 1.6 percentage points of GDP). The contraction of private disposable income, by far the most important factor in the reduction of private savings in this period, was the counterpart of the increase

104

Table 4.1 Domestic savings rates, Mexico 1980–91

	1980	1981	1982	1983	1984	1985	1986	1987	1988	1989	1990	1991
In % of nominal GDP												
Domestic savings	22.2	21.4	22.4	24.7	22.5	22.4	17.8	22.3	19.3	18.8	19.2	17.9
Public savings	7.1	2.1	4.7	7.0	6.3	5.8	4.1	7.0	1.2	2.6	6.0	6.6
External	4.1	3.2	5.0	6.2	5.5	4.4	0.5	1.6	-0.2	0.0	1.3	0.8
Domestic	3.0	-1.1	-0.3	0.8	0.8	1.4	3.6	5.4	1.4	2.6	4.7	5.8
Private savings	15.1	19.3	17.7	17.7	16.2	16.6	13.7	15.3	18.1	16.2	13.2	11.3
Private disposable income	80.2	83.7	79.3	78.6	79.3	81.1	81.8	80.6	87.5	86.5	84.1	83.1
Avg propensity to consume	.832	.787	.835	.807	.817	.818	.866	.848	.806	.818	.853	.869
Inflation tax	2.0	1.9	5.5	3.1	2.1	2.2	3.2	3.6	1.4	0.6	1.0	0.5
Real private income per capita (index 1980=100)	100.0	109.4	97.1	87.8	87.5	89.3	78.5	79.2	82.1	85.7	80.5	81.8

Sources: Banco de México, *Indicadores Económicos*; Presidencia de la República, *Criterios Generales de Política Económica*

in the share of public external savings (the public sector foreign exchange balance in domestic currency) as well as in the share of foreign disposable income in GDP. Both of these were largely a consequence of the sharp peso devaluations in this period. These exchange rate adjustments also explain why, in this period, the domestic savings rate did not fall despite the reduction in private savings; the resulting income transfers from the private to the public sector tended, on the contrary, to increase the economy's average propensity to save. This was the case in 1983, when the real exchange rate was at its peak.[4]

A second shock took place with the oil price collapse in 1986. Initially, the terms of trade reduction represented a negative shock to public savings, since the fall in oil revenues sharply curtailed public disposable income.[5] But through new exchange rate and fiscal adjustments, the shock was transmitted to the private sector. First, the peso depreciation dampened the effects of the loss of oil revenues on the real domestic currency value of the government's foreign exchange balance. Together with the lower foreign interest rates in this period, these exchange rate effects explain why the fall in external public savings (3.4 percentage points of GDP) was much less than the decline in oil exports at constant exchange rates (of the order of 7 per cent of GDP). In addition, the fiscal adjustments following the oil crisis generated an increase of 3.1 points in public domestic savings. The private–public income transfers involved in both the exchange rate and fiscal adjustments led, however, to a 2.1 point decline in the private savings rate in 1986–7, associated with the sharp increase from 0.82 to 0.86 in the average propensity to consume. Since the fiscal measures almost offset the loss in public external savings, the resulting fall in domestic savings was of a similar size.

In 1988, the first year of the stabilization programme known as the 'Economic Solidarity Pact', the downward trend of private savings was temporarily reversed. The private savings rate recorded an impressive recovery, largely associated with the spectacular increase in real interest payments on domestic government debt. Indeed, the very high real interest rates that prevailed during the stabilization period (30 per cent per year in 1988) had the effect of increasing the share of private incomes in GDP and also of reducing the propensity to consume, probably as a result of the distributional consequences of the income transfers involved. Since 1989, as the initial uncertainty and credibility problems of the stabilization effort receded, the domestic real interest rate returned to normal values and with it private incomes and the propensity to consume both returned to their pre-1988 values. However, since the stabilization programme successfully reduced the inflation tax by around 3 percentage points of GDP, compared to 1987, the private saving rate actually declined below its 1986–7 value. At the same time, public savings did not increase between 1987 and 1991 – because the fiscal adjustments of the stabilization programme were offset by the fiscal effects of the real peso appreciation which accompanied it. The net outcome was the sharp decline in the national savings rate in the recent period (see Table 4.1).

Looking now at the three periods as a whole, the fall in the national savings rate can be seen as a result of the sharp decline in private savings, with the increase in domestic public savings compensating for the fall in external government saving following the 1986–7 loss of oil export revenues. In turn, the major factor behind the contraction in the private savings rate was the increase in the average propensity to consume. The reduced share of private income in GDP and the virtual elimination of the inflation tax (compared to the early 1980s) played a secondary role.

The increase in the propensity to consume may reflect the boom in consumer durable purchases associated with the liberalization of consumer goods imports in late 1987. These purchases had been repressed during most of the 1980s as a result of restriction on consumer loans in the banking system and on imports of consumer goods.[6] However, the increase in the propensity to consume had, to a large extent, already taken place by 1986–7, when it reached a value of 0.86 (compared to 0.81 in 1980–1).[7] This suggests that the major factor behind the decline of private savings may have been the decline in real private income. The behaviour of the propensity to consume has been closely related to that of private real income per capita and, as shown in Table 4.1, its increase in the past decade appears to have been determined, in particular, by the sharp real income contractions that took place during the debt crisis and the 1986 oil price collapse.[8]

Deterioration of the structural trade balance

Table 4.2 shows the external adjustments that took place throughout the 1980s in response to the debt crisis, the oil price shock and during the trade liberalization cum real appreciation episode since 1988.

Table 4.2 External adjustments in three periods, Mexico (billion US$)

	Changes within the period			
	1981–4	1984–7	1987–92	1981–92
Trade balance[a]	16.9	−4.1	−25.2	−12.4
Oil exports	2.0	−8.0	−0.1	−6.1
Non-oil trade balance	14.9	3.9	−25.1	−6.3
Non-oil exports[b]	2.2	4.9	10.1	17.2
Imports	−12.7	1.0	35.2	23.5
Consumer goods	−2.0	−0.1	7.3	5.2
Intermediate	−5.7	1.0	12.4	7.7
Capital goods	−5.0	0.1	15.5	10.6

[a] Includes non-factor services
[b] Includes *maquiladora* exports
Sources: Presidencia de la República, *Criterios Generales de Política Económica*;
Banco de México, *Indicadores Económicos*

The adjustment to the debt crisis involved a massive turnaround in the trade balance, of the order of US$17 billion from 1981 to 1984. Except for a modest increase in oil and non-oil exports (of the order of US$2 billion), the external gap brought about by the capital account shock was largely closed through a sharp import compression. The overwhelming presence of oil in the export structure (over 70 per cent at its peak in 1982–3) largely accounts for this type of adjustment. Given its low supply elasticity, oil export revenues reduced the overall export response to the exchange rate adjustments of the period. Moreover, the adjustment in the non-oil current account, for the same reason, had to be greater and so, too, for a given exchange rate adjustment, did the overall reduction in domestic expenditure necessary to achieve the required current account adjustment.[9]

Analogous reasoning explains why, when oil revenues were severely curtailed by the 1986 crisis, external adjustment had to be very different from that in the preceding period. Since both the private sector trade deficit and the public sector trade surplus were now smaller, so too were the contractionary effects of devaluation on absorption. With a more elastic response of non-oil exports – resulting from past devaluations and an exceptionally high real exchange rate in 1986–7 – and a reduced degree of external credit rationing, the balance of payments adjustment was made less severe and much more efficient, relying on export expansion rather than import contraction.

A sharp reversal of past changes in the trade balance took place in the post-trade liberalization period. After 1989 capital inflows of massive proportions, including direct and portfolio foreign investment together with capital repatriation, allowed the financing of a current account deficit in continuous expansion. The import boom in this period reached such proportions that, despite continued export growth, the decline in the trade balance from 1987 to 1992 exceeded by far the improvement that took place between 1981 and 1984.

By 1992 the economy was thus generating trade deficits that were larger than those of the early 1980s, despite a higher real exchange rate and lower levels of capacity utilization. While part of this structural deterioration was the consequence of the fall in oil revenues – by US$6 billion compared to 1981, or 1.8 per cent of 1992 GDP, another part – also of the order of US$6 billion[10] – must be attributed to the structural decline in the non-oil trade balance. The latter clearly suggests that the increase in imports resulting from import liberalization more than offset the positive effects of trade reform on the performance of non-oil exports. Recent trends in the composition of imports confirm the important role played by the late 1987 liberalization of consumer goods imports: out of the US$6.3 billion decline in the non-oil trade balance, around US$5 billion were associated with the surge in consumer goods imports after 1987.

This interpretation of the shift in the growth–external balance trade-off is summarized and illustrated in Figure 4.2. This shows the decline in the investment rate at a given current account deficit as a result of:

1 A downward shift in the savings–investment balance curve (corresponding to equation (8), page 103), brought about by the fall in external public savings and in the private savings rate.
2 A downward shift in the external balance curve (corresponding to equation (9), page 103) that resulted from the fall in oil export revenues and the structural deterioration in the non-oil trade balance.

The joint outcome has been the observed worsening in the relationship between investment growth on the one hand and the

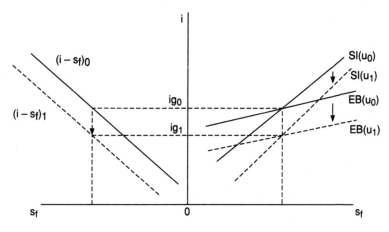

Figure 4.2 The growth–external balance trade-off, Mexico

current account balance on the other, which in Figure 4.1 would be illustrated as an upward shift in the s_f–g curve.

Capital inflows and domestic savings

The shift in the growth–external balance trade-off can also explain a puzzling development of recent years: the extent to which the effects of massive capital inflows on the investment rate have, since 1989, been crowded out by a fall in domestic savings.

As shown in Table 4.3, following the debt crisis in 1982 and the sharp contraction in net capital inflows, the economy was forced to generate substantial trade surpluses. These yielded a current account surplus of 1.7 per cent of GDP on average from 1982 to 1987, compared to an average deficit of 4.3 per cent in 1978–81. This shift of 6 percentage points in the current account balance was largely achieved through a falling investment rate (5.6 percentage points). The national savings rate, in contrast, remained on average roughly at previous levels. After 1988 the current account balance shifted again in the opposite direction, by 1991 reaching a level above pre-debt crisis values. The turnaround was of the order of 6.4 percentage points of GDP and thus similar in size, although of opposite sign, to the shift from 1978–81 to 1982–7.

This time, however, the increase in capital inflows left investment

Table 4.3 Savings and investment rates, Mexico (% of GDP)

	1978–81	1982–7	1988	1989	1990	1991
Gross capital formation	26.0	20.4	20.4	21.4	21.9	22.4
National saving	21.7	22.1	19.3	18.8	19.2	17.9
Public	5.4	5.8	1.2	2.6	6.0	6.6
External	2.5	3.9	−0.2	0.0	1.3	0.8
Domestic	2.9	1.9	1.4	2.6	4.7	5.8
Private	16.3	16.3	18.1	16.2	13.2	11.3
Inflation tax	1.6	3.3	1.4	0.6	1.0	0.5
Foreign saving	4.3	−1.7	1.1	2.6	2.7	4.6

Sources: Banco de México, *Indicadores Económicos*; Presidencia de la República, *Criterios Generales de Política Económica*; OECD 1992

rates well below previous peaks, with most of the increase in foreign savings having as a counterpart a sharp decline in the national savings rate (of the order of 4.6 percentage points by 1991 compared to the 1982–7 average). In fact, had the increase in foreign savings led to an equivalent increase in investment rates – as the contraction in 1982–7 had previously been reflected in falling investment – the latter would have recovered by 1991 the average values of the oil boom period. Instead, the 6.4 point increase in foreign savings had as a counterpart a less than 2 point increase in investment rates. In sum, rather than financing an investment-led recovery, the upsurge in foreign savings in recent years largely led to a crowding out of national savings.

The crowding-out mechanism was the real appreciation of the peso operating against a background of trade liberalization and reduced domestic savings potential. The impact of the real exchange rate on national savings took place through three main channels.

First, combined with a unilateral removal of protective barriers, the real appreciation of the domestic currency tended to increase the trade deficit at given rates of capacity utilization. As import penetration and the associated trade deficit created an excess of savings over investment at the initial level of capacity utilization, the savings–investment balance was restored through a downward adjustment in output and capacity use which reduced domestic savings.

Second, by changing the domestic currency value of the government's foreign exchange surplus, real appreciation eroded the real value in domestic currency of public external savings. This effect amounted to a transfer of income from the public to the private sector which yielded a reduction of national savings to the extent that the sector losing from the transfer had a higher propensity to save than the sector gaining from it.[11]

Third, the real appreciation of the peso played a key role in the success of the stabilization programme of late 1987, and the subsequent decline in the inflation tax. The effects of the fall in inflation tax revenues on domestic savings can be looked at in two ways: either as a fall in the private savings rate (if the inflation tax is included in private income) or, in the context of a real accounting framework where the inflation tax is part of government income, as a transfer of real income from the public to the private sector, leading to a decline in public savings and, as in the previous case, in the national savings rate.

PRODUCTIVITY AND EMPLOYMENT TRENDS

The analysis presented in section two suggests that the slow rate of economic growth in recent years, despite the increase in foreign savings to levels well above historical rates, had its origins in the loss of growth potential brought about by a decline in the domestic savings rate and a structural deterioration of the trade balance throughout the 1980s. At the same time, trade liberalization and other market reforms were pursued with a view to improving the economy's past productivity and external competitiveness performance. Are their effects likely to be significant enough so that, despite lower rates of accumulation, the loss of growth potential suffered during the 1980s can be reversed? This section looks at the pattern and causes of recent productivity trends in manufacturing and the whole economy.

Productivity trends in manufacturing: a review

In recent years, the growth of output per worker in manufacturing made a significant recovery from the low rates of growth that prevailed during the industrial slowdown in the first half of the decade. Although its pace since the last cyclical peak (1985) remains on average below historical performance (2.2 per cent per year compared to 3.5 per cent per year in the 1970s), this recovery gained strength since 1988 and reached an increasing number of industries. In 1990–1 productivity growth was, in fact, proceeding at a faster pace than historical rates and faster even than the recovery of output itself (which by 1991 was showing signs of a significant deceleration). At the same time, the real appreciation of the peso since 1988 more than offset the positive effects of productivity gains on the cost competitiveness of manufacturing, at least when judged from the recent evolution of relative labour unit costs and the spectacular expansion of the manufacturing trade deficit (see Table 4.4).

Ros (1994) examined, for the nine broad components of manufacturing, the behaviour of labour productivity in the 1980s and compared it to historical performance. A summary of the results is presented in Table 4.5, updated to include 1990. The acceleration of productivity growth in recent years appears linked to a variety of factors: the recovery of industrial demand and output growth since 1988; sector-specific policies, including the privatization and shutdown of public enterprises in a number of sectors; and the rapid expansion of imports in the domestic market brought about by the 1985 and 1987 trade reforms as well as by the real appreciation of the peso since 1988.

The role of output growth and sectoral policies was most significant in those sectors with the strongest acceleration of productivity growth since 1985: capital goods and automobiles – with an annual growth rate of 4.2 per cent compared to 3.5 per cent in the 1970s, and the basic metals industry – with 8.5 per cent growth compared to 2.2 per cent in 1970–80. These are also the industries that led the recent process of output expansion. In the automobile industry – by far the largest component of the machinery and equipment sector – industry rationalization was also successfully pursued through a special policy regime established since the late 1970s and involving the protection through licences of the industry's final products,[12] as well as the establishment of foreign exchange budgets for producers of finished vehicles allowing a reduction of domestic content requirements in exchange for the achievement of higher export targets. In the basic metals sector, the productivity increases since 1985 were partly related to the effects of a broader policy of state disengagement in a sector where public enterprises used to have a relatively high share of the industry's output (29.5 per cent compared to 7.2 per cent on average for manufacturing in 1980). This programme started in 1985 and included the shutdown and privatization of several public enterprises in the sector, with the major shutdown (the Fundidora Monterrey steel mill, 8,000 workers) taking place in 1986. The fact that around half of the productivity gains of the 1985–90 period were

Table 4.4 Productivity growth and competitiveness in manufacturing, Mexico

Annual growth rates (%)	1971–80	1981–5	1986–90	1986	1987	1988	1989	1990	1991
Labour productivity[a]	3.5	1.2	2.2	−3.4	2.0	3.2	4.1	4.3	5.6
Output[a]	6.3	1.2	2.7	−5.3	3.0	3.2	7.2	6.1	4.0
Indices 1978=100									
Relative unit labour costs[b]	–	82.6	66.8	51.9	53.5	67.6	77.3	83.9	–
Real exchange rate[c]	–	106.8	109.5	129.1	127.8	102.2	97.4	91.1	–
Real exchange rate[d]	–	110.5	113.7	131.6	128.2	105.6	104.0	99.2	–
Real effective exchange rate[e]	–	91.6	115.6	125.7	136.9	113.1	102.9	99.5	–
Manufacturing trade deficit (% of GDP)	–	3.4	2.1	1.8	−0.1	1.6	2.8	4.6	–

[a] Manufacturing
[b] Mexico's manufacturing/US business sector
[c] US wholesale prices/Mexico's consumer prices
[d] Relative wholesale prices (US–Mexico)
[e] Banco de México, based on consumer prices

Sources: INEGI, *Sistema de Cuentas Nacionales*; Banco de México, *Indicadores Económicos*; Ros 1992

Table 4.5 Output and productivity growth in manufacturing, Mexico

| | Annual growth rates | | | | Percentages | | | | | |
| | Labour productivity | | Output | | Import ratios[a] | | | Export ratios[b] | | |
	1980–5	1985–90	1980–5	1985–90	1980	1985	1989	1980	1985	1989
Food processing[c]	0.7	1.2	2.5	2.2	12.9	4.4	10.2	12.0	11.8	15.5
Textiles, apparel and leather	0.3	0.9	-0.3	-0.7	5.5	2.4	8.5	8.6	8.1	19.1
Lumber, wood and furniture	3.3	-1.3	-0.5	-1.1	6.0	3.1	6.1	2.9	8.2	24.2
Paper	2.4	2.7	2.4	2.7	28.4	14.8	25.9	3.4	4.3	9.1
Chemicals	1.7	2.1	4.6	3.6	43.7	36.9	46.4	14.6	32.6	33.0
Stone, clay and glass	-0.2	0.9	1.1	2.3	6.2	3.1	5.2	4.1	12.1	17.0
Basic metals	-0.1	8.5	0.1	3.7	81.1	37.4	42.3	2.6	11.4	31.7
Fabricated metals, machinery and equipment	0.9	4.2	-1.6	5.3	99.2	56.1	93.9	8.5	23.4	46.3
Automobiles[d]	1.2	6.7	-1.1	14.1	67.6	48.2	75.4	7.3	16.0	28.3
Other manufacturing	0.3	-6.1	1.3	1.4						
Total manufacturing	1.2	2.2	1.2	2.7	40.5	22.9	36.4	9.0	16.7	26.3

[a] Ratio of imports to sector GDP (1980 constant prices)
[b] Ratio of exports to sector GDP (1980 constant prices)
[c] Includes beverages and tobacco
[d] Terminal industry

Sources: INEGI, Sistema de Cuentas Nacionales

achieved in 1986–7 – in sharp contrast to the rest of manufacturing, where productivity had not yet started to recover and at a time when the removal of protection was being largely compensated for by an abnormally high real exchange rate – lends support to this interpretation of the sources of productivity growth in this industry.

Although difficult to disentangle from other effects, including those of a declining real exchange rate since 1988, the contribution of trade liberalization to productivity growth appears to have been positive in a number of cases. In sectors producing capital goods and heavy intermediates, trade liberalization facilitated a greater degree of intra-industry (and intra-firm) specialization in foreign trade, as suggested by the rapid and simultaneous expansion of both exports and imports in some of these industries. In some light manufacturing industries – such as food processing and textiles – trade liberalization shook out less efficient local producers or forced them to modernize, as conveyed by the fact that the recovery of productivity growth took place here in the midst of a slowdown of output growth partly explained by the high rates of import penetration in these sectors. This displacement of local producers resulting from increased exposure to foreign competition led, however, to less beneficial effects in other industries. In the experience of the wood industry and other manufacturing, the result was a worsening of both output and productivity performance whether compared to historical trends or to the period immediately preceding trade liberalization.

A few other studies have examined the recent behaviour of productive efficiency in manufacturing. Hernandez-Laos (1990) and Kessel and Samaniego (1991) are discussed together since the latter essentially updates the former's results for 1988 and 1989. Both studies present residual-based calculations of two-factor (capital and labour) productivity growth for manufacturing as a whole and its nine broad components. Kessel and Samaniego (1991) examine, in addition, the links between productivity performance and trade liberalization since 1985.

Table 4.6 summarizes their results for the manufacturing sector as a whole. The picture that emerges from the table is far more optimistic than suggested by labour productivity trends alone: since 1985 the growth of total factor productivity (TFP), at 3.7 per cent per year, shows not only a sharp recovery from the first half of the 1980s but a much higher rate than in the 1970–80 period (2.2 per cent per year). Based on this recent behaviour and a statistical analysis showing significant structural change in the trend rate of growth of

TFP since 1985, Kessel and Samaniego (1991) concluded that the post-trade liberalization period was accompanied by a sharp increase in the trend rate of growth of productive efficiency in manufacturing.

On a closer examination, however, this inference and the measurement of TFP itself raise strong doubts. As pointed out by Moreno (1992), the structural break with past trends, according to these estimates, took place in 1983 and thus before the 1985 trade reform.[13] Moreover, after 1987 the growth rate of TFP reverted to past trends. In between those years, the acceleration of TFP growth had largely been a consequence of a sharp increase in the growth of capital productivity from 1983 to 1987. Since manufacturing value added was the same in 1982 and 1987, these capital productivity gains (of the order of 35 per cent over five years) are fully explained by the sharp reduction in measured capital input which was falling during this period at a rate of 5.8 per cent per year.

The measurement of capital input by Hernandez-Laos (and adopted without changes by Kessel and Samaniego for the period 1980–7) involved adjusting the net capital stock in manufacturing by an index of capacity use (i.e. measured capital input is the product of the Banco de México estimates of the net capital stock and an index of capacity utilization based on the Wharton peak-to-peak method for measuring potential output). There are two reasons why such estimates of capital input should be taken with strong reservations. The first is simply that the net capital stock estimates (before any adjustment for capacity use) show very implausible behaviour. These estimates, presented also in Table 4.6, indicate a reduction of the capital stock of over 20 per cent from 1982 to 1987, with declines of the order of 6 per cent from one year to the next on three occasions (1984, 1986, and 1987). Alternative estimates of net and gross stocks of non-residential capital for the whole economy (Hofman 1991) show a reduction in the rate of growth of the capital stock in this period but no absolute contractions in any single year.

A second objection is that, even if the manufacturing capital stock had been declining in this period, adjusting the original estimates with a Wharton index of capacity utilization introduces a further problem. This problem is made clear in Table 4.6 – the adopted index of capacity use implicitly assumes that potential output (i.e. productive capacity) was growing at a rate of 1.1 per cent per year over the same period in which the capital stock was shrinking at an annual rate of 4.7 per cent.[14] By failing to consider, in the estimation of potential output, the fact that the capital stock (and thus productive

Table 4.6 Total factor productivity in manufacturing, Mexico

	Annual growth rates											
	1970–80	1980–5	1985–9									
Total factor productivity	2.2	−0.1	3.7									
Labour productivity	3.6	1.2	3.0									
Capital productivity	1.3	−0.8	3.2									
Indices 1980 = 100	1981	1982	1983	1984	1985	1986	1987	1988	1989			
Capital productivity	90.4	82.9	86.7	92.7	96.3	103.5	111.6	112.6	112.9			
Output	106.4	103.5	95.4	100.2	106.3	100.7	103.6	106.9	114.5			
Capital input	117.7	124.9	110.1	108.1	110.4	97.3	92.8	95.0	101.4			
Capital stock[a]	116.0	129.3	125.2	117.9	115.0	108.5	101.5	104.0	110.9			
Capacity use	101.5	96.6	87.9	91.7	96.0	89.7	91.4	–	–			
Potential output[b]	104.8	107.1	108.5	109.3	110.7	112.3	113.3	–	–			
Capital productivity (unadjusted)	91.8	80.1	76.2	85.0	92.4	92.8	102.0	102.8	103.2			

[a] Capital inputs divided by an index of capacity utilization. Values for 1988 and 1989 were extrapolated from the capital input series
[b] Output divided by an index of capacity utilization
Sources: Hernandez-Laos 1990; Kessel and Samaniego 1991; Casar 1989 for index of capacity utilization

capacity itself) was falling in those years, the adjustment of the capital stock by an index of capacity use introduced a downward bias in measured capital input and, thus, an upward bias in the capital productivity estimates.

Unfortunately, in the absence of independent data on capacity utilization, it is not possible to estimate potential output without making some implicit (and arbitrary) assumption about the behaviour of capital productivity itself. We are left, therefore, for lack of a better measure, with the unadjusted estimates of capital productivity. These are shown in Table 4.6. They suggest an acceleration in the growth of capital productivity since 1985 (as well as since 1983), albeit at a much slower pace than the adjusted estimates. Moreover, part of this acceleration, if not most of it, may reflect a genuine increase in capacity utilization since 1985 – by 1989 capital productivity had essentially recovered its 1980 value.

Relying on plant level data and estimates of cost functions for eighteen manufacturing industries, Tybout and Westbrook (1992) examined the evolution of technical and scale efficiency for 1984–9 and their relation to changes in effective protection over this period. A cross-industry analysis of the pattern of productivity changes suggested the following conclusions. First, most sectors showed productivity increases from 1984 to 1989, largely because of gains in technical efficiency rather than in scale efficiency. Second, technical efficiency gains 'show a striking association with changes in exposure to international competition' as measured by effective rates of protection. Third, the association between technical efficiency and protection does not appear to derive from fluctuations in capacity utilization.

Although the extension of the Tybout and Westbrook analysis to 1990 and 1991 – when labour productivity increases further accelerated – could actually strengthen some of the study's results,[15] their conclusions as they stand are in need of some qualifications. These qualifications make their results more consistent with the picture initially presented on industry rationalization and the mixed role that trade liberalization may have played in it.

First, while ten or eleven (depending on whether one includes the beverages industry with a 0.07 per cent gain) among the eighteen industries examined indeed show technical efficiency gains, the mean change in technical efficiency is 11.5 per cent for the whole period (or 2.2 per cent per year) and 3.5 per cent (or 0.7 per cent per year) when one extreme observation is excluded (non-electrical machinery showing a 143.58 per cent improvement). Although the database does not allow for a comparison with past performance, these are far from impressive productivity gains, especially when one considers that these improvements perhaps 'no doubt partly reflect[ed] higher capacity utilization rates towards the end of the period' (Tybout and Westbrook 1992: 37).

Second, the effective protection indicators adopted are based on comparisons of domestic and international prices. As such, and as the authors point out, any association with productivity performance should be interpreted with caution: 'measurement errors in prices can lead to spurious association between protection and productivity measures' and 'measured protection rates are themselves endogenous, and may respond to efficiency changes as well as cause them' (Tybout and Westbrook 1992: 38). This last caveat deserves further consideration because a number of industries showing increases in protection during the period of positive protection at the end of it are also among the industries with fast or very fast rates of import penetration, faster in any case than a number of others showing declining protection rates.

In Table 4.7, the eighteen industries in the Tybout and Westbrook study are ranked according to the rate of import growth in 1984–9 and classified in three groups. While most of the industries showing gains in technical efficiency indeed recorded fast or very fast rates of import penetration, the same applies to those with stagnant or declining levels of technical efficiency. This finding actually applies to a greater extent to the latter than to the former. Half of the industries with stagnant or declining efficiency (beverages, textiles, wood, and tyres and plastics) are in sectors with the fastest rates of import penetration and only one of them (leather and footwear) belongs to a sector of slow import growth. In contrast, while three among the ten industries with significant efficiency gains belong to sectors with very fast import penetration (apparel, metal products and food), three others among those ten industries are in sectors of slow import growth (miscellaneous industries, iron and steel and basic chemicals).

If the speed of import penetration, rather than the change in effective protection rates, was to be taken as the indicator of the change in exposure to foreign competition, the results in Table 4.7 would suggest a more mixed picture on the links between productivity performance and trade regime; a picture in which, as in our previous analysis of labour productivity trends, the beneficial effects

Table 4.7 Technical efficiency, effective protection and import penetration, Mexico

	Change in technical efficiency 1984–9	Change in effective protection[c] (group)	Mean output growth (1984–9)
Group 1[a]			
Beverages	0.07	IV	−0.029
Apparel	5.51	IV	−0.156
Textiles	−1.10	I	−0.078
Metal products	13.62	IV	0.085
Wood	−19.27	III	−0.264
Tyres and plastics	−28.68	II	−0.193
Food	24.46	IV	0.015
Group 2			
Glass	31.10	IV	0.148
Cement/other mineral products	−4.14/5.71	I/IV	−0.082/−0.069
Paper and printing	−19.35	I	−0.032
Transport equipment	7.80	II	0.110
Electrical equipment	−2.42	II	−0.087
Non-electrical machinery	143.58	III	−0.028
Group 3[b]			
Miscellaneous industries	46.04	IV	0.100
Leather, footwear	−17.39	IV	−0.359
Iron and steel	20.65	III	−0.047
Basic chemicals	1.20	III	−0.114

[a] Industries where imports more than tripled from 1984 to 1989
[b] Industries where imports increased by less than 50 per cent from 1984 to 1989
[c] I   = positive to larger positive ERP
     II = positive to smaller positive ERP
     III = positive to negative ERP
     IV = negative to more negative ERP
Source: Tybout and Westbrook 1992

of trade exposure and competitive discipline may at times be offset by the negative effects of import growth on market expansion through output–productivity links.

Clearly, however, import penetration rates may be reflecting the effects of productivity performance as well as increased exposure to foreign competition (i.e. they are no less endogenous in this respect than effective protection rates). Since any negative effects of increased trade exposure on productivity performance would operate through import penetration and output–productivity links, the presumption of a one-way causality going from productivity to import growth would be strengthened if productivity increases across industries were uncorrelated with output growth. Such is not the case, however. The Spearman rank correlation coefficient relating mean output growth rates (Tybout and Westbrook 1992: 26, table 7) and technical efficiency gains is a robust 0.74. Another way of illustrating this is that the mean output growth rates in all of the eight industries showing stagnant or declining technical efficiency were, without exception, negative.

Productivity growth in the whole economy

In contrast to the recent acceleration of productivity growth in manufacturing, no comparable improvement took place in the productivity performance of the whole economy. Despite a higher rate of output growth in manufacturing and a deceleration in the expansion of the labour force, overall productivity levels continued to decline after 1985 and, if anything, the rate of decline has accelerated compared to the first half of the decade.

To examine the sources of overall productivity trends, we follow a variant of a shift-share analysis. The analytical framework is summarized in equation (12), which shows the absolute change in productivity in a given period ($\Delta\pi$) divided into three components:

1 the change due to the increase in productivity in the high productivity (or modern) sectors of the economy ($\Delta\pi^h$, weighted by the sectors' initial employment share, e^h_o).
2 The change due to the productivity increase in low productivity (or traditional) sectors ($\Delta\pi^l$, weighted by their initial share in employment, e^l_o).
3 The change due to the rate of labour transfer (Δe^h) from low to high productivity sectors (weighted by the end of period productivity differential, $\pi^h_1 - \pi^l_1$):

$$(12) \qquad \Delta\pi = \Delta\pi^h \cdot e^h_o + \Delta\pi^l \cdot e^l_o + \Delta e^h \cdot (\pi^h_1 - \pi^l_1)$$

A similar decomposition can be applied to the change in productivity in the modern sectors:

$$(13) \qquad \Delta\pi^h = \Delta\pi^m \cdot e^{mh}_o + \Delta\pi^{oh} \cdot e^{ohh}_o + \Delta e^{mh} \cdot (\pi^m_1 - \pi^{oh}_1)$$

or,

(13') $\quad \Delta\pi^h = \Delta\pi^m \cdot (e^m{}_o/e^h{}_o) + \Delta\pi^{oh} \cdot (e^{oh}{}_o/e^h{}_o) + \Delta e^{mh} \cdot (\pi^m{}_1 - \pi^{oh}{}_1)$

where:

$\Delta\pi^m$ = productivity change in manufacturing

$\Delta\pi^{oh}$ = productivity change in other high productivity sectors

$\pi^m{}_1$ = end of period productivity level in manufacturing

$\pi^{oh}{}_1$ = end of period productivity level in other modern sectors

$e^{mh}{}_o$ = initial employment share of manufacturing in high productivity sectors

$e^{ohh}{}_o$ = initial employment share of other modern sectors in high productivity sectors

Δe^{mh} = change in the employment share of manufacturing within the high productivity sectors

To the extent that $\pi^m{}_1 = \pi^{oh}{}_1$, the third term on the right-hand side of (13') can be neglected. Substituting now (13') into (12), the change in productivity in the whole economy, as shown in equation (14), can be seen as the sum of four contributions coming from productivity growth in manufacturing, other high productivity sectors of the economy, and low productivity sectors, as well as from the rate of labour transfer from low productivity to high productivity sectors:[16]

(14) $\quad \Delta\pi = \Delta\pi^m \cdot e^m{}_o + \Delta\pi^{oh} \cdot e^{oh}{}_o + \Delta\pi^l \cdot e^l{}_o + \Delta e^h \cdot (\pi^h{}_1 - \pi^l{}_1)$

Table 4.8 shows the results of the exercise for 1970–80, 1980–5 and 1985–90, together with some complementary information. To facilitate comparison between periods, the total increase in productivity as well as in each of the four sources is presented as an average annual percentage increase over the productivity level in the initial year (i.e. as the absolute contribution divided by overall productivity in the initial year and by the number of years within each period. Each component can thus be seen as an average growth rate, the sum of which adds up to the average percentage increase in productivity.[17]

During the 1970s each of the four components was making a positive contribution to overall productivity growth. Particularly significant were the rapid productivity increases in traditional or low productivity sectors (agriculture, construction and other services)

Table 4.8 Sources of productivity in the whole economy, Mexico

	1970–80	1980–5	1985–90
Contributions from			
Manufacturing	0.7	0.3	0.5
Other high productivity sectors	1.9	0.0	0.3
Low productivity sectors	1.2	−0.5	−1.1
Labour reallocation	0.6	−0.9	−1.2
Total	4.3	−1.2	−1.4
Annual growth rates			
Labour productivity (whole economy)	3.6	−1.2	−1.4
GDP	6.7	1.9	1.3
Employment			
Whole economy	2.9	3.2	2.8
Manufacturing	3.4	0.1	0.0
Other high productivity sectors	3.9	2.2	0.9
Informal employment (as % of total) (initial/end of period)	15.6/7.6	7.6/13.6	13.6/21.9

Sources: INEGI, *Sistema de Cuentas Nacionales*; Economía Aplicada 1990

and the role of labour reallocation towards high productivity sectors. Both of these are associated with the rapid decline of informal employment – from 15.6 per cent of total employment to 7.6 per cent in 1980 – and together accounted for over 40 per cent of the total increase in productivity. The other major contribution was made by productivity growth in modern non-manufacturing sectors, reflecting the boom of oil output in the second half of the decade and the rapid productivity growth in commerce, probably related to the decline of informal and low productivity activities in this rather heterogeneous sector.

The economic downturn following the debt crisis and the end of the oil boom brought about a sharp reversal of previous trends. Productivity growth in manufacturing and other high productivity sectors stagnated while the contribution of productivity growth in traditional sectors as well as that of labour reallocation effects turned from positive to negative. Indeed, the economic slowdown in the midst of an acceleration in the growth of the labour force – produced by the high rates of demographic growth in the 1960s and 1970s – generated a rapid expansion of underemployment and low productivity informal activities which, by the middle of the decade, had already almost reversed the advances made in this area during the 1970s. The outcome was a decline in overall productivity levels at a rate of 1.2 per cent per year.

After 1985 productivity growth in manufacturing and other high productivity sectors made a positive contribution which, other things being equal, would have led to a 0.5 percentage point increase in the growth rate of overall productivity compared to 1980–5. This contribution, however, was fully offset by the effects of an even faster rate of productivity decline in traditional sectors and labour reallocation away from high productivity sectors. Despite a higher rate of manufacturing output growth and a deceleration in the growth of the labour force in this period, the expansion of employment in high productivity sectors was so slow that informal employment continued rapidly to increase and, thus, lowered overall productivity change below what it would otherwise have been.

Ultimately, the sluggish growth of employment in the modern sectors, manufacturing in particular, and the poor performance of productivity at the economy-wide level, are related to two factors. The first has to do, as in the first half of the decade, with the sluggish growth in the whole economy, resulting from the loss of growth potential examined in section two (pages 104–12). The second is the loss of external competitiveness in manufacturing since 1988. In its absence, the improvement in the productivity performance of manufacturing would have generated a higher rate of manufacturing output growth and encouraged a faster reallocation of resources towards the high and fast-growing productivity sector, both of which would have contributed to a faster rate of change in overall productivity.

Several caveats are in order before concluding. First, the exercise can be very sensitive to the level of aggregation adopted. A higher degree of disaggregation and better identification of high and low productivity sectors would very likely generate higher contributions (positive or negative) from labour reallocation effects and, thus, smaller contributions from sectoral productivity growth rates. Second, the allocation of informal employment to low productivity sectors may have led to a downward bias in the productivity growth of the low productivity sectors and a corresponding upward bias in that of the high productivity sectors outside manufacturing. Third, estimates for total employment make no adjustment for working hours and its growth may be overestimated if the growth of population twelve years and older is less than assumed. This would bias downwards the estimated productivity growth in the 1980s but is unlikely to make any difference to the comparison between the first and second half of the decade. Finally, the exercise makes no reference to the economy's overall productive efficiency as measured by TFP indicators. It should be noted, however, that available estimates of capital productivity for the economy as whole (Hofman 1991) show a steady rise in the capital–output ratio from 1982 to 1989. This increase appears to be associated with the ageing of the capital stock – in the case of the non-residential capital–output ratio which increased from 1.5 to 2.0 – and with the shift in the composition of the capital stock from non-residential to residential investments (which also contributed to an increase from 2.6 to 3.6 in the overall capital–output ratio).

CONCLUSION

The legacy of the crisis and adjustment process of the 1980s has been harsh: a collapse of public and private investment in the wake of the debt crisis, a major loss of fiscal and foreign exchange revenue brought about by the 1986 oil shock, and a severe contraction of the population's real income that followed from the fiscal and exchange rate adjustments to these shocks. While by the early 1990s the foreign exchange and fiscal disequilibria generated by these external shocks had been eliminated, this had been achieved at a severe cost for medium-term growth. In this context, as argued in the introduction to this chapter, the long-term impact and sustainability of trade policy reform will depend on its success in attracting the volume of capital inflows required to finance and sustain a strong investment-led recovery and in improving upon the economy's long-term productivity growth performance.

The analysis presented in this chapter provides no grounds for great optimism. While a massive increase in capital inflows completely reversed the negative resource transfers that the economy had been experiencing from 1983 to 1987, the economy's investment rate failed to recover to a comparable extent and remained well below pre-crisis levels. Despite some encouraging trends in the productivity performance of manufacturing, there are no signs of an improvement in the trend rate of growth of productivity for the economy as a whole.

These developments, it has been argued, are closely linked. Underlying them has been the real appreciation of the peso since 1988, operating against a background of reduced growth potential and the transitional macroeconomic costs of trade liberalization. Real exchange rate effects on savings, together with the short-term effects of trade liberalization on output, explain why the sharp increase in the rate of foreign savings has crowded out domestic savings rather than substantially increasing the investment rate. At the same time, real appreciation, together with trade liberalization, contributed to an acceleration of productivity growth in manufacturing. But in the context of declining external competitiveness of manufacturing and slow overall growth, this acceleration led to a declining employment share of manufacturing and growing numbers of underemployed in the rest of the economy rather than to an improvement in the productivity performance of the whole economy.

The loss of growth potential brought about by the crisis of the 1980s thus remains to be reversed. Its implications for the future prospects of the economy are serious, even in the absence of the severe credit rationing in foreign capital markets that the economy faced in the 1980s. The rate of foreign savings that the economy can absorb in a sustainable manner (i.e. without generating an explosive path in the ratio of foreign liabilities to GDP or exports) is itself dependent on the rate of growth that the economy can achieve for a given rate of foreign savings. The fall in this rate of growth – or rather locus of growth rates, what we have been calling the 'growth potential' of the economy – also reduces the maximum current account deficit that the economy can permanently sustain. At current growth rates (of the order of 3 per cent per year), the present levels of current account deficits (of the order of 6 per cent) are unlikely to be sustainable for a long period of time. A slow growth scenario would make the legacy of the 1980s harder to reverse and, as the recent experience suggests, would also make it more difficult for the potential benefits of trade reform to materialize.

NOTES

1 On the Mexican experience, see Ros 1992, 1994.
2 Changes in the measurement of the balance of payments since 1989 led to an upward revision of worker remittances (an additional 1 per cent of GDP) and to lower estimates of the current account deficit (compared to those based on the old methodology). Thus, on a comparable basis, recent years would lie even further apart from the historical relationship.
3 The specification of the import function thus implies a unit price elasticity for the demand of non-capital goods imports. For simplicity, we omit the effects of domestic demand in the export functions.

4 This effect is the result of the fiscal impact of devaluation, discussed in Krugman and Taylor 1978. Alternatively, the income transfer can be seen as involving the intermediation of the foreign sector, as the sum of an income transfer from the private sector (with a current account deficit) to the foreign sector and an income transfer from the foreign to the public sector (with a current account surplus). Because the expenditure implications of these Hirschman effects are not the same, the net outcome is an increase in the national savings rate.

5 This is the reason why the share of private income in GDP actually increased in 1986.

6 For an analysis of the role of durable goods consumption – which turns out not to be a major determinant of the decline in private savings up to 1990 – see Arrau and Oks 1992. The continued and sharp expansion of consumer credit in recent years suggests, however, that this may have become a more important factor after 1990.

7 However, at the time, its impact on national savings was hidden by the effects of a high inflation tax in 1986–7 and by the fiscal consequences of a heavily depreciated peso which dampened the effects of the oil shock on public savings. It was only after 1988, with the reversal of these fiscal effects by the real appreciation of the peso and the sharp reduction of the inflation tax, that its full impact became clearly visible.

8 For a more detailed defence of this explanation and a discussion of possible alternative hypotheses, see Ros 1992. On the behaviour of private consumption and savings in the 1980s, see also Alberro 1991; Arrau and Oks 1992; and Oks 1992. In addition to the factors already mentioned, the decline in public services, a key element of the fiscal adjustments before 1988, also appears to have led to a substitution of private for public consumption during the 1980s, thus contributing to the decline in the private savings rate (albeit not to the fall in the national savings rate).

9 The reduction of domestic spending was, in fact, induced by devaluation, for in these conditions the exchange rate change was bound to affect external balance through Hirschman and Diaz-Alejandro effects (i.e. through the contractionary effects on private income and spending already mentioned).

10 In fact, somewhat more, since this figure does not correct for the lower real exchange rate and higher capacity utilization of the early 1980s.

11 These effects are the counterpart of the contractionary effects of devaluation already mentioned (see note 4).

12 The automobile industry was, in fact, one of the few that remained protected by import licences throughout the 1980s.

13 Moreno (1992) also suggests that a dummy variable in 1983–9 or in 1984–9 would have equally shown a structural change in the trend rate of growth of TFP. Hernandez-Laos (1990) was also much more cautious, noting that TFP growth after 1985 (i.e. in 1985–7, given his database) was actually less than in the pre-trade liberalization period 1982–5.

14 It may well be that measurement error is less important in the estimates of capacity use than in those of the capital stock. However, the point that the two estimates are inconsistent remains pertinent.

15 On the other hand, the inclusion of data for small-scale plants, which are largely excluded from the INEGI's industrial survey used in the study, could modify the finding regarding the small relative gains in scale efficiency.

16 Any difference between the two sides of equation (14) should therefore be attributed to the neglected term $\Delta e^{mh} \cdot (\pi^m_1 - \pi^{oh}_1)$.

17 The latter is not, however, the compound rate of growth of productivity (also shown in Table 4.8) since it is estimated as a percentage of the initial productivity level (and thus will only coincide with the growth rate for one-year periods).

REFERENCES

Alberro, J. (1991) 'The Macroeconomics of the Public Sector Deficit in Mexico during the 1980s', mimeo, El Colegio de México.

Arrau, P. and Oks, D. (1992) 'Private Saving in Mexico, 1980–90', Policy Research Working Papers, Washington, DC: World Bank.

Banco de México, *Indicadores Económicos* (various issues), México: Banco de México.

Casar, J.I. (1989) *Transformación en el Patrón de Especialización y Comercio Exterior del Sector Manufacturero Mexicano, 1978–87: Ensayos e Investigaciones sobre el Desarrollo Industrial de México*, México: NAFINSA/ILET.

Economía Aplicada (1990) *Manual de Estadísticas*, México: Economía Aplicada, S.C.

Hernandez-Laos, E. (1990) 'Política de Desarrollo Industrial y Evolución de la Productividad Total de los Factores en la Industria Manufacturera Mexicana', report presented to the Fondo de Estudios Ricardo J. Zevada, Universidad Autónoma Metropolitana, Unidad Ixtapalapa.

Hofman, A. (1991) 'The Role of Capital in Latin America: A Comparative Perspective of Six Countries for 1950–89', ECLA Working Paper no. 4.

INEGI, *Sistema de Cuentas Nacionales* (various issues), México: Instituto Nacional de Estadística, Geografía e Informática.

—— (1990) *Estadísticas Históricas de México*, México: Instituto Nacional de Estadística, Geografía e Informática.

Kessel, G. and Samaniego, R. (1991) 'Apertura Comercial, Productividad y Desarrollo Tecnológico', prepared for the Inter-American Development Bank, Washington, DC.

Krugman, P. and Taylor, L. (1978) 'Contractionary Effects of Devaluation', *Journal of International Economics* 8, 3: 445–56.

Moreno, J.C. (1992) 'Multifactor Productivity Growth in Mexico: Some Notes on Recent Research', mimeo, University of Notre Dame.

OECD (1992) *Economic Survey of Mexico*, Paris: OECD.

Oks, D. (1992) 'Stabilization and Growth Recovery in Mexico. Lessons and Dilemmas', Policy Research Working Papers, Washington, DC: World Bank.

Presidencia de la República (1991, 1992) *Criterios Generales de Política Económica*, México: Presidencia de la República.

Ros, J. (1992) 'Ajuste Macroeconómico, Reformas Estructurales y Crecimiento en México', report prepared for the project 'El Rol del Estado en América Latina', with the support of the Fundación CEDEAL.

—— (1994) 'Mexico's Trade and Industrialization Experience since 1960: A Reconsideration of Past Policies and Assessment of Current Reforms' in G.K. Helleiner (ed.) *Trade Policy and Industrialization in Turbulent Times* (170–216), London: Routledge.

Tybout, J. and Westbrook, D. (1992) 'Trade Liberalization and the Structure of Production in Mexican Industries', Working Paper 92–03, April, Department of Economics, Georgetown University.

5

SUSTAINABILITY OF INDUSTRIAL EXPORTING IN A LIBERALIZING ECONOMY

The Turkish experience

Ismail Arslan and Merih Celasun

INTRODUCTION

In the aftermath of her debt crisis in 1978–80, Turkey's trade-oriented adjustment process yielded a substantial amount of restructuring and growth in the greater part of the 1980s. In the context of the prolonged adjustment difficulties in major debtor countries, Turkey's economic recovery was very rapid in the early 1980s, and was followed by well-sustained export-led expansion in the mid-1980s. Given Turkey's import-substitution-based policy stance from the mid-1950s to the late 1970s, a strong post-1980 commitment to greater openness and liberalization attracted considerable research attention in the recent literature. The bulk of this literature covered the 1980 to 1987–8 period, and evaluated its various policy aspects.[1]

Notwithstanding the differences in their focus and analytical framework, recent assessments have commonly noted that Turkey's post-1980 economic performance was strong in external adjustment, but weak in achieving the kind of internal balance that is consistent with the envisaged market-directed and export-led growth path. In particular, the inability to attain price stability created considerable uncertainty as regards the nature of the next policy moves toward stabilization, hampering longer horizon investment projects needed to sustain industrial exporting in the 1990s.

Against the background of the 1980–7 adjustment experience, the post-1988 Turkish economic scene featured new policy contexts and systemic developments, which were not clearly anticipated and explored in earlier studies. These include an almost completely liberalized capital account regime, a sharp reversal of wage trends, and further deterioration of public finance. Furthermore, a free trade agreement was signed (in 1991) with the European Free Trade Association (EFTA) with a commitment to reduce customs duties to levels applicable to imports from the European Union (EU). Turkey's association agreement (and additional protocol) with the EU foresees the formation of a customs union in 1996. Although the preparatory work towards a Turkey–EU customs union is surrounded by political uncertainty, the moves in this direction will entail further tariff reductions as well as new constraints on the subsidy system. All these recent shifts in policy premises imply a considerable loss of autonomy in the conduct of macroeconomic, trade and industrialization policies in the future.

This chapter is concerned with the major issues surrounding the sustainability of industrial growth and exporting in Turkey. Against the backdrop of major indicators of economic performance, section two (pages 132–45) brings out the recent reversal of real exchange rate and wage trends, and examines their impact on trade balance, public finances and domestic saving. Section three (pages 145–53) reassesses export performance with a particular emphasis on the role of cost competitiveness. In section four (pages 153–61), the investment incentive system is discussed, and the pattern of capital formation in manufacturing is analysed with respect to its major determinants. The implications of the new policy context are recapitulated in section five (page 162).

FROM SHARP EXTERNAL ADJUSTMENT TO EMERGING INSTABILITY IN EXPORT-LED GROWTH

Major indicators: an overview

For purposes of policy reappraisal, four episodes may be differentiated in Turkey's recent economic history from the mid-1970s to the early 1990s:

- foreign-financed boom in the mid-1970s;
- debt crisis in 1978–80;
- export-oriented adjustment and liberalization in 1980–7;
- macroeconomic instability from 1988 onwards.

Panel A in Table 5.1 assembles the major indicators to bring out the differential performance in the successive policy episodes. Compared with the dismal conditions in 1978–80, the 1980–7 policy phase was characterized by an above-average (developing country) growth performance accompanied by rapid and sustained export expansion (in real terms nearly 22 per cent per year). Panels B and C in Table 5.1 show the rise in trade ratios, and the increase in the shares of manufacturing in total exports, value added, and employment.

Table 5.1 Economic performance and restructuring, Turkey

	1976–7	1978–80	1981–7	1988–91	1992[a]
A Average annual growth (%)					
GNP	5.9	0.5	5.5	3.7	5.9
Exports (volume)	6.7	−5.5	21.7	4.9	8.3[b]
Imports (volume)	6.1	−6.0	13.2	10.4	8.7[b]
Employment	3.1	−2.6	2.0	2.1	−0.2
Wholesale price index	22.8	72.4	35.1	58.5	62.1
		1980	1988	1991	1992[a]
B Share in GNP (%)					
External trade (goods)[c]					
Exports		5.0	16.5	12.5	13.3
Imports		13.6	20.2	19.3	20.2
Trade balance		−8.0	−3.7	−6.8	−6.9
Saving[d]					
Private		16.0	17.5	21.3	19.5
Public		8.2	8.8	0.7	−0.6
Total domestic		24.2	26.3	22.0	18.9
Foreign saving (CAB)		4.5	−2.3	1.7	3.7
C Share of manufacturing (%)					
Exports		36.0	76.7	77.8	83.2
GDP		25.0	32.4	29.5	29.3
Employment		11.8	13.5	14.1	14.3
Capital stock		28.9	25.2	–	–

[a] Preliminary data
[b] In current US dollars
[c] In current price terms
[d] At constant 1988 prices. CAB denotes current account balance.
Source: Authors' calculations based on State Institute of Statistics trade and price data, and State Planning Organization labour and national accounts data

In contrast tc the favourable parameters of trade-oriented re-structuring in 1981–7, we also note the fall in the share of manu-facturing in the total economy-wide capital stock. This shows the absence of a strong investment boost to manufactured exports at the aggregate level, notwithstanding the fact that the observed changes in capital formation patterns (within manufacturing) favoured current export industries as analysed in section four (pages 153–61).

Given the initial conditions of low utilization rates of existing productive capacities, the post-1980 export expansion seems to have benefited strongly from real exchange rate depreciation as suggested by Figure 5.1. Within the context of the general equilibrium price system, the counterpart of currency depreciation (i.e. the rise in the relative price of tradables) was the steep fall in non-agricultural real wages despite some noticeable gains in labour productivity. The real devaluations-cum-wage repression resulted in a sharply reduced real unit cost of labour in terms of trade partners' currencies from 1980 to 1988, as also shown in Figure 5.1.

The restructuring success of the 1981–7 period was not, however, associated with substantial progress in achieving price stability. In the latter period, the inflation rate still averaged around 35 per cent per year, which nevertheless represented a sizeable reduction from the very high inflation rate in 1978–80. The view that fiscal deficits were the source of this inflation is forcefully articulated by Anand and van Wijnbergen (1989), empirically supported by Rodrik (1990), and widely shared within the policy community. The financial liberalization of the period also contributed to the erosion of the base for the inflation tax, which had been persistently required as a residual source in financing fiscal deficits. A heavy reliance on price adjustments (of the exchange rate, interest rates and state enterprise products) also generated highly variable cost-push elements contrib-uting to inflationary dynamics.

Finally, Table 5.1 draws attention to the growing macroeconomic instability in the post-1988 period. The average inflation rate in 1988–91 increased to around 60 per cent per year, accompanied by high variability of output growth, which tended to slow down in conjunction with the reduced rate of expansion of merchandise exports. While the Gulf War and the embargo against Iraq produced unfavourable exogenous effects, the post-1988 economic perform-ance was mainly affected by significant changes in the domestic policy context.[2] These were:

134

Figure 5.1 Exchange rate, labour cost and labour productivity, Turkey 1979–90

1 The deepening of external financial liberalization.
2 Wage explosion.
3 Deterioration in public finance.

These are each briefly discussed in the remaining part of this section.

External financial liberalization

The process of post-1980 Turkish economic liberalization proceeded in a gradual but quite credible fashion, broadly following the sequencing supported by conventional wisdom (Boeri 1991; Celasun

1994). Trade reforms initially removed quantitative restrictions (QRs) in 1981, eliminated licensing in 1984, and then realigned and reduced tariffs from 1988 onward. The internal financial liberalization was introduced at an early stage (1980–1) by deregulating domestic interest rates.[3] From 1984 on, significant intermediate steps were taken towards external financial liberalization by granting considerable freedom allowing:

1 Residents to borrow in international markets, and to transfer capital and hold assets abroad.
2 Non-residents to issue liabilities or to hold assets in domestic markets.
3 Residents and non-residents to open foreign exchange (FX) deposits in domestic banks.[4]

The underlying objectives were to provide greater flexibility in trade financing and to prevent and/or reverse capital flight in a setting which promoted FX earnings in the private sector.

The post-1984 relaxation of controls over capital flows generated a rapid rise in FX holdings of residents, which intensified currency substitution in the domestic economy. As the stock of FX assets increased, the exchange rate became an asset price as well as, as previously, the price of trade flows in the current account. In the context of the growing interdependence among capital flows, differential interest rates and expected changes in the exchange rate, it became evident that new mechanisms were needed to ensure a more orderly operation and coordination of domestic financial markets.

To regain some degree of indirect control over exchange rates and domestic interest rates, the Central Bank established interbank markets for domestic currency in terms of foreign exchange in 1988. Encouraged by the rapid growth and operational effectiveness of these interbank markets, the policymakers introduced further measures to accelerate capital account liberalization in August 1989, and subsequently adopted the IMF rules for full convertibility in April 1990.

As could be expected from a variety of liberalization episodes elsewhere (e.g. post-1988 Mexico and more recently Argentina), the sweeping deregulation of capital movements resulted in a sizeable real appreciation of the currency, cumulatively by 20 per cent in 1989–90. In conjunction with reductions in import tariffs, currency appreciation provided wider scope for large upward adjustments in real wages, which had been heavily repressed during 1980–8. With the sharp rise in domestic demand, imports nearly exploded in 1990, yielding a huge rise in the merchandise trade deficit as shown in Figure 5.2. The trade deficit increased to US$9.3 billion in 1990 from the annual average of US$3.4 billion in 1988–9. The real appreciation of the currency was halted in 1991, a year which featured Gulf crisis related uncertainties in financial markets, and weakened domestic demand and imports. Helped by a populist fiscal stance after the October 1991 elections, domestic demand and output recovered, boosting imports and raising the trade deficit from about US$7.5 billion in 1991 to US$8.2 billion in 1992.

The modes of financing of Turkey's post-1989 trade deficits become apparent from an examination of the external accounts data shown in Table 5.2. The large differences between trade deficits and

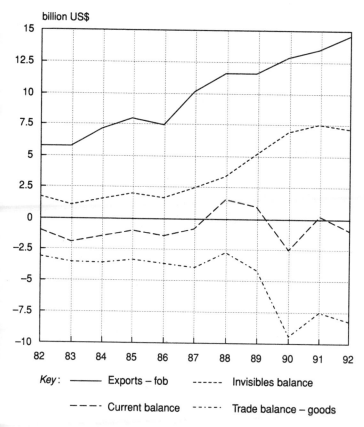

Figure 5.2 Current account indicators, Turkey 1982–92

Table 5.2 External capital flows and related indicators, Turkey 1986–92 (million US$)

	1986–7 average	1988–9 average	1990	1991	1992
A Balance of payments					
Trade balance (goods)	-3,808	-3,420	-9,342	-7,454	-8,157
CAB before grants	-1,196	1,232	-3,380	-1,626	-1,449
CAB after grants	-1,136	1,279	-2,625	258	-943
Capital account	2,008	-89	4,037	-2,397	3,648
Foreign direct investment	116	509	700	783	779
Portfolio investment	214	1,382	547	648	2,411
of which public sector issue of bonds	89	1,020	572	618	2,762
Medium and long term (net)	1,247	-547	-210	-808	-938
Short-term flows	431	-1,433	3,000	-3,020	1,396
Change in:					
Assets	-629	-529	-409	-2,563	-2,438
Credit extended	-548	-109	156	-811	-327
Bank reserves	-82	-420	-565	-1,752	-2,111
Liabilities	1,060	-904	3,409	-457	3,834
Credit received	836	-1,085	2,520	590	4,091
Deposits	225	181	889	-1,047	-257
Errors, omissions and counterpart items	8	637	-104	1,110	-1,221
Change in official reserves	-880	-1,826	-1,308	1,029	-1,484
B Indicators of currency substitution (%)					
Foreign deposits/GNP	3.7	5.2	5.0	7.4	9.6
Time deposits/GNP	14.5	12.0	12.2	11.7	11.8
Reserve money/GNP	8.5	7.6	6.8	6.4	6.0

Notes: CAB denotes current account balance. The term 'grants' refers to official transfers in invisible accounts. A (−) sign indicates an increase in short-term assets and official reserves. The annual averages of monetary aggregates are used in the computation of indicators in Panel B
Source: Central Bank, authors' calculations

current account balances (CABs) underline the growing significance of invisible receipts in the balance of payments. It should be noted, however, that Turkey also benefited in 1990–2 from the official transfers granted by the allies in connection with its role in the Gulf War. Table 5.2 shows, therefore, CAB estimates before and after such official grants. The difference between the trade balance and CAB before grants corresponds to net exports of factor and non-factor services, which showed a positive response to the deregulation of external accounts. Notwithstanding the favourable performance of net service exports, the CAB before grants turned from a surplus position in 1988–9 into a deficit position from 1990 on; this was the product of the sharp rise in trade deficits due to the greater penetration of goods imports.

The capital account items documented in Table 5.2 indicate a number of significant trends in external finance. It is clear that Turkey did not benefit during 1988–92 from positive net flows of medium- and long-term credits because of its large debt repayments. The immediate impact of switching to full convertibility was a steep rise in short-term inflows in 1990 in the form of credits and bank deposits. In 1991, though, the capital movements proved to be highly sensitive to changes in market conditions and uncertainties in domestic financial policies in a pre-election political context, and there was a net outflow of about US$3.0 billion. Such a net short-term capital outflow could not be offset by other items in the capital account in 1991, leading to the drawdown of official foreign exchange reserves by more than US$1.0 billion.

In response to the new administration's attempt (after the 1991 elections) to bring down domestic real interest rates, the net short-term capital outflow continued in early 1992; but this outflow was reversed later, resulting in a net inflow of US$1.4 billion over the year with a strong stimulus provided by higher rates of Treasury borrowing after April 1992. In a setting of large fiscal deficits (about 12.6 per cent of GNP in 1992), high domestic real interest rates (22 per cent) and slight real depreciation (2.4 per cent), commercial banks borrowed in short-term foreign exchange markets (credit received was US$4.0 billion in 1992), converted these into domestic currency and invested in government securities. According to conservative estimates, banks had a short position in foreign exchange of over US$3.5 billion in early 1993.

In the presentation of the capital accounts in Table 5.2, the portfolio investment flows reflect mainly public sector bond issues in international capital markets, which were not tapped heavily during the Gulf crisis. However, bond issues by the public sector expanded later, reaching US$2.7 billion in 1992. Furthermore, as shown in Table 5.2, foreign direct investment (FDI) became an increasingly significant item in the balance of payments, but its relative size still falls short of the levels obtained in other middle-income countries such as Mexico. In the early 1990s the sectoral shares of manufacturing and services in total FDI permits were about 55 and 40 per cent, respectively.

A further observation relates to the currency substitution induced by the rapid expansion of FX holdings by residents. Panel B in Table 5.2 shows the significant rise in FX deposits (to nearly 10 per cent of GNP in 1992 from 3.7 per cent in 1986–7) and the stagnating size of domestic deposits. Together with high and variable inflation, currency substitution contributed to the fall in demand for reserve money (to 6 per cent of GNP in 1992 from 8.5 per cent in 1986–7), lowering the base for seigniorage revenue. The monetary financing of even a small part of the fiscal deficits had therefore become a highly inflationary policy option.

The expansion of currency substitution posed another dilemma for the policymakers. The government's ability to reduce domestic real interest rates was severely constrained by the possibilities of FX hoarding by residents, which could quickly destabilize the FX market. In the absence of current account surpluses, the openness of the capital account therefore necessitated the maintenance of above-normal levels of official international reserves (at a high cost in the form of greater foreign borrowing and larger debt stock) to preserve stability in the FX market in the face of the prospect of speculative behaviour through FX hoarding and/or short-term capital movements.

At this juncture, it is instructive to draw attention to certain broad issues that seem to be common to the economic performance of Turkey and Mexico, both of which pursued similar strategies of intensified external liberalization in the post-1988 period. In Chapter 4 Ros provides a forceful assessment of the growth–external balance trade-off observed in recent Mexican experience. In the mid-1970s Mexico and Turkey had both experienced high GDP growth rates in the context of wide trade deficits (Celasun and Rodrik 1989: ch. 2). However, as the recent data show, both countries faced a decline in their post-1988 growth rates despite the widened trade imbalances.

In his penetrating analysis, Ros attaches prime importance to the real appreciation of the currency, which produced an adverse impact on internal and external balance. In particular, Ros emphasizes the negative effects of real appreciation and capital inflows on domestic savings. His principal argument is that if a fall in net exports (due to trade liberalization) is combined with a fall in domestic savings, the internal and external balance would be restored at lower rates of capacity utilization and investment, causing a slowdown in the growth process.

In its broad analytical spirit, the latter argument is plausible for adjusting economies experiencing trade liberalization, expansion of capital inflows and real appreciation. As Ros points out, the real appreciation reduced Mexican domestic savings mainly through a decline in the inflation tax and the lower peso value of oil export revenue for the public sector. In the Turkish case, the public sector was a net importer rather than a net exporter, and strongly benefited from real appreciation, especially through the reduced fiscal burden of external debt service valued in domestic currency. Nonetheless, the public sector component of Turkish domestic savings sharply declined from 1988 onward mainly due to surging real wages in a more contestable and populist political environment.

From wage repression to wage explosion

As noted earlier, the downward flexibility of real wages was an important structural characteristic of the adjustment process from 1980 to 1988. Under restrictive institutional arrangements in this period, real wages in the formal urban sector were maintained at about 30–40 per cent below the levels obtained in the pre-crisis period (Boratav 1990; Senses 1992). The falling share of labour in total income was widely recognized as a social cost of adjustment with potentially destabilizing features.

The economic effects of real wage restraint have been mainly perceived and discussed as micro-level phenomena. Lower wages definitely enhanced the capacity of firms to absorb cost shocks originating from real devaluations and deregulated interest rates. Lower labour costs increased the competitiveness of exporting firms especially in labour-intensive industries.

In turn, the macro-level effects of real wage reductions have not been sufficiently emphasized in recent literature on the Turkish economy. However, considerable evidence has been provided by Celasun and Rodrik (1989) and Celasun (1994) on the linkage between domestic saving and real wage movements in the Turkish economy. This linkage is particularly strong in the public sector, which employs about 40 per cent of formal wage earners (including civil servants) and more than 20 per cent of total non-agricultural labour. The lowered cost of labour services purchased by the government improves the public sector's capacity for resource mobilization, and results in larger public saving with a positive impact on total domestic saving. Higher domestic saving implies lower domestic absorption, which provides scope for export expansion. This is exactly what took place in the earlier part of the 1980s, as documented by Celasun (1994). At the sectoral level, lower labour income reduces domestic demand mainly in consumption goods industries, which have relatively the highest export orientation, as emphasized by Taskin and Yeldan (1992).

In conjunction with the rapidly liberalized domestic political process and wage settlement arrangements after the 1987 elections, it was expected that real wages would recover under the growing influence of labour unions. With the broad support of public opinion, the wage round of 1989 attempted to compensate workers for their losses in the 1980s. As aptly observed by Onis and Webb (1992), the wage round of 1991 was more aggressive in the sense that unions aimed 'to secure the maximum real wage increase'. From 1988 to 1991 the index of real gross wages (inclusive of social benefits) increased from 100 to 229 for the private sector and from 100 to 288 for the public sector, as shown in Table 5.3.

The impact of the post-1988 wage hikes on factor shares are also shown in Table 5.3 for the top 500 industrial firms in Turkey. The figures show that private firms were better equipped to absorb wage shocks than public firms, but their profits dropped sharply in 1991. For public firms, the share of wages (in net value added) increased from 35 per cent in 1988 to 130 per cent in 1991, causing unsustainably large losses (negative profits) with a vastly unfavourable impact on public finance.

Post-1988 deterioration of public finance

The Turkish public sector deficit (PSBR) increased from 6 per cent of GNP in 1988 to 14 per cent in 1991. A thorough analysis of Turkey's public finance is certainly beyond the scope this chapter. In the present discussion, we are mainly interested in identifying the fundamental causal factors for the post-1988 fiscal deterioration. In

Table 5.3 Factor shares in 500 largest industrial firms and real wages, Turkey

	1984–7 average	1988	1989	1990	1991
A Factor shares[a]					
Private firms					
Wages	34.9	31.8	39.1	48.5	55.8
Interest payments	37.3	38.4	30.4	24.8	30.7
Rents	0.7	0.5	0.5	0.5	1.0
Profits	27.1	29.3	30.0	26.2	12.5
Total	100.0	100.0	100.0	100.0	100.0
Public firms					
Wages	45.9	35.4	55.5	76.0	130.4
Interest payments	23.3	50.1	40.4	38.4	68.4
Rents	0.2	0.2	0.2	0.3	0.4
Profits	30.6	14.3	3.9	−14.7	−99.2
Total	100.0	100.0	100.0	100.0	100.0
B Real gross wages[b]					
(Index: 1988 = 100)					
Private sector	102	100	130	152	229
Public sector	114	100	146	184	288

[a] Factor shares sum to net value added, which excludes depreciation
[b] Gross wages are before taxes, including social benefits
Source: Journal of the Istanbul Chamber of Industry (August 1992) for factor shares; State Planning Organization for wage data

our view, widening fiscal deficits pose a major threat to Turkey's industrial restructuring and sustained export-led expansion in the 1990s, because they diminish – through various channels – available funds for private industrial investment (Snowden 1992).

In Table 5.4 we present the estimates for the basic revenue and expenditure items, measured as percentage of GNP from 1988 to 1991 in such a way as to decompose the sources of increase in the public sector deficit. This presentation shows that the overall public sector deficit increased in this period despite the restraints on investment and transfer expenditures, and an increase in the tax/GNP ratio. The two main sources of deficit widening are (a) a fall in public sector factor income; and (b) a rise in public consumption expenditures.

Table 5.4 Post-1988 deterioration in public finance, Turkey (% of GNP)

	1988	1989	1990	1991	Change 1988–91
Public revenue					
Taxes	18.5	20.0	21.6	23.1	+4.6
Non-tax revenue	2.1	1.8	1.8	1.8	−0.3
Factor income[a]	7.9	6.5	4.5	0.5	−7.4
Total	28.5	28.3	27.9	25.4	−3.1
Public expenditure					
Current	8.7	11.3	14.0	15.9	+7.2
Investment	10.9	9.9	12.0	10.5	−0.4
Transfers[b]	12.3	11.6	10.3	10.5	−1.8
Inventory revaluation fund	2.9	2.6	2.2	3.0	+0.1
Total	34.8	35.4	38.5	39.9	+5.1
Public sector deficit	6.3	7.1	10.6	14.5	+8.2
General government[c]	3.5	4.5	5.3	10.1	+6.6
State enterprises[d]	2.8	2.6	5.3	4.4	+1.6
General government					
Primary deficit	−1.4	−0.3	0.4	4.8	+6.2
Interest bill	4.9	4.8	4.9	5.3	+0.4
Total deficit	3.5	4.5	5.3	10.1	+6.6
Personnel expenditures (Central Government)	5.7	8.1	10.5	12.4	+6.7

[a] Public sector income from property, including mainly the operational surpluses of state enterprises and institutions
[b] This expenditure item is measured net of intra-public-sector transfers, and comprises mainly domestic and foreign interest payments of the Central Government, direct subsidies and capital transfers to the private sector
[c] General government includes Central Government, external budgetary accounts and local governments
[d] The deficit of state enterprises is measured after transfer payments (i.e. subsidies) from the Central Government
Source: State Planning Organization, authors' calculations

In Turkey's official planning presentations, public sector factor income consists mainly of the operating surpluses of public enterprises and institutions. As shown earlier in Table 5.3, the massive drop in this revenue item largely reflects the impact of real wage hikes in state-owned enterprises and operations. The bottom line in Table 5.4 also shows that the increase in central government's personnel expenditures (for civil servants) explains the bulk of the rise in total public consumption expenditure. These estimates illustrate clearly the massive impact of the post-1988 wage and salary adjustments on the overall fiscal balance in Turkey. In this context, it should also be noted that the tax burden on gross wages is high, and the rise in the tax/GNP ratio reflects to a considerable extent the response of income taxes to wage hikes in the private and public sectors.

The impact of the post-1988 wage increases on saving performance in the public sector may also be noted. As shown previously in Table 5.1, the share of public saving in GNP dropped to 0.7 per cent in GNP in 1991 from 8 per cent in 1988 in response to diminishing public sector factor income, and rising public consumption expenditure. Consequently, the overall domestic saving ratio declined sharply in the post-1988 period.

The foregoing analysis is not intended to provide a basis for a definitive judgement on wage policy, which has important implications for social peace and political stability. The authors' intent, rather, is to show the vulnerability of fiscal balance and domestic saving to sharp changes in real wages, which also have a bearing on export performance as examined in the next section.

EXPORT GROWTH AND TRADE REFORMS

Export performance and cost competitiveness

Recent econometric studies by Arslan and van Wijnbergen (1990) and Uygur (1992) provide strong evidence on the prominent role of real exchange rate policy in Turkey's post-1980 export expansion. In this chapter we use econometric techniques to throw more light on cost competitiveness as an explanatory factor in export performance.

Before we discuss our regression results, we examine the findings of a constant-market-share analysis (CMSA) undertaken by the OECD (1992) as shown in Table 5.5. The OECD analysis attributes the differential growth of Turkish and world exports to a regional composition effect, a product mix effect and a residual, which presumably reflects changes in competitiveness. As expected, the findings show that Turkish export growth in 1980–5 was achieved in an inhospitable world trade environment, but benefited quite significantly from changes in regional composition and most prominently from gains in competitiveness. From 1985 to 1987 accelerated world demand coupled with the continuing positive residual effect became the major pull factors. From 1987 to 1990 Turkish export growth lagged world export growth concurrently with losses in Turkish competitiveness as borne out by the price data given in panel B in Table 5.5.

Table 5.5 Export performance and wage–price movements, Turkey

	1981–2	1984–5	1987–8	1988–90
	1979–80	1982–3	1985–6	1987–8
A Constant market share analysis				
Growth of Turkish exports	42.1	14.7	19.1	6.1
Growth of world exports	0.7	3.9	15.8	10.9
Difference	41.6	11.2	3.8	−5.3
Regional composition effect	9.2	−3.9	−3.6	0.7
Product mix effect	−0.3	−0.6	−0.5	−1.3
Residual	34.9	15.1	7.6	−4.8
	1988	1989	1990	1991
B Prices				
1 Nominal				
Export prices (TL)	70	50	34	57
Wholesale prices	70	64	52	57
Unit labour cost (TL)	57	106	71	87
2 Real exchange rate (appreciation −)	5	−7	−14	3
3 Relative cost position of Turkish labour[a]	−4	43	44	38

[a] Real unit labour cost in terms of trade partners' currencies
Sources: OECD 1992 for Panel A and B.1 data; authors' calculations for Panel B.2 and B.3 estimates

To focus on the issue of international competitiveness, we have calculated a new time series for real (productivity-adjusted) unit cost of Turkish manufacturing labour expressed in major trading partners' currencies; this series was inspired by Hansen (1991: 415–19). By extending the database of Arslan and van Wijnbergen (1990) to the year 1990, regression estimates (using annual data) are obtained for Turkish exports to the Middle East oil-exporting countries (RXO) and to the rest of the world (RXDC), which are reported in Table 5.6.

The regression results confirm the significant price responsiveness of Turkish exports in both trading regions. They are also significantly

Table 5.6 Regression estimates for Turkish exports, 1975–90 (t-values in parentheses)

		Coefficient		
A Dependent variable: LRXDC				
1	Constant	−13.17(−5.28)	Adj.R**2	0.89
	LRELP	−1.53(−2.85)	D-W	1.09
	LDCRG	3.10(14.13)	SEE	0.21
2	Constant	−5.09(−3.13)	Adj.R**2	0.90
	LRW	−0.49(−3.11)	D-W	1.37
	LDCRG	3.37(12.08)	SEE	0.21
3	Constant	2.01(0.93)	Adj.R**2	0.95
	LREXR	−1.04(−5.27)	D-W	1.70
	LDCRG	2.36(7.48)	SEE	0.14
4	Constant	1.79(1.61)	Adj.R**2	0.90
	LRW	−0.63(−3.99)	D-W	1.41
	LDCM	2.02(13.04)	SEE	0.20
5	Constant	7.08(5.06)	Adj.R**2	0.90
	LREXR	−1.15(−6.08)	D-W	1.72
	LDCM	1.37(8.92)	SEE	0.13
B Dependent variable: LRXO				
6	Constant	12.00(3.89)	Adj.R**2	0.95
	LREXR	−4.54(−18.45)	D-W	1.36
	LORM	2.17(4.90)	SEE	0.27

Key:
LRXDC = Log of real exports to countries other than Middle East oil-exporting
 countries
LRELP = Log of relative prices (Turkish export prices over nine developed country
 import prices)
LDCRG = Log of nine developed country real GDP growth
LRW = Log of real unit cost of labour in trade partners' currencies
LREXR = Log of real exchange rate (depreciation down)
LDCM = Log of nine developed country real import growth
LRXO = Log of real exports to Middle East oil-exporting countries
LORM = Log of real imports of Middle East oil-exporting countries
Source: Based on extended database of Arslan and van Wijnbergen 1990

elastic to real income (or import) growth in both areas. The analysis verifies the very favourable impact of the import explosion in the oil-exporting countries in the early 1980s in the aftermath of the 1979 oil-price shock, especially in the context of flat demand in OECD countries as was also shown by the CMSA estimates.

These regression estimates underline the central role of real exchange rates in Turkey's export performance in the 1980s. The findings also strongly support our contention that wage competitiveness has been a crucial factor in Turkey's exporting process as it explains, together with the OECD income effect, about 90 per cent of the variations in the 1976–90 sample period.

In these regressions, we have not been able to incorporate export subsidy variables because of data limitations for the pre-1980 period. However, Uygur's (1992) study provides helpful evidence on the subsidy effects based on regressions using quarterly data for more recent periods. Uygur reports that direct export incentives had a moderately significant impact in the earlier phase of the export drive, but their influence tended to disappear in the latter part of the 1980s.

The present analysis provides additional support to the available cross-country evidence that an appropriate exchange rate is an essential ingredient of 'successful' industrial exporting (Helleiner 1994). As Helleiner aptly emphasizes, the exchange rate is basically a macroeconomic policy instrument, and should preferably not be subsumed under the heading of trade policy. (Strictly, trade policy is concerned with the structure of external incentives, namely import tariffs and restrictions, and export subsidies.) In the Turkish context, we have shown that real wage reduction and real currency depreciation moved in tandem to ensure the competitiveness of Turkish exports in the 1980s.

Trade policy reform and its sectoral impact

As extensively described elsewhere, Turkey's trade reforms progressed in a gradual manner, and produced no major 'shocks' to the industrial structure.[5] Following the 1978–80 debt crisis, which featured an intensive use of quantitative restrictions (QRs) for imports, the sequencing of trade liberalization may be reviewed in the context of three successive policy phases, corresponding to the 1981–3, 1984–8, and post-1989 periods.

The 1981–3 period had seen the removal of import quotas in 1981, but still featured a strong reliance on import licensing and high tariffs for protection. Export subsidies reached their peak in this period, particularly in 1983.

During 1984–8 the major reform was the elimination of import licensing in 1984 by a switch to a negative list for imports, which included only a few items (e.g. arms, ammunition, etc.). In this period, the ratio of actual tariff collections to total imports rose from 7.4 per cent in 1984 to 12.5 per cent in 1988, reflecting mainly the more intensive use of extra-budgetary fund levies (surcharges), which were earmarked for special public spending programmes and partly for the financing of incentive schemes. Export incentives declined in 1984–8 from their high levels in 1981–3.

Import tariffs were substantially reduced and somewhat realigned in 1989–90, partly to serve as an instrument of anti-inflationary policy (in conjunction with an appreciating real value of the currency). Following minor tariff adjustments in 1991–2, a new import regime was introduced in early 1993 (at the time of finalizing this chapter). Under the new import regulations, imports are no longer subject to a number of taxes and surcharges other than customs duty and a Mass Housing Fund (MHF) levy. Before this reform initiative, Turkey's tariff regime was a complicated system of at least six types of duties and levies.[6] The average import-weighted tariff rate (including levies and taking into account duty exemptions) was expected to decrease from 12 per cent in 1992 to 9 per cent in 1993.

The major components of the export subsidy system may be classified as follows:

- direct cash payments;
- credit subsidies;
- customs duty exemptions;
- various tax allowances, including reductions in corporate tax liabilities;
- foreign exchange allocation and retention schemes, which lost their significance in the mid-1980s.

The relative weights of direct cash payments (mainly tax rebates) and credit subsidies were high in the early 1980s. In 1985–6 tax rebates were replaced by value-added tax exemptions in the context of Turkey's acceptance of the GATT subsidy code. From 1989 onward, tax allowances became the larger part of export subsidies, while the supportive role of the Turkish EXIMBANK gained importance in export financing.

As in other developing countries, the practice of customs duty exemptions complicates the evaluation of movements in protection rates and anti-export bias measures (Helleiner 1994). If statutory (scheduled) tariffs are taken as reference data (i.e. ignoring duty exemptions), protection was high for the pre-1989 period, but declined markedly in 1990–1 (Togan 1992). If collected tariffs are used, protection rates fell sharply in 1989. Taking into account the impact of the removal of import restrictions, Krueger and Aktan (1992) estimate that the overall anti-export bias (measured by the ratio of the effective exchange rate, EER, for imports to the EER for exports) declined from 2.01 in 1981 to 1.08 in 1989.

The available estimates for the structure of protection and export subsidies are given in Table 5.7 together with indicators of export propensity and import penetration for major sectors within manufacturing. These estimates show the significant export response (from a very low export base) of import-competing investment goods and intermediate goods to altered incentives in the early 1980s. Although the intermediate goods sector showed a sustained export response to new policies in 1983–8, its export propensity stagnated afterwards. The export propensity of investment goods fell in the late 1980s with the more rapid decline of subsidies in this sector. Notwithstanding its relatively higher rates of protection and lower rates of subsidy, the consumption goods sector became progressively more export-oriented, mainly reflecting Turkey's high comparative advantage in labour-intensive textile and clothing industries.

A more disaggregated breakdown of manufactured exports presented in Table 5.8 shows the sustained predominance of labour-intensive textiles and clothing in manufactured exports. The growing mismatch between Turkey's export mix and the OECD import mix is shown by OECD (1991) and Boeri (1991).

Trade policy toward the mid-1990s

A further observation on Turkey's trade policy relates to the future position of import tariffs and export subsidies in the context of the envisaged customs union with the EU and the EFTA–Turkey free trade agreement signed in 1991.

Turkey initiated tariff harmonization with the EU in 1973.[7] This process implied moving toward zero tariffs against EU imports and transition to the Common External Tariff of the EU against imports from non-EU countries. Products were placed either on a twelve- or twenty-two-year list, implying a complete alignment with the EU by

Table 5.7 Sectoral structure of protection, export subsidies and trade orientation in manufacturing, Turkey (%)

	Consumption goods	Intermediate goods	Investment goods	Total manufacturing
A Protection				
Nominal (statutory)				
1983	129	58	62	82
1988	88	38	88	62
1990	52	26	38	36
1991	53	22	33	34
Effective (statutory)				
1983	178	73	90	104
1988	25	102	209	100
1990	79	52	73	63
1991	51	41	65	48
Nominal (actual)				
1985	35	17	24	22
1989	15	8	14	11
Effective (actual)				
1985	46	20	26	25
1989	17	8	17	12
B Export subsidy				
1983	33	51	68	47
1984	23	36	41	32
1986	13	32	26	25
1988	13	30	32	24
1990	14	26	20	21
C Export propensity				
1978	11	2	1	6
1983	16	8	8	11
1988	25	15	10	18
1990	27	14	7	17
D Import penetration				
1978	1	15	35	13
1983	1	15	36	16
1988	4	20	36	19
1990	8	23	35	22

Sources: Togan 1992 for export subsidy and statutory-protection rates; Ozhan and Tanrikulu 1989 and OECD 1992 for actual protection rates, which are based on collected tariffs; and State Planning Organization for trade-orientation estimates

Table 5.8 Sectoral mix of manufactured exports, Turkey (million US$)

	1980	1983	1986	1989
Consumption goods	633	1,969	2,518	4,422
Food, beverages, tobacco	209	670	667	817
Textiles, clothing	424	1,299	1,851	3,605
Intermediate goods	313	1,311	2,055	3,815
Leather	50	192	345	604
Forest products	4	15	52	16
Chemicals	76	120	350	734
Petroleum products	39	232	178	254
Rubber, plastics	16	77	141	313
Non-metallics	76	189	185	291
Basic metals	52	486	804	1,603
Investment goods	101	378	751	849
Metal products, machinery	30	122	263	228
Electrical machinery	11	69	130	234
Others[a]	60	187	358	387
	1,047	3,658	5,324	9,086

[a] This category may include some intermediate goods
Source: Authors' classification based on data from Taskin and Yeldan 1992

1995. Because of its external debt difficulties, Turkey postponed its obligations in 1977–8 and the process remained stalled until 1988. In 1988 Turkey resumed its process of duty alignment with the EU and announced its intention to fulfil all remaining obligations at an accelerated pace by 1995, with the provision that the MHF levy would be gradually phased out at the end of 1998. The 1993 import regime entailed notable duty reductions as part of the process to reach the targets set for 1995. Within the framework of the free trade agreement with EFTA, Turkey also has a commitment to reduce customs duties to levels applicable to EU imports.

The domestic policy implications of a possible EU–Turkey customs union have not been adequately researched nor sufficiently debated in Turkey. A customs union with the EU – if it is established – is likely to involve, as the EFTA–Turkey agreement (Article 18) actually stipulates, severe constraints on the choice of export incentive schemes, which have been flexibly applied in recent periods.

A recent multi-sectoral general equilibrium analysis for Turkey takes the actual tariff and subsidy structure of 1989 as a point of departure, and finds that 'harmonization to the EU tariff structure can be a welfare-enhancing policy if accompanied by a policy of removing or reducing export subsidies' (Harrison *et al.* 1992: 3). In our view, the general validity of the latter finding needs to be explored more fully under variant sets of real exchange rate, labour cost and external account conditions, especially in the light of sharply widened trade deficits in 1990–2 as shown earlier in Figure 5.2.

In many cases, the evolving nature of arrangements for trade with the EU and EFTA countries, and the implied potential loss of autonomy over trade policy, have important implications, in particular, for the possibilities of more effective use of non-trade policies at the micro-level. These are mainly investment incentives, institution building for export financing, foreign direct investment, promotion of R&D, standardization and technology-related activities, labour retraining, encouragement of small–medium size enterprises and improved infrastructure.[8] In the next section, we attempt to provide a broad evaluation of the investment incentive system, which has been used as a strong policy instrument to direct sectoral developments.

INVESTMENT INCENTIVES AND ALLOCATIONAL PATTERNS

The investment incentive system and its cost to the government

From the late 1960s on, investment incentives were structured and implemented by a centralized and special administrative unit. These incentives provided economic subsidies to investors in addition to the normal benefits allowed by the regular corporate tax code. The incentive regime was specified and announced on an annual basis, and was subject to considerable variation over time. Upon a highly crude, but quite rapid, evaluation of proposed investment projects, the centre issued 'incentive certificates', which entitled investors to have access to a variety of fiscal and credit benefits. These certificates were issued mainly to private sector projects, but could be granted to public sector agencies in specific cases.

In the presence of major distortions in the economy (e.g. high non-preferential interest rates, high levels of protection and a high tax burden on financial transactions), the general presumption has been that investment subsidies were to some extent justified on economic grounds. Besides providing subsidies to correct existing distortions, the incentive regime featured a strong dose of corporate tax deductions and sometimes direct cash grants to stimulate investment in desired directions. The arbitrary nature of above-normal incentive benefits induced widespread rent-seeking activity, and created vested interests in the maintenance of the complicated incentive regime as a whole.

The multiplicity of objectives also limited the possibilities for development of the investment incentive system in more efficient directions. The objectives included regional development, sectoral promotion, encouragement of scale economies, technological improvement, increased export orientation and broadened ownership. In the light of such diverse objectives, it is practically impossible to conduct social cost–benefit analysis to assess policy options. Unlike in the East Asian model, the incentive system did not produce an effective pattern of industrial targeting, backed up by forward-looking sectoral programmes. In fact, the system became more generalized in the late 1980s by its adoption of a negative list, which specifies subsectors and project characteristics not eligible for incentives. Under the recently revised system, however, the differentiated pattern of incentives continues to hold.

The structure and magnitude of investment incentives have been differentiated mainly by sector (or by subsector), region, production scale and market orientation. Because of the virtual absence of data on implementation results, and the lack of transparency of the system, the economics of investment incentives have not been researched properly.

On the basis of a number of hypothetical (but presumably representative) projects, the World Bank (1989) made an attempt, however, to quantify the present value of incentive benefits, differentiated by sector and region, as a percentage of fixed investment cost on an after-tax basis. The results are summarized in Table 5.9, which also indicates the nature and relative significance of the major components of investment incentives. The value of incentives shows a high degree of regional and sectoral differentiation. In developed regions, where industrial activity is concentrated, manufacturing received more benefits than agriculture. Although investment subsidies were highest in least developed (priority) regions, they were not able to attract new investments in these areas, because of their locational disadvantages in terms of infrastructure, marketing and skilled manpower.

The investment incentive estimates shown in Table 5.9 may also be differentiated according to whether they contribute to (a) a firm's total income (cash grants); (b) cost reductions (e.g. low-cost credit,

Table 5.9 Estimated present value of investment incentives, Turkey (mid-1980s) (percentage of fixed investment cost on after-tax basis)

Incentives	#1	#2	#3	#4	#5
A Benefits provided by incentive administration					
Cash grant[a]	–	3.5	10.0	–	10.0
Domestic machinery grant[a]	1.5	1.5	1.5	2.3	1.1
Preferential credit subsidy[b]	7.9	9.5	15.5	12.0	12.0
Customs duty exemption[b]	12.0	12.0	12.0	7.2	3.6
Tax, fee exemption and postponement[b]	9.6	9.6	9.6	7.0	2.0
Investment allowance[c]	9.8	13.0	32.5	13.0	32.5
B Benefits provided by regular tax code					
Accelerated depreciation[c]	3.2	3.2	3.2	3.6	4.8
Export tax reduction[c]	5.4	5.4	5.4	5.4	–
Total	49.4	57.7	89.7	50.5	66.0

Key:
#1 Manufacturing – developed region
#2 Manufacturing – normal region
#3 Manufacturing – priority I region
#4 Agriculture – developed region
#5 Tourism – normal region

[a] Increases firm's income
[b] Provides cost reduction
[c] Decreases corporate-tax liability
Source: World Bank 1989: Table VIII

customs duty exemptions, various indirect tax concessions); or (c) reductions in corporate tax liabilities (e.g. investment allowances plus normal benefits from the regular tax code). Cost-reducing incentives were intended to provide compensation for existing distortions; the net value of remaining incentives was about 20 per cent of manufacturing investment cost in developed regions.

Against the backdrop of available data on sectoral and regional distribution of incentive certificates, their likely realization rates, and rough calculations for the values of incentives, the World Bank (1989) estimated the total net present value of investment incentives (in the mid-1980s) as 1.9 per cent of GNP per year. As the study points out, the budgetary cost of the investment incentive regime may be slightly lower than this figure, because the interest subsidy to the investors was overestimated by assuming that the cost of preferential credit creation by the Central Bank was equal to the market borrowing rate of the Treasury.

Taking the available estimate for the budgetary cost of investment incentives, we may arrive at the total cost (to the government) of investment and export incentives. In the mid- and late 1980s, the share of manufactured exports in GNP was on the average 10–12 per cent, while the export subsidy rate varied around 20–25 per cent. Thus, the overall budgetary cost of investment and export incentives appears to have been around 4 to 5 per cent of GNP levels. In this period the tax/GNP ratio was less than 20 per cent.

These admittedly rough calculations clearly illustrate the high cost of Turkey's micro-level incentive mechanisms, which also lacked transparency in their application. They placed a heavy burden on the public sector budget, which also had to cope with rising debt service. It is no wonder that the policymakers strove to maintain a firm grip on public sector wages to generate a satisfactory amount of resources for public investment. From 1989 on, as discussed in section two (pages 132–45), this grip was loosened, as one would expect in the context of a more liberal political process, requiring a more rational design of the incentive systems under tightened budget constraints.

If we look at the inner rationality of investment incentives, a number of points emerge for future policy consideration. The post-1989 reductions in customs duties and their planned harmonization with the EFTA and EU by the mid-1990s will sharply diminish the need for concessions in this area. The need for various tax and fee exemptions will be lessened by the contemplated move further to reduce indirect taxes on financial transactions, which is expected to enhance financial intermediation. Direct cash payments are potentially effective instruments, but have been subject to misuse in the Turkish context, as they require firm-level political decisions. They may partly be transformed to augment resources for preferential credits, and the government has already taken steps in this direction.

Under reduced protection, cash grants may be used as effective tools to support R&D activities and labour training schemes in selected industries. Similarly, tax allowances (corporate tax exemptions proportional to the cost of investment) should be retained, albeit at lower rates with less variability, because they encourage firms to be more efficient in the earlier years of investment to generate taxable income. They have the added advantage of being neutral in their impact on the choice of factor proportions in new production. They strongly disfavour, however, new firms which may not be able to generate sufficiently large positive profits in the earlier life of investments to benefit from investment allowances.

Given the tightness of the budget constraint, we feel that the central thrust of new policies should be toward increasing the availability of medium- and long-term preferential credit to manufacturing by lowering the excessive shares of housing and agricultural sales cooperatives. In a longer term perspective, the challenging task is to attain lower real interest rates for non-preferential credit, and achieve lower rates of inflation for a better investment climate. The latter is, however, an essentially macroeconomic phenomenon.

In the discussion of investment incentives, a further observation relates to the share of manufacturing in the issue of incentive certificates in the 1980s. In value terms, the latter share declined to a 35–40 per cent level in the mid-1980s from 70 per cent in the latter part of the 1970s. This share recovered in the late 1980s, and rose to about 60 per cent in 1990–1, possibly in response to increased capital inflows under the capital account liberalization. In the issue of certificates, the shares of tourism, infrastructure and housing were more prominent in the mid-1980s. The available data on the sub-sector mix of investment certificates indicate that capacity stretching and technology upgrading projects were favoured by manufacturing firms applying for incentive benefits.

Patterns of fixed investment in manufacturing

The investment slowdown in manufacturing has been widely crit-icized as an unsuccessful part of the post-1980 restructuring process. In this part of the chapter, we present the available evidence on manufacturing investment, and then examine the inter-industry pattern of capital accumulation in relation to its presumably import-ant determinants.

Table 5.10 presents the broad trends in domestic fixed investment. At the economywide level, the share of public sector investment in GNP remained high in 1980–5 compared with the falling share of the private sector in this period. This reflects the strong saving effort of the public sector in the early stabilization phase of the adjustment process. As these estimates show, the public sector had rapidly cut back its investment programmes in manufacturing in order to be able to release capital resources for infrastructure sectors with a particular emphasis on projects that were complementary to the newly launched export drive (e.g. rehabilitation of ports, energy and communications systems). Given the low rates of capacity utilization in manufacturing, such a reallocation had an appealing rationale. This point is often missed in critiques of the post-1980 economic performance. In a similar vein, the share of manufacturing in total private investment had also fallen, but not as drastically as in the case of the public sector. In the 1980s private investment had shifted to services (such as transport, tourism and, increasingly, housing), mainly in response to more favourable demand conditions and supportive government policies.

Table 5.10 Time pattern of fixed investments, Turkey

	1975	1980	1985	1990
Share in GNP (%)				
Total investment	31.5	26.6	25.1	24.4
Private investment	14.7	10.3	9.7	14.0
Public investment	16.8	16.3	15.4	10.4
Share of manufacturing (%)				
Total investment	40.7	34.7	22.0	19.0
Private investment	46.0	35.3	33.5	29.9
Public investment	36.0	34.3	14.8	4.5
Index of real investment level				
Total manufacturing	100	81.8	61.4	68.9
Private manufacturing	100	61.5	68.3	117.6
Public manufacturing	100	104.6	53.7	14.6
Memo item:				
Production capacity				
utilization in manufacturing (%)	n.a.	51.0	72.7	71.7

Source: State Planning Organization

The estimates presented in Table 5.11 show the breakdown of real (total) manufacturing investment by major industry groups for three successive five-year intervals. The share of intermediate goods remained high in 1980–4 as in 1975–9, because of the continuity of long-gestation projects. Over the 1984–9 period, we observe, however, a structural shift toward consumption goods and investment goods industries.

Table 5.11 Sectoral structure of manufacturing investment, Turkey
(public and private)

Industries	Five-year totals (%)		
	1975–9	1980–4	1985–9
Consumption goods	22.4	20.0	26.4
Intermediate goods	61.0	66.8	53.5
Investment goods	16.6	13.2	20.1
Total	100.0	100.0	100.0
Memo item: Five-year total manufacturing investment (billion TL, constant 1988 prices)	37,832	25,759	20,099

Source: State Planning Organization

A more disaggregated breakdown of allocational trends is shown in Table 5.12 for private manufacturing. The allocational shifts in the post-1980 period seem to have favoured exporting industries more than import competing industries.

The annual variations of subsector investments make it difficult, however, to draw firm conclusions as to the driving forces of manufacturing investment. By making use of newly available semi-official capital stock series, we provide a classification of manufacturing industries in Table 5.13 on the basis of the growth rate of capital stock from 1983 to 1988. The incentive signals and medium-term growth prospects were more clear in 1983–8 than in the turbulent conditions of the early 1980s. The industries are then further classified on the basis of their growth rates of output and exports, and high or low rates of effective protection (based on 1985 actual collected tariffs). The industries are also categorized with respect to their high or low capacity utilization rates in 1983.[9]

The classification of industries given in Table 5.13 is suggestive of some crude inferences, among which are the following:

1 High capital growth took place mainly in industries with above-average growth of exports and/or output.
2 High effective protection was associated with high capital growth, particularly in high output growth industries.
3 High capital growth industries had generally high capacity utilization rates as their initial condition.
4 Symmetrically, low capital growth industries had low effective protection and low initial capacity utilization rates.

Table 5.12 Allocational shifts in private manufacturing investment, Turkey (%)

Industries	1980	1983	1986	1989
Consumption goods	18.2	35.2	35.8	34.1
Food	4.6	5.9	6.2	7.7
Beverages, tobacco	0.6	4.5	1.2	1.1
Textile, clothing	13.0	24.9	28.4	25.3
Intermediate goods	59.8	43.9	38.7	44.3
Leather	0.0	0.3	2.2	0.7
Forest products	0.3	0.3	0.5	1.1
Paper, printing	3.7	1.5	3.0	3.9
Chemicals	17.2	16.2	5.5	8.1
Petroleum products	1.4	1.1	1.4	0.7
Rubber, plastics	1.1	12.2	2.8	5.8
Non-metallics	17.8	9.0	17.0	14.3
Basic metals	18.2	3.3	6.4	9.7
Investment goods	22.1	20.9	25.6	21.6
Metal products	2.8	3.5	4.5	5.2
Machinery	3.5	6.7	5.8	3.6
Electrical machinery	1.8	5.1	7.0	4.4
Transport equipment	14.0	5.1	8.0	8.0
Other	0.0	0.5	0.3	0.4
Total	100.0	100.0	100.0	100.0
Memo item: Real investment level (billion TL, 1988 prices)	2,440	2,411	3,085	2,851

Source: State Planning Organization

The foregoing assessment provides no clues as to the age, quality and efficiency characteristics of the manufacturing capital stock, all of which are critically important. Nevertheless, it shows that capital reallocation within manufacturing responded well to short- and medium-term signals encouraging export-led expansion in the mid-1980s. Given the shortage of available investment resources, the overall effect of the incentive systems on capital use may be marked favourably in a medium-term perspective. However, the observed patterns of investment show the limited nature of any deeper and longer horizon restructuring of the manufacturing capital stock for sustained industrial exporting in the remainder of the 1990s.

Table 5.13 Growth of sectoral capital stock in relation to its major determinants, Turkey

	High gK		Low gK	
	High gX	*Low gX*	*High gX*	*Low gX*
A High gE				
High ERP	Textiles (HC) Rubber, plastics (HC)	Metal products (LC)		
Low ERP	Leather (LC) Chemicals (HC) Electrical machinery (LC)		Basic metals (LC)	Machinery (LC)
B Low gE				
High ERP	Non-metallics (HC) Transport equipment (HC)			Beverages, tobacco (LC)
Low ERP			Forest products (LC) Petroleum products (HC)	Food (HC) Paper, printing (HC)

Key:
High (low) gK – above (below) average growth of capital stock in 1983–8
High (low) gX – above (below) average growth of gross output in 1983–8
High (low) gE – above (below) average growth of exports in 1983–8
High (low) ERP – above (below) average effective rate of protection (actual) in 1985
HC, LC – above (below) average rate of capacity utilization in 1983
All averages are for manufacturing sector (public and private)
Source: Authors' analysis based on State Planning Organization data on output and exports; Maraslioglu and Tiktik 1991 data on capital stocks; Ozhan and Tanrikulu 1989, estimates for protection

CONCLUSION

In this chapter we have been primarily concerned with the major policy issues surrounding Turkey's sustained industrial growth and exporting in the 1980s. We have shown that wage–cost competitiveness performs almost as well as the real exchange rate in explaining, in combination with real growth in major export markets, export performance. Against the backdrop of this empirical evidence, we have drawn attention to the considerable loss of policy autonomy in exchange rate determination after the liberalization of the external capital account in 1989–90. In a similar vein, we have examined the sharp reversal of real wage trends in the post-1988 period under more liberal wage settlement arrangements in an increasingly contestable and populist political environment. These trends imply falling cost competitiveness of Turkish exports.

In addition to these new policy contexts, we have also noted the post-1988 reductions in import tariffs, which will be further lowered (and virtually eliminated in most instances) in the context of the free trade agreement with EFTA and more complete alignment with the EU. These new external arrangements will eventually place constraints on the export subsidy system.

Thus, the emerging loss of autonomy and/or flexibility in exchange rate policy, trade policy and the wage determination process gives rise to a new set of issues, which require careful assessment.[10] In order to secure the benefits of openness in trade and finance, and avoid large transitional costs, institutional adaptations seem to be needed to achieve fiscal stabilization, financial deepening and more stable distributional arrangements. At the micro-level, our analysis suggests that the investment incentive system should not be dismantled in the new policy context, but should be reformed so as to place greater reliance on medium- and long-term preferential credits for new exporting industries, and direct support to R&D, technological and labour training activities.[11]

ACKNOWLEDGEMENTS

The authors are indebted to Gerry Helleiner for encouragement and valuable suggestions. Helpful comments by Sebnem Akkaya, Ahmet Tiktik, and participants at the UNU/WIDER Conference on Trade and Industrialization, Phase II (Paris, 24–27 November 1992) are appreciated. The usual disclaimers apply. The views put forward in this chapter are personal and do not reflect those of the respective institutions of the authors.

NOTES

1 See Aricanli and Rodrik 1990 for a variety of contributions to recent literature on the Turkish economy.
2 These recent developments have been closely connected with shifting patterns of Turkey's labour market arrangements and political economy, which are evaluated in well-informed studies by Senses 1992, Onis and Webb 1992, and Waterbury 1992. Our assessment of the post-1988 economic policy context is based on available data as of the end of 1992, using the State Planning Organization version of the national accounts which may be revised in 1993–4.
3 For the scope and impact of internal financial liberalization, see Akyuz 1990. Snowden 1992 provides evidence on the unfavourable impact of fiscal deficits and high intermediation costs on the ability of banks to fund private investment and shows the increased scope for equity finance. For an econometric analysis of private investment behaviour, see Conway 1990.
4 These observations draw heavily on Altinkemer and Ekinci 1992, and UNCTAD 1991: 129–39. Altinkemer and Ekinci provide a thorough treatment of institutional developments and Central Bank policies leading to liberalized capital accounts in Turkey.
5 Krueger and Aktan 1992 provide a comprehensive review and documentation of the trade regime, and give estimates for effective exchange rates of commodity imports and exports. In an input–output framework, Togan 1992 estimates protection and subsidy rates, domestic resource costs, and anti-export measures. Export subsidies are also estimated by Uygur 1992 and Aktan 1992. As a background to their general equilibrium analysis, Harrison et al. 1992 present updated data on recent trade policy changes.
6 These were customs duty, wharf tax, stamp duty, municipality tax, the Mass Housing Fund levy and the Support and Price Stabilization Fund levy.
7 For a broad perspective on Turkey–EC economic convergence, see Hine 1992.
8 At the micro-level, a proper treatment of non-trade policies for industrial exporting requires additional research. See Helleiner 1992: 1–17; 1994) for an incisive assessment of related issues. In this context, foreign direct investment (FDI) acquires crucial importance. See Balasubramanyan 1992 for Turkey's FDI policies, which contain redundant incentives.
9 Our analysis of capital stock growth patterns is inspired by a recent study by World Bank (1989), which employed different sets of indicators and data.
10 For a comprehensive discussion of policy issues connected with openness in trade and finance in developing countries, see Akyuz 1991.
11 The future use of medium- and long-term preferential credit facilities will

have to be consistent with the guidelines and provisions of the EFTA–Turkey agreement on matters concerning state aid for sectoral restructuring and regional development.

REFERENCES

Aktan, O. (1992) 'Liberalization, Export Incentives and Exchange Rate Policy: Turkey's Experience of the 1980s', paper presented to conference on 'The Turkish Economy Since Liberalization', 3 October 1992, Ankara, Bilkent University.

Akyuz, Y. (1990) 'Financial System and Policies in Turkey', in T. Aricanli and D. Rodrik (eds) *The Political Economy of Turkey* (98–131), London: The Macmillan Press Ltd.

—— (1991) *Trade and Finance: Policy Dilemmas in Structural Adjustment*, Geneva: UNCTAD.

Altinkemer, M. and Ekinci, N.K. (1992) 'Capital Account Liberalization: The Case of Turkey', paper presented at the MEEA meeting, 25 January 1992, New Orleans.

Anand, R. and van Wijnbergen, S. (1989) 'Inflation and the Financing of the Government Expenditure: An Introductory Analysis with an Application to Turkey', *World Bank Economic Review* 3, 1: 17–38.

Aricanli, T. and Rodrik, D. (eds) (1990) *The Political Economy of Turkey*, London: The Macmillan Press Ltd.

Arslan, I. and van Wijnbergen, S. (1990) 'Turkey: Export Miracle or Accounting Trick?', Working Papers WPS 370, Washington, DC: World Bank.

Balasubramanyan, V.N. (1992) 'Foreign Direct Investment in Turkey', paper presented to conference on 'The Turkish Economy Since Liberalization', 3 October 1992, Ankara, Bilkent University.

Boeri, T. (1991) 'Problems in Implementing Structural Reforms in Developing Countries: The Experience of Turkey in the 1980s', Centro Studi Luca d'Agliano–Queen Elizabeth House, Development Studies Working Papers No. 35.

Boratav, K. (1990) 'Inter-Class and Intra-Class Relations of Distribution under "Structural Adjustment": Turkey during the 1980s' in T. Aricanli and D. Rodrik (eds) *The Political Economy of Turkey* (199–229), London: The Macmillan Press Ltd.

Celasun, M. (1994) 'Trade and Industrialization in Turkey: Initial Conditions, Policy and Performance in the 1980s' in G.K. Helleiner (ed.) *Trade Policy and Industrialization in Turbulent Times*, London: Routledge.

Celasun, M. and Rodrik, D. (1989) *Debt, Adjustment and Growth: Turkey*, Book IV in J. Sachs and S. Collins (eds) *Developing Country Debt and Economic Performance: Country Studies*, Vol. 3 (615–808), Chicago and London: The University of Chicago Press.

Conway, P. (1990) 'The Record on Private Investment in Turkey' in T. Aricanli and D. Rodrik (eds) *The Political Economy of Turkey* (78–97), London: The Macmillan Press Ltd.

Hansen, B. (1991) *The Political Economy of Poverty, Equity and Growth: Egypt and Turkey*, Oxford: Oxford University Press.

Harrison, G.W., Rutherford, T.F. and Tarr, D.G. (1992) 'Piecemeal Trade Reform in Partially Liberalized Economies, An Evaluation for Turkey', Working Papers WPS 951, Washington, DC: World Bank.

Helleiner, G.K. (ed.) (1992) *Trade Policy, Industrialization and Development: New Perspectives*, Oxford: Clarendon Press.

—— (1994) 'Introduction' in G.K. Helleiner (ed.) *Trade Policy and Industrialization in Turbulent Times*, London: Routledge.

Hine, R.C. (1992) 'Turkey and the European Community: Regional Integration and Economic Convergence', paper presented to conference on 'The Turkish Economy Since Liberalization', 3 October 1992, Ankara, Bilkent University.

ISO (1992) *Istanbul Sanayi Dergisi* [Journal of Istanbul Chamber of Industry], August.

Krueger, A. and Aktan, O. (1992) *Swimming Against the Tide: Turkish Trade Reform in the 1980s*, an International Center for Economic Growth publication, San Francisco: ICS Press.

Maraslioglu, H. and Tiktik, A. (1991) *Turkiyede Uretim, Sermaye ve Istihdam, 1968–88* [Output, Capital and Employment in Turkey, 1968–88], Ankara: DPT (State Planning Organization).

OECD (1991) *Turkey, Economic Survey (1990/91)*, Paris: OECD.

OECD (1992) *Turkey, Economic Survey (1991/92)*, Paris: OECD.

Onis, Z. and Webb, S.B. (1992) 'Political Economy of Policy Reform in Turkey in the 1980s', mimeo, Bogazici University and the World Bank.

Ozhan, G. and Tanrikulu, K. (1989) *Turkiye Sanayiinde Koruma Oranlari* [Protection Rates in Turkish Industry], Ankara: DPT (State Planning Organization), IPB–UPVD.

Rodrik, D. (1990) 'Premature Liberalization, Incomplete Stabilization: The Ozal Decade in Turkey', National Bureau of Economic Research, Working Paper No. 3300, Cambridge.

Ros, J. (1995) 'Trade Liberalization with Real Appreciation and Slow Growth: Sustainability Issues in Mexico's Trade Policy Reform', this volume (Ch. 4).

Senses, F. (1992) 'Labor Market Response to Structural Adjustment and Institutional Pressures', ERC/1992–1, Ankara: Department of Economics, Middle East Technical University.

Snowden, P.N. (1992) 'Financial Liberalization in Turkey since 1980: Stabilization, Bank Regulation and the Contribution of Equity Finance', paper presented to conference on 'The Turkish Economy Since Liberalization', 3 October 1992, Ankara, Bilkent University.

Taskin, F. and Yeldan, E. (1992) 'Export Performance and Growth in the Turkish Manufacturing Industry', paper presented to conference on 'The Turkish Economy Since Liberalization', 3 October 1992, Ankara, Bilkent University.

Togan, S. (1992) 'Trade Liberalization and Competitive Structure in Turkey During 1980s', paper presented to conference on 'The Turkish Economy Since Liberalization', 3 October 1992, Ankara, Bilkent University.

UNCTAD (1991) *Trade and Development Review*, Geneva: UNCTAD.

Uygur, E. (1992) 'Trade Policies and Economic Performance in Turkey in the 1980s', paper presented to conference on 'The Turkish Economy Since Liberalization', 3 October 1992, Ankara, Bilkent University.

Waterbury, J. (1992) 'Export-Led Growth and the Center-Right Coalition in Turkey', *Comparative Politics* 24, 2, January: 127–45.

World Bank (1989) 'Turkey: Issues and Strategy for the Industrial Sector', mimeo, Washington, DC: World Bank.

6

THE DEVELOPMENT OF MANUFACTURING FOR EXPORT IN TANZANIA

Experience, policy and prospects

Benno J. Ndulu and Joseph J. Semboja

INTRODUCTION

Tanzania's industrialization process, like that of many other developing economies, stagnated after an initial period of vigorous growth. The early stages of import substitution were accompanied by a rapid growth of the manufacturing sector, raising its contribution to GDP from 4 per cent at independence (1961) to a peak of 12 per cent in 1977. This expansion was not, however, sustained subsequently. Forced de-industrialization resulted in a drastic fall of the sector's share in GDP to a low of 7 per cent in 1985. A key reason for this drastic downturn was import compression, which forced steep cuts in capacity utilization and a slowdown in capacity expansion. This is similar to what Seringhaus (1991) described as the 'typical' case: an initial burst of industrial growth resulting from manufacturing to fill domestic demand created by displaced imports which is subsequently not sustained due to a drastic reduction in import capacity. The role of reduction and instability of import capacity in constraining growth has been demonstrated in several other studies, including those by Leff and Sato (1987), Helleiner (1986), and Ndulu (1986, 1991).

In Tanzania's case the fall in real import capacity, starting in the late 1970s, was due to the combination of a decline in the volume of exports, a steep decline in the barter terms of trade, and a fall in net foreign resource inflows (Ndulu and Lipumba 1990). The negative impacts of the general import compression on the process of industrialization were exacerbated by a lopsided allocation of the scarce foreign exchange in favour of the expansion of unusable capacity at the expense of support for the utilization of existing capacity (Ndulu 1986; Doriye and Wuyts 1992).

The manufacturing sector during this period did not make a significant transition from import substitution to export expansion. The sector made little contribution towards meeting its own high import requirements; nor did it contribute significantly to the diversification of the country's export base. Diversification is particularly important in view of the vulnerability of the Tanzanian economy to instability in primary commodities markets as well as to the downward trend of the prices of many of these commodities.

Numerous empirical studies have attempted to confirm the orthodoxy that export-oriented policies lead to better growth performance than import substitution policies, including those by Balassa (1978, 1990); Michaely (1977); Krueger (1978); Bhagwati (1987); Ram (1985); and the World Bank (1987). The classic argument is that policies which do not discriminate against exports allow exploitation of comparative advantage; permit greater capacity utilization, exploitation of scale economies, and employment generation as a result of an expanded market opportunity; and generate technological improvements in response to foreign competition (Balassa 1978: 181). It is also argued that barriers to imports for protection purposes are effectively a tax on exports because they raise domestic resource costs for exports and appreciate the real exchange rate, thereby reducing international competitiveness and the incentive to export (DeRosa 1990). Although both tariff and non-tariff barriers are considered in this regard, the latter are particularly singled out for criticism, especially in the case of Sub-Saharan Africa.

The critique of the orthodoxy is also strong. The gist of the counter-argument is the lack of strong empirical evidence to support the link between export performance and growth (Helleiner 1986), the problem of the lumping together of the effects of trade and macroeconomic policies (Rodrik 1992), and the failure to account adequately for important exogenous factors in poor performance episodes, or for the roles of such factors as institutional arrangements and export know-how in longer term performance. A comprehensive critical review of the orthodoxy and its evidence as well as a detailed analysis of other important and relevant aspects of trade strategy is found in Helleiner (1990, 1994). While trade policy and the macroeconomic environment are generally recognized as important, particularly in the initial stage, the transition from import substitution to export expansion entails several other strategic measures. These include the creation of competitiveness as a generic requirement of exporters, reduction or removal of barriers to exporting, and creation of export incentives and assistance to potential and actual exporters, particularly on the supply side and with respect to market penetration (Seringhaus and Rosson 1991; Keesing and Lall 1992). Constraints to entry and exit in developing countries may also limit industrial rationalization (restructuring) in accordance with a country's comparative advantage and thus exploitation of the economies of scale emphasized in so much of the literature (Rodrik 1992).

Our concern in this chapter is to investigate three major issues related to the development of manufacturing for export in Tanzania. First, to what extent did policies to support import substitution stifle the sector's export orientation? Second, what role did commercial policy and the macroeconomic environment each play in influencing the incentive structure and supply response of exports? Third, what impacts did both export promotion measures and liberalization of trade and exchange policies have on the reorientation of the manufacturing sector towards exporting and on the raising of its productivity? In the case of the last issue we caution the reader as to the brevity of the liberalization episode, approximately six years, and therefore the difficulty of assessing impacts.

The second section (pages 169–78) reviews briefly the export performance of the manufacturing sector over time. The third section (pages 179–88) assesses the links between the import substitution strategy pursued in Tanzania and export orientation. Section four (pages 188–97) evaluates the impact of incentives on the export of manufactures. Here we attempt to distinguish the effects of trade and macroeconomic policies. Section five (pages 197–206) evaluates export promotion efforts in relation to the constraints faced by exporters and the liberalization measures pursued after 1986.

EXPORTS OF MANUFACTURES: A REVIEW OF PERFORMANCE, 1966–90[1]

Export diversification was one of the notable features in Tanzania's economic recovery in the late 1980s. Manufactured exports played a major role in this diversification through their significant growth over the period. Although the high rate of diversification was partly on account of slower recovery of traditional exports,[2] the growth of non-traditional exports dominated the change. These included horti-cultural products, marine products, exotic wildlife and products, a variety of manufactures, and gold produced by small-scale pro-spectors.

Table 6.1 presents the extent and structure of export diversi-fication for the period 1966–90. It provides several definitional distinctions of the categories. From Table 6.1 it is clear that non-traditional exports exclusive of minerals doubled their share in total official exports in the five-year period, from 21 per cent in 1986 to 42 per cent in 1990. If one includes gold, this share reached about 50 per cent in 1992. The share of manufactured exports in non-traditional exports (excluding minerals) also increased significantly over the period. This increase was particularly great if petroleum products are excluded. Relative even to the pre-crisis best perform-ance (1976–80), the share of manufactures increased by approxi-mately 25 per cent.

Table 6.2 summarizes the main performance indicators for exports of manufactures at the sectoral level. The indicators include the growth rate of exports measured in dollars, the share of manufactures in total exports and the share of exports in the total output of manufactures. Output is measured in constant PPP (purchasing power parity) US dollars to facilitate comparison over time, in view of the major depreciation of the shilling in the last five years of the period. (PPP dollars were obtained by appropriate adjustment of the official nominal exchange rate to maintain parity with a 1966 base year.)

Three main phases can be distinguished in the performance over the period 1966–90. The first phase, 1966–80, was characterized broadly by a continuous growth of exports hand in hand with output. This raised the share of manufactures in total exports from an average of 13.5 per cent during 1966–70 to 15.6 per cent during 1975–80. During the 1966–70 period, the growth rate of manu-factured exports was led, with the commissioning of the oil refinery in 1966, by petroleum and petroleum products. Exports of non-oil manufactures declined during that period. Growth subsequently was led by non-oil manufactures. In terms of export orientation, however, the share of exports in the total output of manufactures declined continuously over the period. The more rapid growth of output compared to exports went essentially to meet increasing domestic demand partly created by displaced imports.

The second phase, 1981–5, coincided with the period of rapid

Table 6.1 Export diversification in Tanzania, 1966–90 (%)

		1966–70	1971–5	1976–80	1981	1982	1983	1984	1985	1986	1987	1988	1989	1990
Share of manufactured exports in total exports	(a)	7.5	8.7	11.2	9.2	8.5	11.5	8.5	11.4	11.2	18.1	19.4	24.1	22.5
	(b)	13.5	14.5	15.7	11.0	11.2	15.3	14.4	16.2	12.6	20.2	22.7	28.1	26.7
Share of non-traditional exports in total exports	(c)	24.9	23.5	25.6	29.6	30.9	24.0	22.2	24.0	21.0	35.7	35.4	40.8	42.1
	(d)	35.9	32.2	32.6	38.8	39.4	35.5	31.0	31.6	24.7	42.0	39.7	43.9	48.8
Share of manufactured exports in non-traditional exports	(e)	21.1	27.1	35.5	23.8	21.5	32.3	27.5	36.2	45.4	43.1	48.8	54.8	46.1
	(f)	31.0	37.3	45.3	31.2	27.3	47.8	38.3	47.6	53.5	50.8	54.7	59.0	53.6
	(g)	53.3	61.3	62.3	37.2	36.4	63.6	64.6	67.5	59.9	56.5	63.9	68.7	63.5
	(h)	37.0	44.7	48.8	28.4	28.5	43.0	46.4	51.4	50.8	48.0	57.0	63.8	54.7

Notes:
(a) Manufactured exports not including petroleum
(b) Manufactured exports including petroleum
(c) Non-traditional exports not including minerals
(d) Non-traditional exports including minerals
(e) Manufactured exports not including petroleum; non-traditional exports including minerals
(f) Manufactured exports not including petroleum; non-traditional exports not including minerals
(g) Manufactured exports including petroleum; non-traditional exports not including minerals
(h) Manufactured exports including petroleum; non-traditional exports including minerals

Sources: Bank of Tanzania, Economic and Operations Report, various issues; Economic Research Bureau, Tanzania Economic Trends: A Quarterly Review of the Economy 4, 3 (October 1991) and 4, 4 (January 1992); United Republic of Tanzania, Economic Survey; Foreign Trade Statistics, various issues; Annual Trade Report, various issues

Table 6.2 Summary performance indicators for the export of manufactures, Tanzania 1966–90 (%)

	1966–70	1971–5	1976–80	1981–5	1986–90
Share of manufactures in total exports	13.5	14.5	15.6	13.1	21.1
Growth rate of total manufactured exports	20.74	13.51	17.49	−11.20	19.94
Growth rate of total manufacturing output (except petroleum)	−1.85	19.12	25.50	−15.13	23.72
Share of exports in total manufacturing output	16.8	12.4	8.0	4.6	17.9
Growth rate of manufacturing output in PPP$[a]	−0.5	20.9	12.9	−8.1	3.9
Growth rate, manufacturing GDP	10.00	4.81	0.43	−4.89	2.53

[a] Output in PPP$ at 1966 prices computed as: output (in Tshs)/PPPNOER, where PPPNOER is the nominal exchange rate that would maintain purchasing power parity with major trading partners, with 1966 as a base

Sources: Bank of Tanzania, *Economic and Operations Report*, various issues; Economic Research Bureau, *Tanzania Economic Trends: A Quarterly Review of the Economy* 4, 3 (October 1991) and 4, 4 (January 1992); United Republic of Tanzania, *Economic Survey*, various issues; *Foreign Trade Statistics*, 1986, 1987; *Annual Trade Report*, various issues

de-industrialization. Manufactured exports declined rapidly. The annual average rate of decline for the period was 11.2 per cent. Exports of manufactures other than petroleum declined at an even faster rate (−15.1 per cent). The difference is explained by the fact that oil product exports to land-locked neighbours were partly contractual. The share of manufactures in total exports declined to an average of 13.1 per cent as a result of their even more rapid decline than that of other exports. The manufacturing sector's export orientation declined even more steeply as the share of exports in output declined to a very low 4.6 per cent.

The third phase, 1986–90, coincided with the period of economic recovery when growth in the export of manufactures rebounded strongly. The growth rate of manufactured exports, inclusive of petroleum products, averaged 20 per cent per year. Excluding petroleum products, the average growth rate was even higher at an average of 24 per cent annually. This very high growth rate was partly a result of starting from the very low base of the crisis period. However, it also very much exceeded the output growth rate. This explains the very large recorded jump in export orientation with the share of exports in total output reaching a historical record of nearly 18 per cent. With other categories of exports recovering more slowly, the share of manufactures in total exports rose significantly to an unprecedented average of 21.1 per cent for the period.

Since 1990 a decline in the value of manufactured exports has been recorded, despite continued modest real growth in manufacturing sector output. The rapid increase in the export orientation of the sector registered during 1986–9 could not be sustained. Perhaps a plausible explanation for this slowing down lies in the limited scope of export expansion, which was based mainly on substitution out of domestic consumption of exportables induced by higher export profitability with a more or less unchanged production structure.[3]

Tables 6.3 and 6.4 present the structure of manufactured exports, and the export orientation of subsectors. The structure is presented for two different subperiods, 1978–87 and 1985–90, because the components of the categories are different for the two sources of data. One is able, however, to get a reasonably consistent picture of the relative shares of the major subsectors. The same applies to the data on export orientation. The 1985–90 categorization does not cover all food items, excludes processing of tobacco for export from the relevant subsectors, and adds these to a much larger 'other manufactures' category. Table 6.5 presents export orientation for sixty-six firms in similar sectoral categories for which data covering the period 1985–90 exist.

Five main subsectors dominate the contribution to exports of manufactures. Tobacco manufactures (dominated by processing of raw tobacco for export); manufacture of food (including grain milling); textiles and garments; petroleum and industrial chemicals (dominated by petroleum); and china, pottery, glass and non-metallic products (dominated by cement). Paper and paper products became a significant contributor after the commissioning of the only pulp and paper mill in 1985. Over the period of recovery the rise in the relative shares of non-metallic products, sisal fabrics, food products and even leather and leather products is particularly notable. In terms of export orientation the broad trends for the sector as a whole are reflected in the subsectors too.

Table 6.3a The structure of manufactured exports by subsector, Tanzania 1978–87 (%)

	1978	1979	1980	1981	1982	1983	1984	1985	1986	1987
Food products	17.75	23.48	13.76	18.26	9.95	18.67	5.27	6.53	11.70	10.93
Beverages and tobacco	24.92	12.33	9.30	18.58	23.74	18.79	14.24	16.38	26.65	19.19
Petroleum products, dyes and paints, processed oils and other chemicals	11.87	13.74	17.35	17.20	19.06	20.54	31.24	34.79	12.01	17.32
Textiles yarn and fabrics	13.69	24.07	27.01	12.74	16.79	15.40	18.80	10.90	16.89	26.12
Other processed minerals and materials	30.48	24.52	30.82	30.15	26.62	23.22	26.51	27.71	29.33	22.66
Machinery and transport equipment	1.28	1.86	1.76	3.08	3.84	3.38	3.93	3.69	3.41	3.79
Totals	100.00	100.00	100.00	100.00	100.00	100.00	100.00	100.00	100.00	100.00

Sources: United Republic of Tanzania, *Foreign Trade Statistics*, various issues; *Annual Trade Report*, various issues

Table 6.3b The structure of manufactured exports by subsector, Tanzania 1985–90 (%)

	1985	1986	1987	1988	1989	1990
Food products	9.52	8.68	7.35	10.15	11.19	11.54
Beverages and tobacco	25.00	28.95	18.77	18.27	12.49	6.47
Petroleum products, dyes and paints, processed oils and other chemicals	29.94	18.78	17.81	24.18	19.74	19.69
Textiles yarn and fabrics	23.06	28.80	20.88	22.52	26.29	25.65
Other processed minerals and materials	5.64	10.79	20.20	16.57	18.24	19.42
Machinery and transport equipment	2.35	2.08	2.09	1.97	2.61	2.56
Other manufactures	4.50	1.92	12.91	6.32	9.44	14.68
Totals	100.00	100.00	100.00	100.00	100.00	100.00

Sources: Bank of Tanzania, *Economic and Operations Report*, various issues; United Republic of Tanzania, *Economic Survey*, various issues; *Annual Trade Report*, various issues

Table 6.4a Manufacturing sector export orientation by subsector, Tanzania 1978–87 (% share of exports in output)

	1978	1979	1980	1981	1982	1983	1984	1985	1986	1987
Food products	9.33	16.32	10.19	8.41	3.60	6.18	1.75	2.32	4.54	9.72
Beverages and tobacco	36.87	27.62	20.58	28.14	16.81	11.26	12.08	14.55	20.27	33.44
Petroleum products, dyes and paints, processed oils and other chemicals	11.95	20.40	30.08	16.31	15.45	15.13	20.16	26.49	7.57	25.02
Textiles yarn and fabrics	11.15	19.26	19.57	6.26	6.36	5.34	8.58	5.46	7.11	25.19
Other processed minerals and materials	11.56	11.22	13.88	9.32	7.44	5.39	6.31	7.23	5.93	10.51
Machinery and transport equipment	1.36	2.55	2.25	2.59	2.61	2.20	4.19	3.01	1.81	4.59
Total manufacturing sector	11.65	14.51	14.37	9.42	7.56	6.71	7.59	8.06	6.77	15.51

Sources: United Republic of Tanzania, Economic Survey, various issues; Bank of Tanzania, Economic and Operations Report, various issues; United Republic of Tanzania, Foreign Trade Statistics, 1986, 1987; Annual Trade Reports, various issues

Table 6.4b Manufacturing sector export orientation by subsector, Tanzania 1985–90 (% share of exports in output)

	1985	1986	1987	1988	1989	1990
Food products	2.11	2.91	6.80	13.21	19.68	24.32
Beverages and tobacco	13.86	19.01	34.04	28.39	26.39	16.40
Petroleum products, dyes and paints, processed oils and other chemicals	14.23	10.22	26.78	33.86	37.33	44.64
Textiles yarn and fabrics	7.21	10.46	20.95	19.56	30.89	36.13
Other processed minerals and materials	0.92	1.88	9.75	10.00	14.80	18.89
Machinery and transport equipment	1.19	0.95	2.63	4.74	8.53	10.02
Total manufacturing sector	5.03	5.84	16.14	18.65	24.94	30.18

Sources: United Republic of Tanzania, *Economic Survey*, various issues; Bank of Tanzania, *Economic and Operations Report*, various issues; United Republic of Tanzania, *Annual Trade Reports*, various issues

Table 6.5 Export orientation for selected set of sixty Tanzanian firms by subsector, 1985–90 (% share of exports in output)

	1985	1986	1987	1988	1989	1990
Food products	–	–	–	–	0.08	0.01
Beverages and tobacco	13.22	12.66	19.35	13.06	20.38	3.09
Textiles and clothing	2.56	0.66	10.77	8.26	8.42	7.08
Leather and leather products	7.92	5.22	8.65	17.86	15.31	20.22
Wood and wood products	–	0.33	5.64	10.23	6.98	5.73
Paper and paper products	–	–	–	–	–	–
Petroleum and chemical products	9.62	3.92	6.96	5.25	9.60	4.73
Rubber and plastic products	–	0.09	–	–	0.59	2.31
Pottery, glass and non-mineral products	3.24	3.18	3.79	11.79	13.24	12.41
Metallic products	0.00	0.05	1.90	3.01	0.56	0.45
Machinery	1.45	3.65	5.08	6.69	3.64	3.08
Miscellaneous manufactures	13.96	6.60	11.00	1.39	0.92	1.18
Totals	4.71	3.95	6.62	5.80	7.48	4.08

Source: Computed from data from the Bank of Tanzania

IMPORT SUBSTITUTION, EXPORT ORIENTATION AND PRODUCTIVITY CHANGES IN THE MANUFACTURING SECTOR

Import substitution and export orientation

Table 6.6 presents the relationship between import substitution and export orientation in Tanzania's manufacturing sector for the period 1966–90. There is a negative correlation between the extent of import substitution and export orientation for the period as a whole. The index of import substitution rose persistently between 1966 and 1985 and then fell precipitously during 1985–90, partly as a result of the import liberalization initiated in 1984 with the 'own funds' imports scheme, initially for a limited range of goods and subsequently expanded; and partly due to the new incentives for export sales by local manufacturers.

The decline in export orientation during 1970–80 occurred in spite of the high rate of output growth for the same period. This trend suggests product development and cost structures that were biased towards sales in the protected domestic market. The subsequent decline in output during 1981–5 and the stringent squeeze on imports generated shortages in manufactures, raised scarcity premiums for the products in the domestic market, and hence further raised the relative attractiveness of domestic sales. In response, the proportion of total output exported fell steeply, reflecting an even faster reduction in export sales than the decline in total sales.

The sharp rebound in export orientation after 1985, as argued earlier, was the result of a much faster growth in exports, averaging 20 per cent annually compared to the 3.9 per cent growth in real output. A strong shift from domestic to export sales was achieved during this period. It appears that the response to the change in policy environment, now more favourable to exports, was dominated by manufacturers who were already established in the domestic market and now had low costs by world standards. A consistent data set for sixty firms shows that the number of firms exporting increased by about 60 per cent, from fifteen in 1985 to twenty-three by 1990. In addition, those firms already exporting increased their shares of total export sales.

Table 6.7 presents the export participation rates of the sixty firms, for the period 1985–90. We consider 1985 as the pre-regime shift year, and the subsequent period as the one where various measures

179

Table 6.6 Export orientation, import substitution and output growth, Tanzania (%)

	1966–70	1971–5	1976–80	1981–5	1988–90
Share of exports in total manufacturing output	16.8	12.4	8.0	4.6	17.9
Import substitution index[a]	36.5	38.7	46.9	51.9	30.9
Growth rate of output in PPP$	–0.5	20.9	12.9	–8.1	3.9

[a] Import substitution index is measured as production of manufactures for domestic use (output less exports) as a proportion of total domestic supply (output plus imports). All merchandise imports have been counted as manufactures, including cereals which are a product of grain milling

Sources: Bank of Tanzania, *Economic and Operations Report*, various issues; United Republic of Tanzania, *Economic Survey*, various issues; *Annual Trade Report*, various issues

Table 6.7 Export participation and types of exporter, Tanzania 1985–90

	1985	1986	1987	1988	1989	1990
A Export participation rates (sixty firms)[a]						
Total no. of producing firms	53	56	58	58	56	54
Total no. of exporting firms	15	19	20	21	26	24
Total no. of non-exporters	38	37	38	37	30	30
Proportion of producers exporting (%)	28	34	34	36 46	43	
Share of exports in total sales (%)	4.7	3.9	6.4	5.8	6.9	6.4
B Classification of exporters						
Old exporters[b]	15	15	15	15	15	13
New exporters[c]	0	4	5	7	12	11
New exporters/total exporters	–	21	25	33	46	48
Share of new exporters in total export values (%)	–	0.62	5.1	7.0	5.3	7.4

[a] Within the period five firms either resumed or started production; in 1984 two firms, and in 1990 four firms did not have their production recorded
[b] All those exporting prior to regime shift (1985 or earlier). Two of these did not export in 1990
[c] Includes those exporting for the first time or that resumed exporting after 1985
Source: Computed from data from the Bank of Tanzania

were put in place to improve incentives to export. The overall response of the firms to the changes is represented by the rise in export share of total sales, from 4.7 per cent in 1985 to 6.9 per cent in 1989. (The decline recorded in 1990 is the result of two producers not registering their exports.) Participation in exports grew from 28 per cent of the firms in 1985 to 43 per cent in 1990. The proportion of 'new' exporters (those firms that did not participate in exportation by 1985) grew from 21 per cent in 1986 to 48 per cent in 1990. However, in value terms, the share of new exporters in the total reached a peak of only 7.4 per cent in 1990. The rise in overall export orientation was thus dominated by old exporters' expansion of sales.

With the exception of paper and paper products, the other notable sectors with high rates of growth of export orientation were already established domestically. These included textile, clothing and sisal fabrics, which together more than tripled their export orientation from 7.2 per cent in 1985 to 36 per cent in 1990; processed minerals and other materials, leather and leather products, food products, as well as machinery and transport equipment. New exporters were scattered across sectors but were predominantly in wood products, canned fruit and vegetables, sisal bags and fabrics. Exporters in the group of sixty firms performed better in real output growth terms than non-exporters. Their weighted average growth rate was approximately 2 per cent during 1985–90 compared to –5 per cent for the non-exporters.

Notable changes in the structure of products were also observed during the most recent period. In the case of textiles and leather products, for example, the shift was towards less-finished products, to take advantage of their relative international cost competitiveness and higher adaptability to the more stringent end-use tastes in the export market. More specifically, in the case of textiles, export of grey fabrics rather than finished fabrics became dominant (TEXMAT 1989). Relative to international costs, locally produced grey fabric became more competitive than finished fabric. The additional import costs for dyes in the face of a rapidly depreciating shilling partly explains this shift.

Import substitution, export orientation and productivity changes

Several explanations have been offered in the literature for the negative relationship typically found between import substitution and export orientation in the manufacturing sector. These can be divided into four main categories:

1 The different nature of products and supply requirements for the domestic and export markets.
2 The higher costs engendered by input production under protection eroding export competitiveness.
3 The erosion of incentives for exporting compared to sales for the domestic market.
4 The greater know-how required for penetrating and enlarging shares in export markets.

We shall here confine ourselves to the first two explanations. The third and fourth will be taken up under sections four and five, respectively.

Keesing and Lall (1992: 178) underscore the problem of the different nature of products and supply requirements under import substitution and export orientation. The standards of finish, styling, quality, packaging and supply reliability are very much more stringent in the extreme 'buyers' markets for exports compared to the protected 'suppliers' markets locally. Moreover, markets for standardized products are small compared to the fast-growing markets for made-to-order products. Flexibility and know-how required to meet this larger segment of the market is unlikely to be developed under a dominantly import substitution environment. It can be acquired through learning by experience with deliberate support in export marketing.

In a study by Wangwe (1992), 50 per cent of the firms surveyed emphasized product quality improvement and the modernization of the production process to respond to the demands of export markets to be their key concerns in industrial restructuring and rehabilitation. The study notes that under protection, firms pursued short-term output expansion objectives at the expense of creating technological capabilities. It further argues that in the absence of competitive pressure, product quality and development of core capabilities to support competitive strategies were de-emphasized. Thus it is not surprising that the recent rise in Tanzania's export orientation was dominated by standardized products of established manufacturers. Achievement of a shift to new product designs and ultimately a capacity to meet high quality orders reliably will take time and deliberate strategies. In our opinion this is perhaps the single most important hurdle in the process of developing manufacturing for export.

The infant industry argument for import substitution is mainly predicated on achieving technical efficiency under protection as scale in production is realized and technological capabilities are created. It would thus be expected that the resultant cost competitiveness achieved under protection would subsequently provide a springboard into exporting. To the extent that protection tends to 'crowd in' too many firms producing at too low levels of output, technical efficiency is not, however, achieved. Ndulu and Semboja (1994) have presented evidence on the lack of significant realization of technical efficiency under the import substitution strategy in Tanzania.

In the case of the textile and beverages subsectors, for example, Mbelle (1988), using frontier production functions, showed that cost savings ranging between 21 per cent and 66 per cent in 1976 and between 21 per cent and 57 per cent in 1984 could have been achieved through using the most efficient firms to produce the same levels of output. In a later study Mbelle and de Valk (1990) showed that technical efficiency deteriorated steeply between 1980 and 1985 before improving slightly by 1988 in the case of the textile industry. A subset of the firms could have produced the same level of output using 85 per cent, 50 per cent, and 58 per cent of inputs during 1980, 1985, and 1988 respectively. Moreover, the decline in capacity utilization during the period of severe import compression further hampered the realization of technical efficiency by restricting the scale of output. Large differences in the level of productivity across firms (sustainable under protection) persisted. It is widely hoped that the weeding out of inefficient firms in the recent effort of parastatal restructuring, divestiture and trade liberalization will foster rationalization of industry structure in the future.

Table 6.8 presents cost efficiency trends for the manufacturing sector and subsectors during the 1980s to indicate approximately the sector's response to both trade restraints and liberalization, and macroeconomic measures. Cost efficiency here is measured as unit cost divided by an aggregate index of input prices. It is thus the inverse of productivity trends, a decline showing an improvement in cost efficiency.

The aggregate input price index is measured using the Tornquist method. This method uses the weighted average of GDP price deflators for costs of primary inputs, and for imported inputs the import price index consisting of trade-weighted unit value indices

Table 6.8 Cost efficiency trends, manufacturing sector, Tanzania 1980–90 (1980 = 100)[a]

	1981	1982	1983	1984	1985	1986	1987	1988	1989	1990
Food products	99.82	107.83	98.01	108.71	107.98	89.74	63.53	51.80	40.51	35.37
Beverages and tobacco	110.32	163.73	100.63	108.15	105.63	78.41	76.27	55.26	44.44	38.98
Petroleum products, dyes and paints, processed oils and other chemicals	84.43	75.27	84.30	93.65	100.85	75.16	74.27	47.03	37.72	33.05
Textiles yarn and fabrics	103.08	130.38	91.68	100.87	105.40	86.10	116.46	52.77	41.13	35.89
Other processed minerals and materials	106.50	126.98	123.39	146.47	142.70	108.29	107.48	68.87	53.94	47.10
Machinery and transport equipment	99.07	98.39	95.53	100.70	98.01	79.18	51.97	48.42	38.00	33.17
Miscellaneous manufactures	28.02	90.10	193.26	230.09	220.03	170.73	110.93	534.52	84.33	73.28
Totals	103.04	110.19	112.41	126.38	126.47	99.38	94.23	61.70	48.46	42.30

[a] Index of unit cost divided by an aggregate index of input prices
Sources: Bank of Tanzania, Economic and Operations Report, various issues; United Republic of Tanzania, Economic Survey, various issues; Annual Trade Report, various issues

for manufactures of trading partners, multiplied by the exchange rate. The weights for the two component price indices are the share of value added in gross output and the residual. It is assumed that changes in prices of imported inputs and exportable raw materials are dominated by changes in the exchange rate, which is particularly realistic after 1986. The real output index is measured in terms of PPP dollars.

The results show a reduction in cost efficiency between 1980 and 1985, probably a result of the decline in capacity utilization and continued wasteful utilization of 'subsidized' inputs. Subsequently, however, after 1985 in response to the rapid depreciation of the exchange rate, firms appear to have saved on costs of both imports and exportables. In contrast to the continued technical inefficiency at the industrial level, improved allocative efficiency appears to have been prompted in response to changes in input prices. These results are only indicative, and should not be taken as conclusive.

In the specific case of the textile sector, Mbelle and de Valk (1990) show that some compression of input coefficients was achieved in response to the rise in input costs in the 1980s. The labour coefficient declined very slightly from 0.35 to 0.32 between 1980 and 1988, probably since labour costs either stagnated or declined in real terms. The coefficient for domestic inputs (mostly exportables) declined significantly by 36 per cent from 0.14 in 1980 to 0.09 in 1988. In the case of imported inputs, the coefficient decreased by a significant 43 per cent, from 0.14 in 1980 to 0.08 in 1988. The capital cost coefficient, however, doubled over the same period probably from the continued pressure of capacity underutilization and as a counterpart to the reduction in the other coefficients.

This broad characterization of productivity/efficiency trends glosses over significant differences in performance at firm level within the same industry. We therefore undertook a microeconomic analysis using available audited accounts, supplemented by our own survey for ten textile firms and five leather-producing firms. The selection of the two industries was based on three considerations: first, the availability of data and previous coverage by other studies (Mbelle 1988; Mbelle and de Valk 1990); second, significant differences in competitive efficiency of the two industries based on the results of a 1987 World Bank survey (leather industries generated negative value added at world prices, World Bank 1987); and third, the significant contribution of the textile industry to industrial output and value added. The included firms account for more than 60 per cent of output in each industry.

The productivity/efficiency indicators included output per worker, capacity utilization rates, and cost efficiency. Output per worker (in physical units) and cost efficiency were measured as indices with 1987 as a base, and the capacity utilization rate was measured as the percentage of actual output to capacity. Four main findings can be noted.

First, there was wide variation in the generally continued poor performance in capacity utilization. Average rates of capacity utilization in textiles, though significantly higher than those for leather industries in the post-liberalization period, on the whole remained at levels significantly lower than in the first half of the 1980s. A partial recovery after a steep decline was observed in four out of the ten textile firms. Three out of the five leather plants showed an accelerated decline in capacity utilization in the second half of the 1980s, and an additional one was stagnant.

Second, in terms of output per worker, out of the seven textile firms for which data are available, six registered rather strong productivity growth in the post-liberalization period. In the leather goods sector, however, only one firm showed an improvement in labour productivity. The rest showed either continued deterioration or stagnation, but in all cases much lower levels in productivity compared to the first half of the 1980s.

Third, there appears to be improvement in cost efficiency in the textile industry even in the cases where no significant improvement in capacity utilization was recorded. This was most likely due to a reduction in the utilization of high cost imports through a shift towards a less import intensive product mix and a more efficient use of cotton, as noted earlier by Mbelle and de Valk (1990). In any case, it is clear that unit costs increased by less than input prices. In the case of the leather industries where the product mix range is more limited, unit costs appear to have increased faster than input prices as a result of the continued steep decline in capacity utilization.

Fourth, the strong exporters in textiles also registered relatively high labour productivity growth and capacity utilization rates in the last six years.

From the analysis above it appears that there is still wide dispersion of performance across firms and that there is wide scope for industrial restructuring. The poorest performers, particularly in the leather industry, are facing increased pressure from the liberalization process, as indicated by their continued decline in production, and are probably threatened with closure. Industry rationalization appears to be largely within firms, and spearheaded by adjustments to product mix and savings in input use, in response to the steep rise in the domestic prices of imported and exportable inputs.

DETERMINANTS OF EXPORT ORIENTATION AND EXPANSION IN TANZANIA'S MANUFACTURING SECTOR

Policy stance and incentives to export

We focus here on two main policies that affect incentives to export: trade policy and macroeconomic policy. Quantitative restrictions (QRs) on imports are normally considered under trade policy. As Rodrik (1992) emphasizes, the tendency of a restrictive regime to coexist with macroeconomic instability has often led to confusion between the effects of macroeconomic policy and those of trade policy. In part, this confusion results from the pervasive use of import restraints for balance of payments management purposes during periods of sustained external imbalances in place of exchange rate policy. In such cases trade policy is often equivalent to macro-economic policy. By contrast, in periods of liberalization the typical pattern has been to replace macroeconomic management-based quantitative import restrictions with exchange rate management, and confine trade policy to its 'pure' forms, mainly tariffs.

The distinction between the effects of quantitative restrictions and those of macroeconomic policies on incentives to export is often difficult to make in Tanzania's case because of the extensive use of QRs for balance of payments management purposes. The intensity of application of import controls has varied with foreign exchange availability and such changes have been predominantly used in place of variations in the exchange rate. In this section we shall analyse their impact. First, however, we highlight the extent to which they affect import flexibility, relative profitability of the export and domestic markets, and international competitiveness. Measures aimed at alleviating the resulting export constraints will be discussed in section five (pages 197–206).

Import controls in Tanzania were selectively applied in the 1960s. They became a permanent feature of trade and exchange arrangements in the 1970s. In times of foreign exchange crisis, as in the first oil crisis of 1973–5 and the crisis period of 1978–86, they were predominantly used to protect foreign exchange reserves. In addition to reducing import flexibility during periods of tightening of import controls, they had two other anti-export bias effects. Restrictions effectively acted as implicit tariffs, limiting domestic supplies and raising the attractiveness of domestic sales due to price increases. The associated tightening of exchange controls also reduced access to foreign exchange from official sources, leading to a rise in the premium on foreign exchange in the parallel market and implicit taxation of those exporting through official channels (Ndulu and Semboja 1994). Oil imports and non-competitive (project-aid tied) imports of capital goods had the first claim on the official foreign exchange supply; during periods of large hikes in oil prices, the implicit tariff effects on import substitutes were particularly amplified since the share of export earnings in total available foreign exchange, which could be more flexibly allocated to competing imports, then declined (Doriye and Wuyts 1992).

Significant changes were made from 1984 onwards in terms of reducing import controls and thereby raising import flexibility. An 'own-funds' imports scheme was introduced in 1984. This scheme provided for automatic licensing for importation of goods for which the importers provided their own foreign exchange. In addition, beginning in 1986, a growing proportion of external finance became united to projects, allowing for its broader use for import support. Starting in 1988, the Open General Licence (OGL) system with automatic licensing for some imports was introduced. A significant proportion of funds for programme support was channelled to this window, accounting for 18 per cent (in 1990) and 27 per cent (in 1991) of the value of all import licences issued. Although at the beginning the positive eligibility list under this facility was largely confined to industrial raw materials, spares and medical items, it was gradually expanded and then converted to a negative list of a few items (some luxuries and 'prohibited' goods) that were ineligible. Another scheme allowed exporters to retain portions of their foreign exchange earnings for their own 'free' use. The proportion of import licences issued under these schemes increased rapidly from 19.4 per cent of the total in 1984 to 60.3 per cent by 1991. Correspondingly, the convertibility of the shilling increased over this period, as shown by the decline in the parallel market premium, to a large extent as a result of the pursuit of an active official exchange rate policy.

To the extent that import restrictions influence the equilibrium

189

real exchange rate, we can determine their influence on incentives to export and hence their impact on export performance. This requires controlling for other influences on the movement of the equilibrium exchange rate, to separate their relative impacts. DeRosa (1990) uses this link to estimate the effects of protection on the real exchange rate and hence on international competitiveness and the incentive to export. Barriers to import are considered a tax on exports since they raise the domestic resource cost of exports. Having estimated the influence of protection on the real exchange rate, DeRosa proceeds to simulate the effects of protection on exports. The exercise is undertaken in two stages. One is to estimate export responsiveness to real exchange rate changes. The other is to measure the influence of trade policy on the real exchange rate. While the influence of tariffs can be attributed wholly to trade policy, non-tariff barriers to imports, as pointed out earlier, cannot so easily be categorized since they were often used for balance of payments management.

Macroeconomic influences, whether policy induced or caused by exogenous factors, have an important impact on manufactured export performance – through two channels. They influence the incentive to export and thus the export orientation of the sector. They also affect the export base (i.e. the output level) through their influence on capacity utilization.

In the short term, the excess of domestic credit expansion over real growth and foreign inflation not compensated for by nominal depreciation of the exchange rate was found to be the most important source of real appreciation of the shilling in Tanzania during the 1980s (Ndulu 1993). Monetization of a widening fiscal deficit (i.e. macroeconomic policy) was the major reason for this excess during the first half of the 1980s. Controlling for this, other 'fundamentals', including trade policy (tariff and non-tariff barriers), external terms of trade, and net foreign resource inflows, have been found (elsewhere) to influence the longer term movement of the equilibrium real exchange rate (Edwards 1987a, 1987b, 1988, 1989, 1990; Dornbusch 1974; Elbadawi 1989; Cottani et al. 1990; Khan and Ostry 1991).

Below we undertake three econometric investigations. First, we estimate the responsiveness of export orientation in the manu-facturing sector to the real exchange rate. We consider the real exchange rate to be a summary statistic reflecting the combined effects of trade and macroeconomic policy and other exogenous economic fundamentals on the incentive to export. Second, we estimate export supply (volume) responsiveness to the real exchange rate and output. Third, we estimate the determinants of the real exchange rate to enable us to assess the impact of trade policy and import restrictions on the incentive to export.

Responsiveness of manufactured exports to incentives

The response of Tanzanian exports to price incentives is estimated on the basis of the simple model used by Balassa (1990: 391). On the demand side, Tanzania is assumed to be a 'small' country, able to sell all it can offer to the international market at prevailing prices. The supply of exports is influenced by changes in relative prices between traded and non-traded goods (here proxied by the real exchange rate (RER) measured as the trade-weighted relative inflation-adjusted price of foreign exchange), and a domestic capacity variable (here measured as the sector's real GDP).

In view of the possible existence of correlation between exports and domestic capacity, we first estimate the responsiveness of manufactured exports using the export–output ratio (RATO) as the dependent variable. This ratio represents the export orientation of the manufacturing sector. Since the relevant variables, expressed in logs, were each found (using the conventional tests) to be non-stationary and not co-integrated, equation (1) was estimated in rates of change between successive years for the period 1966–90 with the following results (t-statistics in brackets):

$$\text{d log RATO} = -0.03 + 1.64 \text{ d log RER} + 0.50 \text{ d log GDP} \quad (1)$$
$$\phantom{\text{d log RATO} = } (-0.49) \ (3.52) \phantom{\text{ d log RER} + 0.50 } (0.50)$$

$$R^2 = 0.49 \qquad \text{Adj.}R^2 = 0.41 \qquad F = 6.02 \qquad DW = 2.30$$

The results indicate that the responsiveness of manufactured exports to changes in the profitability of exports relative to domestic sales is very high. The estimated elasticity exceeds 1.6. Domestic capacity appears to have a small and insignificant impact on export orientation, confirming our earlier observation that the high output growth period of the 1970s, though accompanied by absolute export expansion, did not lead to a rise in the ratio of exports to output. Again, the steep rise in the ratio after 1985 was not matched by similar growth in output.

Since we are also interested in the responsiveness of the actual volume of exports (REXPO) to incentives, we include here an estimated equation for supply responsiveness in volume terms. Real exports are measured as dollar values of manufactured exports deflated by an index of weighted average unit prices of trading partners. Domestic capacity is expected to have a positive and significant influence here as the base for exports. As noted above, the small country assumption is invoked so that Tanzania is assumed to be able to sell all it can export at the prevailing world market prices. A partial adjustment model is used to allow for non-instantaneous completion of response within the period.

The following results are obtained for the period 1966–90 (t-statistics in parentheses):

$$\log REXPO = \qquad\qquad\qquad (2)$$
$$-14.1 + 1.85 \log GDP + 0.68 \log RER -0.12 \log REXPO (-1)$$
$$(-2.1) \ (2.07) \qquad\qquad (2.40) \qquad\qquad (-0.50)$$

$$R^2 = 0.70 \qquad Adj.R^2 = 0.63 \qquad F = 10.4 \qquad DW = 2.1$$

As expected, both the incentive to export and the export base (output) significantly influence the volume of manufactured exports. The included variables explain 70 per cent of export performance. The real exchange rate impact is statistically significant with an estimated elasticity of 0.68. The mean adjustment period is about 1.1 years. We also tried a specification in log changes to correct for any trend spurious correlations; the elasticity for the real exchange rate was higher in this version, at 0.97, and statistically significant, although as expected the R^2 was lower (0.47).

The relative impact of trade and macroeconomic policy

In this section we assess the relative impacts of trade and macroeconomic policy on export performance. This is done by first estimating the influence of these policies on the determination of the real exchange rate. The relative impacts of these policies on export performance is then estimated utilizing the estimates of supply responsiveness to the real exchange rate.

Following Edwards (1987a, 1987b, 1988), Cavallo and Cottani (1985), Elbadawi (1989) and Ndulu (1993), we distinguish between two sets of factors which determine the real exchange rate – real and monetary factors. Two basic equations are involved. The first postulates that changes in the official real exchange rate (ORER) in the short run around its equilibrium level (ERER) are caused purely by excess aggregate demand (X), which is the domain of macro-economic policy:

$$ORER_t = ERER_t + bX_t + e_t \qquad (3)$$

Second, the equilibrium exchange rate itself changes in response to changes in the relevant fundamentals (F). ERER is not observed but its fundamentals are, and hence an estimate for it can be obtained:

$$ERER = f(F_t) + u_t \qquad (4)$$

A reduced form for the determinants therefore is:

$$ORER_t = f(F_t) + bX_t + u_t \qquad (5)$$

The above specification allows us to separate the purely macro-economic policy effects from other fundamentals. The included fundamentals affecting ERER are three: the external terms of trade, a proxy for import restrictions, and the effective tariff rate. Although foreign resource inflow is often included as a fundamental affecting ERER, we have excluded it after finding it, in prior estimation, to have an insignificant influence. To the extent that foreign resource inflows are mainly used for imports, their effect on the price of non-tradables is insignificant. In Tanzania's case, during the 1970s and early 1980s project finance was largely for procurement of capital goods abroad. More recently, the bulk of external aid has been for import support. To the extent that the flows predominantly contribute to the relaxation of import restrictions (an endogenous trade liberalizing effect) they would have an offsetting effect to that of raising aggregate demand.

The 'classical' effect of the terms of trade (TOT) deterioration in a 'small' country is to cause a real depreciation in the value of the currency, and vice versa in the case of improvement in the terms of trade. However, if one takes into account the second round effects of terms of trade change, the net effect may be ambiguous (Edwards 1987a, 1987b; Elbadawi 1989). In an economy with exchange controls, a terms of trade improvement may induce a trade liberal-ization effect leading to a depreciation rather than appreciation of the real exchange rate (Ndulu 1993). An associated rise/fall in real income may also offset the 'standard' effect which is presumed to dominate in the classical case (Khan and Ostry 1991).

The tightness of quantitative import restrictions is proxied here by the parallel market premium on foreign exchange (PREM), expressed as a percentage of the official rate. The premium is also, of course, linked to the currency inconvertibility arising from foreign exchange controls. It is assumed that a tightening of controls raises excess demand for foreign exchange in the marginal segment of the market for foreign exchange, and hence raises the premium. A relaxation of controls will lower the premium and lead to a depreciation of the real exchange rate to clear the likely deficit. As has been seen, import restrictions may be considered to be trade policy; however, when used for balance of payments management, although their protective effect exists, they constitute macroeconomic policy, substituting for exchange rate policy (Collier and Joshi 1989). Another way of looking at the premium is to consider it as an implicit tax on exporters (Pinto 1989). Exporters surrender their earnings at the official exchange rate and buy imports at domestic prices that are assumed fully to adjust to the parallel rates. Such import pricing existed in Tanzania, particularly after 1984 (Ndulu 1993). A rise in the premium increases the implicit tax on exporters, which in turn discourages exports and leads to a likely widening of the current account deficit, requiring a depreciation of the real exchange rate to close it.

The effective tariff rate (i.e. import duties paid as a proportion of import value – IMPTAX) is employed to represent explicit trade policy. Tariff liberalization (reduction in effective tax rates) will lead to real depreciation. The assumption here is that the substitution effect between tradables and non-tradables will dominate the real income effect from tax cuts. In any case, the likely increase in the trade deficit with liberalization will require a real depreciation to close it.

Macroeconomic policy effects on the real exchange rate are measured through their impact on aggregate excess demand (MACRO). The excess of domestic credit growth over nominal depreciation of the exchange rate, the real GDP growth rate, and foreign inflation measures expansionary macroeconomic policy. We assume that credit expansion (largely from fiscal deficits) in excess of real growth directly measures domestic inflationary pressure. The dominance of the transactions demand for money makes it plausible to assume a stable demand for money that rises with real income. This variable (MACRO), unlike the others discussed here, is expressed in terms of growth rates (proportionate changes).

Using appropriate tests, we confirmed that the variables in the model are non-stationary and are not co-integrated. To avoid spurious correlation, the equation was estimated in first differences (of logs). However, we have also included the log of levels equation (corrected for first order serial correlation) for purposes of comparison. A partial adjustment specification of equation (3) is adopted. The results are presented below.

$$\log \text{RER} = 2.17 \quad -0.033 \log \text{TOT} (-1) -0.157 \log \text{PREM} \quad (6)$$
$$(1.03)(-0.124) \qquad\qquad (-2.30)^*$$

$$-0.184 \log \text{IMPTAX} -0.218 \text{ MACRO} + 0.724 \log \text{RER} (-1)$$
$$(-1.12) \qquad\qquad (-2.499)^* \qquad\qquad (2.01)$$

$$R^2 = 0.92 \qquad \text{Adj.}R^2 = 0.89 \qquad F = 31.682 \qquad DW = 1.79$$

$$d \log \text{RER} = 0.012 \quad -0.018 \, d \log \text{TOT} (-1) -0.149 \, d \log \text{PREM} \, (7)$$
$$(0.520)(-0.08) \qquad\qquad (-2.34)^*$$

$$-0.132 \, d \log \text{IMPTAX} -0.193 \, d \text{ MACRO} + 0.509 \, d \log \text{RER} (-1)$$
$$(-0.83) \qquad\qquad (-2.44)^* \qquad\qquad (2.82)^*$$

$$R^2 = 0.61 \qquad \text{Adj.}R^2 = 0.50 \qquad F = 5.40 \qquad DW = 1.81$$

(*significant at 5 per cent or less)

The models perform quite well statistically in spite of the brevity of the sample period (1966–90). All fundamentals have the correct signs. The terms of trade coefficient is small and insignificant, probably because of the offsetting second-round effects discussed earlier. Explicit import taxes exert no significant effect on the real exchange rate since such import restrictions, particularly in the late 1970s and the 1980s, were dominated by quantitative restrictions. The coefficient for the parallel market premium has the right sign and is statistically significant; this can be seen as supportive of the view that QRs constitute an implicit tax on exports. Macroeconomic policy also exerts a most significant influence on the real exchange rate over the sample period.

On balance, the macroeconomic influence on the real exchange rate and hence on export competitiveness and the incentive to export appears to be dominant. Using the estimated effects of trade and macroeconomic policies on the real exchange rate and the responsiveness of exports to changes in the exchange rate, we next estimate (approximately) the relative effects of each on the exports of manufactures. We assume here for simplicity that quantitative restrictions on imports are a shared burden of both macroeconomic and trade policies. During periods of foreign exchange scarcity, controls are assumed to be tightened primarily for balance of payments management purposes – macroeconomic policy, and during other times for predominantly protective purposes – trade policy.

Table 6.9 presents our approximation of the relative impacts of trade and macroeconomic policy effects during three periods: 1970–9, 1980–5 and 1986–90. Pure trade policy, represented by effective tariff rates, not only had statistically insignificant impact coefficients but also, for the whole 1970–90 period, showed a surprising decline (with some fluctuations) in protection, mainly as a result of an increasing trend to tax exemptions.

During the 1970–9 period, an expansionary macroeconomic stance,

Table 6.9 Macroeconomic and trade policy effects on export supply response: manufacturing sector, Tanzania

		Pure macroeconomic policy effects (MACRO)	Pure trade policy effects (IMPTAX)	Mixed trade and macroeconomic effects (PREM)
(a)	Impact coefficient	−0.132*	−0.09	−0.102*
(b)	Policy shift			
	1970–9	0.24	−0.04	0.20
	1980–5	0.08	−0.01	0.52
	1986–90	−0.36	−0.08	−0.25
(c)	Impact on exports			
	1970–9	−0.032	0.004	−0.020
	1980–5	−0.010	0.001	−0.053
	1986–90	0.05	0.007	0.026

* Statistically significant impact coefficient

Notes:

(a) The impact coefficient is measured as the product of the influence of relevant policy on the real exchange rate and the supply responsiveness to the real exchange rate, e.g. [(d REXPO/d RER) · (d RER/d MACRO)]

(b) Policy shift is measured by the average change in MACRO, IMPTAX and PREM respectively. A positive average MACRO describes an expansionary macroeconomic policy stance (the excess of domestic credit growth over real growth, nominal exchange rate growth and foreign inflation on average for the period). IMPTAX and PREM are shown as their respective average growth rates for the period

(c) Impact on exports measures the response of manufactured exports to macroeconomic policy shifts, changes in average import tariff rates, and import restrictions (as measured by the premium) respectively. It is the product of the impact coefficient and policy shift, i.e. (a) times (b)

as measured by MACRO, was the dominant source of the real currency overvaluation, that was mainly the result of the maintenance of a stable nominal exchange rate in spite of changes in the fundamentals, particularly during 1973–5 and the late 1970s. The fiscal deficit impact was particularly great in the last two years of the latter period. Import restrictions also tightened during 1970–9, more for protective than for balance of payments management purposes (except during the first oil crisis period, 1973–4). On balance, however, macroeconomic policy dominated the explanation of the contraction of export supply, via its influence on the overvaluation of the shilling. The continued expansion of manufactured exports during the period, in spite of the decline in export orientation shown earlier, was mainly the result of output expansion in the manufacturing sector.

During the 1980–5 period tightened import controls (measured in the table by PREM), mainly to protect reserves, dominated other influences on the appreciating real exchange rate and the rapid contraction of exports of manufactures. Pure macroeconomic policy continued to be expansionary. Thus macroeconomic policy again dominated export incentives and export performance.

The dramatic recovery of the growth of manufactures after 1986 was again primarily attributable to the influence of macroeconomic policy. The macroeconomic policy stance as measured here was at that time significantly contractionary, mainly via massive nominal depreciation of the currency, and partly via a decline in the growth rate of domestic credit net of real growth. The parallel market premium for foreign exchange fell significantly during this period in response to the real depreciation of the official rate; a significant reduction in import restrictions appears also to have contributed to the reduction in the premium.

EXPORT PROMOTION MEASURES AND EXPORT PERFORMANCE

During the 1980s the government of Tanzania introduced several measures to promote export expansion. These measures can be categorized into two main groups. The first were measures to compensate for the penalties on exporters resulting from the pursuit of expansionary macroeconomic policies and import controls. The compensation was either in the form of increased profitability of exports or enhanced import flexibility for the earners of foreign exchange. Key among these measures were export retention schemes, export rebates, duty drawbacks, and selective subsidies to exporters.

The second were proactive measures aimed at (a) reducing bottle-necks to exporting and (b) enhancing core capabilities of exporters to respond flexibly to the demands of export markets. In the former case the key measures were public support to facilitate financing of exports and the streamlining of export procedures to reduce time costs of exporting. In the latter case the proactive measures were aimed at improving access to information on markets, performance awards to encourage strong performers, and similar supports for technological and quality improvement. The proactive measures were also mainly financed through public resources.

The distinction between the two groups of measures is not merely in terms of their main objectives. The importance of the compensatory measures declines with reduction in the anti-export bias due to macroeconomic and trade policy reforms. However, proactive measures will continue to be of critical importance for enhancing export capabilities in the long term. Indeed, as our interviews with exporters have confirmed, enhancing core capabilities and facilitating access to information are fundamental for sustained export expansion.

Below we describe in detail the key promotional measures adopted, evaluate their effectiveness, and suggest further improvements in the design and implementation of the various schemes.

Compensatory measures

Measures to alleviate the impact of import restrictions

In section four (pages 188–97) we noted the effect of import restrictions as a tax on exporters. There are other significant negative impacts such restrictions have on the supply of exports. They impinge on the flexibility of exporters to respond to demands that are changing in character and to offer timely delivery, and thus to maintain or increase market shares. The various retention schemes elaborated below were primarily geared to enhance the flexibility of exporters in securing inputs and spare parts for export production. But they also raised the profitability of exporting by allowing retained earnings to be used for importing scarce consumer goods to be disposed of locally at prices inclusive of the scarcity premium. In this sense, the retention scheme was a *de facto* multiple exchange rate instrument used preferentially to ameliorate the negative effects of taxation of exporters through an overvalued currency. A significant proportion of retained earnings was used for enhancing profitability rather than for imported inputs. Between 1987 and 1990, for example, 40 per cent of total retained earnings was used to import consumer goods (Bank of Tanzania 1992). Of all export promotion measures, the retention schemes have been the most popular with exporters.

Four types of retention schemes have been operated for varying time periods. We take up each of them in turn.

The Seed Capital Revolving Scheme (SCRS)

The SCRS was introduced in January 1985 to provide seed capital in foreign exchange for the importation of inputs to initiate production for export. The participating companies had to pay 100 per cent cash cover in Tanzanian shillings (Tshs) for the allocation. Part of the export earnings from this scheme is allocated to the exporters for seed capital (required to purchase the next round of input requirements). Of the remaining, 45 per cent is retained by the exporter for emergency spare parts and importation of inputs for production for domestic consumption, and the rest is transferred to the Board of External Trade (BET) Seed Capital Account to be used by other eligible manufacturing exporters (15 per cent) and the national foreign exchange pool (40 per cent).

In later years the popularity of the SCRS declined. First, it forced producers to export, whereas later more flexible alternative sources of foreign exchange existed (e.g. the open general licence (OGL) facility). Second, whereas the SCRS was essential during the mid-1980s when foreign exchange was the binding constraint, more recently the binding constraint for most exporters was the cash cover on Tanzanian shillings. Since banks limited the level of financing to the proportion of foreign exchange earnings shared between the national pool and the Seed Capital Fund, the users of the scheme faced reduced access to local bank credit. The scheme seemed to perform well during 1985–9 when the number of beneficiaries rose from eighteen to fifty-one, generating US$14 million in non-traditional exports (Board of External Trade 1990) but began to face problems thereafter as the number of inactive exporters and cost inefficient producers rose (Bank of Tanzania 1992).

Since the initial, as well as subsequent, foreign exchange allocations were based on imported input requirements, the scheme tended to encourage the use of imported inputs.

Commodity Exchange Programme (CEP)

This programme, which came into force (with Swedish support) in late 1983, allowed Tanzanian exporting industries to acquire inputs (mainly from Sweden) in exchange for goods. The aims were to improve capacity utilization and product quality for export products through improved supplies of imported inputs and technical assistance. The retention rate was 100 per cent.

The programme's performance was not impressive. Its export proceeds rose relatively slowly from US$0.6 million in 1984–5 to US$1.6 million in 1988–9, compared to the CSRS whose proceeds rose from US$0.36 million in 1985 to US$6.7 million in 1988 (Board of External Trade 1989; Bank of Tanzania 1992). Clearly the complexities of barter trade limited growth to the minimum required to import essential inputs from specified origins. Furthermore, existing alternative sources of financing offered more attractive and flexible terms.

Foreign investment retention

Under the terms of the National Investment (Promotion and Protection) Act 1990, the government introduced a retention scheme which permitted foreign investors to retain up to 50 per cent of their net foreign exchange earnings. Such funds were to be used for importation of inputs and settlement of external obligations (e.g. debt servicing, profits, and dividend payments), and kept in external accounts under the supervision of the Bank of Tanzania. It is too soon for an assessment of its impact.

General Retention Scheme (GRS)

The GRS, introduced in 1986, allowed exporters to retain a specified percentage of their export earnings for the importation of essential inputs, spares, and incentive goods. The funds could also be used to service foreign debt. Until 1989 the retention rates were 50 per cent for non-traditional and 10 per cent for traditional exports. Subsequently, after the introduction of OGL, the retention for traditional exports was scrapped and that for non-traditional exports scaled down to 35 per cent. The rate of utilization (actual retention/retainable amount) for non-traditional exports rose from 1.4 per cent in 1985 to 10 per cent in 1987 and to 20 per cent in 1988, and then jumped to 42.3 per cent in 1991 (Bank of Tanzania 1992). The rate was expected to rise in response to the introduction of *bureaux de change* and exporters' right, from March 1992 on, to exchange retained earnings at the *bureaux* exchange rate. The utilization of this scheme by exporters of manufactures was quite low. Other non-traditional exporters used it more actively.

Measures to improve the financial profitability of exporters

The export incentive schemes discussed in the previous subsection were primarily aimed at improving flexibility in securing imported inputs and spare parts. These measures focused on foreign exchange availability and allocation. However, as previously noted, improvements in the availability and allocation of foreign exchange gave rise to another problem, namely, availability and allocation of the local currency required not only to raise the required cash cover for imports but also to finance the locally available inputs to match the rising demand (as capacity utilization rose).

The local cash squeeze was aggravated by several other reform measures. First, currency devaluation raised the debt service burden in local currencies and the costs of imported inputs and spare parts. Second, as part of the reforms, interest rates on domestic credit were raised from 9.5 per cent in 1984 to 31 per cent in 1988, recording real positive rates beginning in 1989. Third, the imposed credit ceilings continued to hurt the non-agricultural sector since much of the credit continued to be allocated to agricultural marketing institutions. Fourth, many of the high debt–equity entities no longer qualified for credit as financial institutions began to apply commercial criteria. Finally, within the context of export retention, retained export proceeds did not form the basis for determining bank credits since the banks had no control over these funds.

The government adopted further measures aimed at minimizing the impact of some of these financial constraints. The most important ones include the Export Rebate Scheme (ERS), the Duty Drawback Scheme (DDS), and the subsidy to exporters of cotton products and financial services. We elaborate on each below.

Export Rebate Scheme (ERS)

The export rebates, introduced in mid-1981, ranged between 5 and 25 per cent of the FOB value of exports (depending on the duty and sales tax rates of the imported inputs used for export production and the import intensity of the activity) and were aimed at offsetting losses which exporters incurred in foreign competitive markets *vis-à-vis* the lucrative domestic market. The scheme disbursed Tshs 35 million in 1982 and Tshs 81 million in 1984 to manufacturing exporters, representing less than 8 per cent of the value of manufactured exports. Within the manufacturing sector the scheme mainly benefited exporters of tea, sisal, textiles and leather products, and radiators (World Bank 1987; Board of External Trade 1989). The rebates were computed on the basis of the value of exports and imported inputs. Thus, activities which were both import intensive and inefficient in the use of these inputs were not penalized. Further problems arose with the use of the value of exports as the base for computing the rebate.

The Duty Drawback Scheme (DDS)

The DDS was introduced in mid-1988 to replace the ERS as a refund scheme for all the duties and taxes paid on imported inputs used for export production, and also on imported products exported in the same state. This scheme, like its predecessor, faced the problem of verification of the end use of imported inputs for exports, as well as the practical difficulties of computing appropriate import intensities and efficiency levels of exporting firms in order to discourage wasteful utilization of imports. With the scrapping of duties for intermediate imports altogether in 1992, the rationale for this scheme was weakened.

Selective input price subsidy to exporters: cotton products

In 1985 the government raised the producer price of cotton significantly, leading to a rapid rise in the price of cotton lint paid by the domestic textile manufacturers. At the same time, international market prices for cotton lint fell, making the domestic textile manufactures uncompetitive *vis-à-vis* their foreign counterparts. The government therefore introduced a temporary 'refund' (in fact, a subsidy) system under which exporters of cotton products were refunded the difference between the local purchase price of cotton lint and the international market price at the prevailing exchange rate.

Subsidized credit

Since August 1985 exporters of manufactured goods benefited from a preferential interest rate (World Bank 1987: 24). By November 1988 all export finance facilities were to be charged an interest rate of 26.5 per cent instead of the commercial rate of 31 per cent (National Bank of Commerce 1990). However, many exporters were not aware of the concession.

Proactive measures

Information on markets

Lack of knowledge about potential buyers – their tastes, demand stability, popular designs, quality specifications – created a crucial information gap for exporters. Furthermore, knowledge about competitors and the opportunity cost of exporting was also lacking. Such information is critical for a decision on whether to export or sell locally. Yet the kind of cost–benefit analysis that has to be undertaken requires more information gathering than many individual producers can afford.

The Board of External Trade initiated a Contract Promotion Programme (CPP), the elements of which included demand (or export potential) studies, trade missions, and trade fairs to assist potential exporters. Many export potential studies were comprehensive and useful. For example, a demand study on wooden furniture and wood products found that Tanzania's furniture contained too much moisture for European requirements. Local producers were advised accordingly and kilns were acquired.

Many of the demand studies were followed by trade missions to potential buyers. During 1984–8 trade missions visited other countries in Africa, the Middle East, and Western Europe. In some of these missions orders were secured.

Trade fairs also played an important promotional role. The Dar es Salaam International Trade Fair which takes place annually in July has attracted both local and foreign firms and traders. During 1980–8, twenty-six countries from Africa, Eastern and Western Europe, the USSR, Asia (including Japan and China) and Cuba participated. During the same period, Tanzanian exporters participated in fifty-eight different trade fairs abroad. At the fairs, orders were made on Tanzanian products (Board of External Trade 1990). Although trade fairs and missions provide important opportunities for contact between Tanzanian exporters and potential importers of their products, no studies have yet been done to assess their cost effectiveness and establish whether they pay their way.

Procedural issues

Tanzania Trade Facilitation Organization (TANPRO) was established in 1981 as part of the export incentive package to rationalize procedures for export documentation. Prior to its formation exporters had to go through cumbersome procedures and plenty of paperwork. The process was costly and time-consuming and the average waiting time prior to exporting was six months. This acted as a disincentive to exporters.

Many important documents have been aligned in accordance with the UN Layout Key and paperwork has been reduced and procedures shortened significantly. Average waiting time is now one week.

Promotional measures

Export credit guarantee scheme

The pre-shipment finance guarantee offered by the Bank of Tanzania covers the lending institution (usually commercial banks) for up to 75 per cent of the loss resulting from insolvency or default of the exporter/borrower and enables the lending institutions to offer export finance, thus enabling exporters to compete more effectively by offering attractive terms of payment to the foreign buyers. The National Bank of Commerce (NBC) allows credit up to 80 per cent of the value of expected proceeds. If the customer is under a retention scheme, NBC finances up to 80 per cent of proceeds not retained.

The comprehensive shipment guarantee which would have covered the exporter against the risk of non-payment by the buyer and the political risk of restrictions on remittances has been rendered irrelevant by the use of the Letters of Credit (LC) system. However, even confirmed and irrevocable LCs do not guarantee payment to the exporter (National Board of Commerce 1992).

The Presidential Award

This award was introduced in 1981 in recognition of exemplary export performance. The privileges associated with award winners include: improvement of the exporters' image, and trust and confidence in him/her; use of the award for promotional purposes; and preferential treatment in the allocation of foreign exchange. The significance of the latter has diminished with the introduction of other sources of finance, especially the OGL.

Business Travel Fund

The Business Travel Fund provides foreign exchange for business travel abroad, covering the cost of tickets and subsistence allowance.

Measures to enhance core capabilities of exporters

Once information on exporting is made available, through mail, trade missions and/or research, it has to be translated into action. Many times importers' specifications and research results have demanded quality improvements, change in design and/or specific taste requirements. Such demands have often required changes in the technology in use or acquisition of an entirely new technology.

The old age of machines is one of the most quoted causes of low productivity and inability to respond to changing demands and rising costs in the manufacturing sector in Tanzania. Old machines frequently break down, and use inputs inefficiently. Furthermore, old technology often cannot easily be modified to match the constantly changing tastes/fashions and quality/standard specifications. These changes can only be made at high cost. New investments were largely directed at setting up new plants, and rarely at rehabilitating or upgrading the technology of old ones.

One of the major challenges in the development of manufactured exports is how to develop an appropriate technology for the export sector. This area has not been sufficiently addressed by policymakers.

Lessons and future outlook

Tanzanian export promotion schemes have recorded some successes. These include facilitation of export documentation; providing information on markets, facilitating matches (between customers and exporters), and promoting competition among domestic producers; and improving flexibility in terms of securing imported materials for production purposes.

However, the schemes were applied indiscriminately without consideration of the performance differences among producers/exporters, encouraging some firms to export at very high cost and encouraging import intensive activities, thus aggravating import compression effects on output and growth. They did not place sufficient emphasis on the development of appropriate technology for the export market.

Ongoing trade and macroeconomic reform calls for a different approach to export promotion. Programmes which are aimed at compensation for distortions caused by trade and macro mismanagement are no longer relevant since the distortions have been significantly reduced. The changed environment requires programmes which are aimed at developing export capacity and competence. There is therefore a need to have more selective target-oriented programmes which focus on a few efficient producers/exporters – improving their accessibility to technological information and its acquisition, and assisting them to develop products to meet the challenges of changing demand. Such programmes will be more cost-effective.

CONCLUSION

The manufacturing sector in Tanzania has not yet achieved a significant transition from import substitution to export expansion. Indeed, given the sector's high dependence on imports for production, its contribution to net foreign exchange generation remains low and stagnant. The rapid expansion of exports by the sector during 1986–90, though certainly encouraging, has to be viewed in relation to the very weak performance of the prior economic crisis period (of the early to mid-1980s). One must also be concerned as to whether the expansion rate is sustainable, since signs of stagnation have appeared.

The recent macroeconomic and trade reforms played a dominant role in the restructuring of incentives for the export of manufactures. The steep real currency depreciation, in particular, made export sales significantly more profitable than domestic sales and induced a rapid expansion of exports through substitution out of domestic consumption of exportables, with a more or less unchanged production base and structure. Exports of manufactures were expanding at an average rate of 20 per cent during the period compared to a real growth rate of 3.9 per cent for the manufacturing sector. The short-run response to this change in incentive structures was dominated by firms established under the import substitution strategy, particularly those with some flexibility to change their product mix toward items which are more cost competitive and adaptable to demand requirements in the export market. The government's export promotional measures were largely to offset the negative effects of the previous distortions in macroeconomic and trade policies. Some proactive measures aimed at facilitating exportation and building export capability were pursued but in a rather ad hoc and unambitious way.

A sustained transition to an export orientation of Tanzania's manufacturing sector will require, in addition to appropriate macroeconomic and trade policies, strengthening core export capabilities of firms and reorienting products to meet the requirements of export markets. Product quality improvement and the modernization of the production process to respond flexibly to the demands of the export markets should be the key aims of industrial restructuring and rehabilitation programmes. Targeted and cost-effective public support programmes to improve exporters' accessibility to technological and marketing information should supplement efforts by individual firms.

NOTES

1 This section draws on Ndulu and Semboja 1994.
2 Traditional exports here include the main agricultural products: coffee, cotton, sisal, tea, tobacco, cashew nuts, and diamonds. Although the volume of exports of these products increased significantly over the period, the value of earnings either stagnated or declined due to a fall in world prices.
3 The value of manufactured exports declined drastically by 39 per cent during 1991 and, in spite of a partial recovery in 1992 and 1993, has remained about 30 per cent below the value realized in 1990. The drastic drop has been explained by production bottlenecks associated with power rationing which was in force until the second quarter of 1993. However, the decline in exports has been much more severe than that of production. Recent real appreciation pressures on account of tight money policy and increased capital inflows may have contributed to the increased attractiveness of domestic sales together with expanded domestic demand.

REFERENCES

Balassa, B. (1978) 'Exports and Economic Growth: Further Evidence', *Journal of Development Economics* 5: 181–9.
—— (1990) 'Incentives, Policies and Exports Performance in Sub-Saharan Africa', *World Development* 18, 3: 383–91.
Bank of Tanzania, *Economic and Operations Report* (various issues).

—— (1992) 'Review of Export Performance and Classification Under Foreign Exchange Retention Scheme', mimeo, Dar es Salaam: Bank of Tanzania.

Bhagwati, Jagdish (1987) 'Outward Orientation: Trade Issues' in Vittorio Corbo, Morris Goldstein and Mohsin Khan (eds) *Growth-oriented Adjustment Programs* (257–90), Washington, DC: IMF/World Bank.

Board of External Trade (1989) 'Ten Years of the Board of External Trade, 1979–1989', mimeo, Dar es Salaam: Board of External Trade.

—— (1990) 'The Seed Capital Revolving Scheme', mimeo, Dar es Salaam: Board of External Trade.

Cavallo, D. and Cottani, J. (1985) 'Economic Performance and the Real Exchange Rate in Less Developed Countries', mimeo, Background Paper for the *World Development Report, 1986*. Washington, DC: World Bank.

Cottani, J., Cavallo, D. and Khan, M.S. (1990) 'Real Exchange Rate Behaviour and Economic Performance in LDCs', *Economic Development and Cultural Change* 39: 61–76.

Collier, P. and Joshi, V. (1989) 'Exchange Rate Policy in Developing Countries', *Oxford Review of Economic Policy* 5, 3: 94–113.

DeRosa, D.A. (1990) 'Protection and Export Performance in Sub-Saharan Africa', *Weltwirtschaftliches Archiv* Band 128, Heft 1: 88–124.

Doriye, J. and Wuyts, M. (1992) 'Aid, Adjustment and Sustainable Recovery: The Case of Tanzania', mimeo, The Hague: Institute of Social Studies.

Dornbusch, R. (1974) 'Tariffs and Non-Traded Goods', *Journal of International Economics* 4, 2: 177–85.

Economic Research Bureau, *Tanzanian Economic Trends* (various issues), Dar es Salaam: University of Dar es Salaam, Economic Research Bureau.

Edwards, S. (1987a) 'Exchange Rate Misalignment in Developing Countries', CPP Working Paper, Washington, DC: World Bank.

—— (1987b) 'Tariffs, Terms of Trade and Real Exchange Rate in an Intertemporal Model of the Current Account', NBER Working Paper, Cambridge, Massachusetts: NBER.

—— (1988) 'Real and Monetary Determinants of Real Exchange Rate Behaviour: Some Preliminary Evidence from Developing Countries', *Journal of Development Economics* 29: 311–41.

—— (1989) *Real Exchange Rates, Devaluation and Adjustment*, Cambridge, Massachusetts: MIT Press.

—— (1990) 'Real Exchange Rates in Developing Countries: Concepts and Measurements' in T.J. Grennes (ed.) *International Financial Markets and Agricultural Trade* (56–108), Boulder, Colorado: Westview Press.

Elbadawi, I. (1989) 'Terms of Trade, Commercial Policy and the Black Market for Foreign Exchange: An Empirical Model of Real Exchange Rate Determination', Discussion Paper No. 570 (January, supp.) New Haven: Economic Growth Centre, Yale University.

Helleiner, G.K. (1986) 'Outward Orientation, Import Instability and African Economic Growth: An Empirical Investigation' in S. Lall and F. Stewart (eds) *Theory and Reality in Development: Essays in Honour of Paul Streeten*, New York: St. Martin's Press.

—— (1990) 'Trade Strategy in Medium-Term Adjustment', *World Development* 18, 6: 879–97.

—— (1994) 'Introduction' in G.K. Helleiner (ed.) *Trade Policy and Industrialization in Turbulent Times* (ch. 1), London: Routledge.

Keesing, D.B. and Lall, Sanjaya (1992) 'Marketing Manufactured Exports from Developing Countries: Learning Sequences and Public Support' in G.K. Helleiner (ed.) *Trade Policy, Industrialization and Development: New Perspectives*, Oxford: Clarendon Press.

Khan, M.S. and Ostry, J. (1991) 'Response of the Equilibrium Real Exchange Rate to Real Disturbances in Developing Economies' IMF Working Paper, January. Washington, DC: IMF.

Krueger, A.O. (1978) *Liberalization Attempts and Consequences*, New York: National Bureau of Economic Research.

Leff, N.H. and Sato, K. (1987) 'The Prospects for Higher Savings Rates in Latin America', *Journal of Policy Modelling* 9, 4: 559–76.

Mbelle, A.V.Y. (1988) 'Foreign Exchange and Industrial Development: A Study of Tanzania', unpublished PhD thesis, Gothenburg University.

Mbelle, A.V.Y. and de Valk, P. (1990) 'Textile Industry under Structural Adjustment in Tanzania (1980–1990)', mimeo, Dar es Salaam.

Michaely, M. (1977) 'Exports and Growth: An Empirical Investigation', *Journal of Development Economics* 4: 49–54.

National Bank of Commerce (NBC) (1990) 'NBC/Comments on the Exporters' Problems of a Banking Nature', Dar es Salaam: National Bank of Commerce.

Ndulu, B. (1986) 'Investment, Output Growth and Capacity Utilization in an African Economy: The Case of the Manufacturing Sector in Tanzania', *East African Economic Review* (New Series), 2, 1.

—— (1991) 'Growth and Adjustment in Sub-Saharan Africa', in Ajay Chhibber and Stanley Fischer (eds) *Economic Reform in Sub-Saharan Africa* (287–302), Washington, DC: World Bank.

—— (1993) 'Exchange Rate Management in the Context of Economic Reforms in Sub-Saharan Africa: Tanzania as an Illustrative Case' in Göte Hansson (ed.) *Trade, Growth and Development: The Role of Politics and Institutions* (ch. 12), London and New York: Routledge.

Ndulu, B. and Lipumba, N. (1990) 'International Trade and Economic Development in Tanzania' in J.H. Frimpong-Ansah, S.M. Ravi Kanbur and P. Svedberg (eds) *Trade and Development in Sub-Saharan Africa* (ch. 9), Manchester: Manchester University Press.

Ndulu, B. and Semboja, J. (1994) 'Trade and Industrialization Experience in Tanzania, A Review of Experience and Issues' in G.K. Helleiner (ed.) *Trade Policy and Industrialization in Turbulent Times*, London: Routledge.

Pinto, B. (1989) 'Black Market Premia, Exchange Rate Unification and Inflation in Sub-Saharan Africa', *The World Bank Economic Review* 3, 3: 321–38.

Ram, Rati (1985) 'Exports and Economic Growth; Some Additional Evidence', *Economic Development and Cultural Change* 33: 415–25.

Rodrik, D. (1992) 'Closing the Productivity Gap: Does Trade Liberalization Really Help?' in G.K. Helleiner (ed.) *Trade Policy, Industrialization and Development: New Perspectives*, Oxford: Clarendon Press.

Seringhaus, R. (1991) 'Export Promotion Organization in Developing

Countries: Their Role, Scope and Function' in R. Seringhaus and J. Rosson (eds) *Export Development and Promotion: The Role of Public Organization*, Lancaster: Kluwer Academic Publishers.

Seringhaus, R. and Rosson, J. (eds) (1991) *Export Development and Promotion: The Role of Public Organization*, Lancaster: Kluwer Academic Publishers.

TEXMAT (Textile Manufacturing Association of Tanzania) (1989) 'Tax Issues of Textile Sub-Sector', mimeo, Dar es Salaam: TEXMAT.

United Republic of Tanzania, *Annual Trade Reports* (various issues), Dar es Salaam.

—— *Economic Surveys* (various issues), Dar es Salaam.

—— *Foreign Trade Statistics* (various issues), Dar es Salaam.

—— (1990) *National Investment (Promotion and Protection) Act*, Dar es Salaam.

Wangwe, S. (1992) 'Rehabilitation in the Manufacturing Sector in Tanzania: Approaches, Characteristics and Technological Implications', mimeo, Ottawa: International Development Research Centre.

World Bank (1987) 'Tanzania: An Agenda for Industrial Recovery', mimeo, Washington, DC: World Bank.

INDEX

211